THE SCARED AND THE DOOMED

THE SCARED
AND
THE DOOMED

THE JEWISH ESTABLISHMENT
vs.
THE SIX MILLION

M.J. Nurenberger

MOSAIC PRESS
OAKVILLE   NEW YORK   LONDON

TABLE OF CONTENTS

Introduction
Acknowledgement

CANADIAN CATALOGUING IN PUBLICATION DATA

Nurenberger, M.J. (Meyer J.) — The Scared and the Doomed: the Jewish establishment vs. the six million

Bibliography: p.
Includes index.
ISBN 0-88962-290-6 (bound). — ISBN 0-88962-289-2 (pbk.)

1. Jews — United States — Politics and government. 2. Refugees, Jewish — United States. 3. Holocause, Jewish (1939-1945). I. Title.

E184.J5N48 1985   973'.004924   C85-098980-9

Published by Mosaic Press, P.O. Box 1032, Oakville, Ontario, L6J 5E9, Canada. Offices and warehouse at 1252 Speers Road, Unit 10, Oakville, Ontario, L6L 5N9, Canada.

Mosaic Press acknowledges the ongoing support of the Canada Council and the Ontario Arts Council.

Copyright© M.J. Nurenberger, 1985
Printed and bound in Canada.

ISBN 0-88962-290-6 cloth
     0-88962-289-2 paper

MOSAIC PRESS:

In the United States: Flatiron Book Distributors, 1170 Broadway, Suite 807, New York, N.Y., 10000, U.S.A.

In the U.K.: John Calder (Publishers) Ltd., 18 Brewer Street, London, W1R 4AS, England.

In Australia & New Zealand: Bookwise International, 1 Jeanes St., Beverley, South Australia, 5007 Australia.

BIOGRAPHICAL NOTE

Meyer Joshua Nurenberger was born in Cracow, Poland and was educated in France, Belgium and New York. As a student, he contributed to Belgian newspapers and was a Parliamentary reporter in Brussels. On February 2, 1939, he came to America at the invitation of the New York daily, **The Jewish Morning Journal**, now defunct. In 1947, he became editor of **The Jewish Morning Journal**, the youngest chief executive in the flourishing Yiddish press. He served as U.S. Army correspondent and covered the Nuremberg Trials. He also covered the Eichmann Trial in Jerusalem.

M.J. Nurenberger settled in Canada in 1957 where he established **The Canadian Jewish News**, which he ran until June 1971. He then spent several years in libraries in Jerusalem, Bonn, London and the United States — the F.D.R. Archives, New York, and the National Archives, where he studied more than one thousand documents confirming his theory that the Jews of Europe perished not only because of the indifference of the non-Jewish world, but also because of the bickering among American Jews and the jealousy among its leaders.

Mr. Nurenberger is presently editor and publisher of **The Jewish Times**, a journal of news analysis. He also writes the main weekly editorial column for the New York Yiddish newspaper, **Algemeiner Journal**.

INTRODUCTION

The Scared And The Doomed is essentially a book of memoirs written by a Jewish journalist who during World War II had a front seat in observing what he calls the Jewish Civil War: a strange war between the pseudo-Zionist establishment in North America (and Palestine) and the revolutionaries of the Irgun underground in Eretz Israel and their delegation in Washington and New York. This conflict became the primary cause for the paralysis of organized American Jewry when it was facing the greatest challenge in Jewish history — Hitler's war against the Six Million and their eventual extermination.

The Scared And The Doomed is not written in chronological order. It treats topics and events as they affected a particular situation. The author, who witnessed some of these tragic occurrences and who was involved with the rescue activities of the Irgun Delegation in its battle to save the Jews hijacked by Hitler, plainly relates the story of why American Jews did not respond to the SOS from their brethren overseas. When analysing the events during WWII, one should never forget that of all peoples victimized by Hitler, only the Jews lost the war. Today, forty years after WWII, the world Jewish population is smaller than in 1939. Why? Some of the answers can be found in this book.

The Scared And The Doomed consists not only of personal reminiscences but contains facts based on historical documents which help the reader find answers to the queries of the new generation which asks: What was the attitude of the Jews in the free countries, including Palestine, vis-a-vis the European tragedy?

Forty years after WWII the answer given must be straightforward and sincere, without fear of offending the sacred cows within the Jewish establishment, both past and present. Why did North American Jews, the most powerful Jewish community in history and the best organized, fail to rise to the challenge of the hour? Is it perhaps because they were too well organized, and had too many organizations with too many vested interests, that the holiest task facing that generation was totally neglected? Is it possible that this competition among conflicting factions vying for "power" within the community could have prevented them from hearing the cry of despair from overseas? Were the American Jewish masses aware of their leaders' betrayal of their sacred duty to fight for the survival of the Jews in Europe? Or had they been so misled by professionals that they truly believed their leaders were acting on behalf of the Jews trapped in Hitler's inferno?

Were the leaders scared? Frightened of anti-semitic repercussions on this continent, if the Jewish voice were to be raised too loudly? In this book, the author endeavours to answer candidly. He tells the largely unknown story of the activities of the Irgun delegation in the United States which moved heaven and earth in order to fight the apathy of the organized Jewish community. He also relates the details of the persecution of the members of the Irgun delegation by the Jewish establishment, which co-operated with anti-semitic U.S. State Department officials instead of supporting the campaign for saving the Jews of Europe.

When writing this book the author did not rely exclusively on memory, or even solely on pertinent documents (approximately 2,000 of which he consulted), but also interviewed a number of men and women who had been active in the field of rescue. For the first time this book introduces those non-recognized or forgotten Irgun idealists who fought the battle of the Jews of Europe. When speaking of such men and women, one can apply Winston Churchill's famous evaluation of the RAF: "Never have so many owed so much to so few." Thus from **The Scared And The Doomed** there emerges a picture of the sad events which transpired in the free world during the Hitler era. Who were the Jewish leaders who sabotaged the efforts of the Irgun and the Vaad Hatzalah of the American Orthodox Rabbinate in their efforts to save the European Jews? In retrospect, should they be considered war criminals or villains?

The theme of this book inspires me to conclude with the following verse from an ancient prayer:

. . . . It is known to Thee that I did not write it for my personal honour nor for that of the house of my father, but in order that there will be no more division within the House of Israel . . . .

Toronto, Ontario   V.E. Day 1985

ACKNOWLEDGEMENTS:

In the preparation of this book, I benefitted from the help, advice and encouragement of several individuals:
- My dear friends Hillel Kook (Peter H. Bergson) and Samuel Merlin, who were the wartime leaders of the Irgun Delegation in America;
- The late Dr. Julius Kuhl, who during World War II was one of the most prominent leaders of the Rabbinical Vaad Hatzalah in Switzerland and who, as a Polish diplomat stationed in Berne, actually aided several thousand Jews to escape from Hungary and other Nazi-occupied countries;
- Dr. Reuben Hecht of Haifa, who was Jabotinsky's emissary in the Balkans, and who together with Dr. Kuhl and the Sternbuchs achieved results in the field of rescue;
- My late friend, Irving M. Bunim, the leader of the Young Israel movement in America;
- Leah Belfon, who assisted in the editing of this manuscript;
- My daughter, Atara Beck, who patiently helped me to read and edit the most complicated chapters of this book;
- My daughters, Ilana Ovadya and Cynthia Berke, as well as my grandson, Steven Ovadya, for their help in reading the proofs;
- And my publisher, Howard Aster of Mosaic Press for his special interest in this manuscript.

This book is a result of my involvement with the Irgun Delegation in America. This experience I owe to my late wife, Dorothy C. Nurenberger, co-founder and Acting Editor of the **Canadian Jewish News** until her premature demise in September 1970. Despite all difficulties and the personal persecution suffered by anyone connected with the Irgun, Dorothy encouraged me; and before she passed away she asked me to ensure that someday I write the story of my involvement with the Irgun Delegation in America for the benefit of her children and her children's children. Thus I hope that my daughters Ilana Ovadya, Cynthia Berke and Atara Beck; my sons in-law Elyahu Ovadya, Gary Berke, and Meyer Beck; my grandchildren Steven, Ephraim, Benjamin and Doron Ovadya, Deborah and Jordana Berke, Devora and Dov Beck and their children will find in this book an answer to the question: "Where were you during the years of the Holocaust?"

The cartoon by Arthur Szyk is reprinted from **Answer Magazine** and by permission of its editor Samuel Merlin. Many photos are from the Archives of **Answer Magazine** and the Institute for Mediterranean Affairs, New York, N.Y. Some photos are from the Archives of Herman Landau, Toronto, Ont., and from the Archives of M.J. Nurenberger.

I
Prelude

On February 10, 1939, the Department of State of the United States informed President Franklin Delano Roosevelt of a secret cable sent to Myron Taylor and George Rublee, the American representatives at the Intergovernmental Refugee Committee meetings in London. The wire contained instructions from the then Secretary of State, Cordell Hull, concerning a "program of emigration" of Jews from Nazi-controlled territory, a program "which the German government had indicated its willingness to carry out." In this message, Taylor, who was in charge of the so-called refugee program, was informed by Hull that the U.S. Government wished "to emphasize certain general considerations."

The first consideration was that Taylor and Rublee should "emphasize" to the Refugee Committee that, in negotiations with the Germans, the problem of emigration and resettlement of Catholics, Protestants and others should also be discussed — as if the "Catholics, Protestants and others" were facing a similar danger.

The State Department found the memorandum to Taylor and Rublee, who had negotiated with Germans, "insufficient" because "it relates exclusively to Jews." Yet this was the period of German antisemitic activity when most of the members of the Nazi government still believed that the Jews were a commodity important to the democracies, and that other governments would accept Jewish emigrants.

Among the Nazi leaders, Goehring and Schacht were interested in getting rid of the Jews "in a civilized manner" — as long as some other country would welcome them. Apparently they believed that such a "civilized" policy against Jews would neutralize American public opinion, so the German government appointed a certain Dr. Wohltat to negotiate with the Americans and the British an organized exodus of Jews from German-controlled territory.

Yet the State Department immediately started finding loopholes in the program and kept postponing decisions. In a memo signed by Sumner Welles, then Undersecretary of State, the Department declared unacceptable the condition that a program will be put into effect "only when Germany is satisfied that the countries of immigration are disposed to receive Jews."

Thus, at the very beginning, the State Department threw a monkey wrench into a program that had already been accepted by its representative on the Intergovernmental Refugee Committee.

This memo, aired to London on February 10, 1939, seven typewritten pages long, was complicated enough to demonstrate that the United States was not ready to help alleviate the plight of the Jews. Although the program was only a limited one (it dealt with the immigration of 150,000 persons over a period of five years), the Department still made it clear that as far as immigration into the United States was concerned, "Our immigration laws would not permit the intervention of any agency between applicant and consulate." Thus the entire program was made dependent upon the "regulations." No change!

Does it not sound cynical when, in conclusion, Secretary of State Cordell Hull congratulated Rublee for a "mission accomplished" in Berlin? This was the manner in which the State Department treated any suggestion for evacuation of Jews from Hitler-held territory. Myron Taylor was supposed to act, following the convention in Evian, in 1938, when an intergovernmental committee for refugees was established. There was hope of evacuating the Jews, according to another secret message from Taylor to U.S. Ambassador Bullitt in Paris; the German emigration plans were first "proposed by Schacht," in the name of the German government.

The very tenor, the style, the approach to this problem of saving human lives is characteristic: The life-and-death struggle of the Jews is covered in the euphemism, "refugee situation." But the correspondence shows that there was hope for rescue. Even Mussolini was informed of the problem and, according to American diplomatic representatives, was ready to help evacuate the Jews from Hitler's territory if a country could be found to receive them.

In another document submitted to the president by Sumner Wells, Roosevelt was informed that the American representative Robert Pell "had a long, secret conference with Jewish leaders in Berlin." According to this memo, dated March 8, 1939, the Jewish leaders "are, of course, very nervous and jumpy, and inclined to discount much of what we are doing."

In the same document, the U.S. government was advised that "Goehring wished to go ahead with his (emigration) program, but desires ammunition with which to justify his activities to Hitler."

It seems from this communication that Hitler did not believe any country would take the Jews en masse, despite the negotiations between Americans and Wohltat.

The situation, according to this confidential memo from Pell, was:

(a) "the ammunition (needed by Goehring) is to take the form of the memorandum on settlement projects which I am to take back to Berlin in a fortnight's time;

(b) the Jews became somewhat optimistic when they heard that Goehring "is centralizing the administration of the emigration . . ." But they insisted they have to get their people out, whether there is an easing of the tension or not . . . At any moment an incident might occur which would endanger the very lives of their people."

While the German Jews, according to this secret information transmitted from the embassy to the State Department, were "nervous and jumpy," in the United States the "official" Jewish leaders were busy fighting the Irgun emissaries who were alarming public opinion about the necessity of evacuation.

The German Jewish leaders, according to the State Department files, secretly informed the Americans that there was "illegal" emigration going on — not only towards Palestine (the Irgun shiploads on the Danube and in the Mediterranean), but also boats moving towards Shanghai and the Caribbean.

They warned the Americans that "we could not afford to take chances . . . They were ready to yield to the enticement of shipping companies and let their people emigrate without papers and without a fixed destination . . . they said there are no opportunities for emigration, except the small American quota and limited refugee opportunities in England. The rest of the world had dried up."

The American representative then told the German Jewish leaders that "when they insist upon *force majeure* and reveal their plight to the world in a dramatic fashion, they are doing more harm than good, and that they were defeating American efforts." The Jews were told to be nice, not dramatize their plight.

The State Department representative thus reported the reaction of the Jewish leaders in Berlin to his appeal for calm:

" . . .They laughed in my face . . . after six years of dealing with this problem, they are very hard . . . They do not believe in promises . . . Too many promises have been broken . . . They want action and are in a state of mind where they will force action."

These are only the main points of this statement. Again, it must be stressed that during that period, Irgun emissaries were busy moving "illegal" refugees on boats through the Danube. These emissaries were denounced by official Zionist leaders for obstructing the policy of selective emigration to Palestine. In the United States, the Irgun representatives were prevented from collecting funds by professional Jews in the established organizations. The Irgun emissaries who alarmed the American public were constantly and consistently harassed. How they were able to function baffles me to this day. The British were at war with the potential emigrants to Palestine, and, in every European port, British officials were ordered to disrupt any activity on behalf of the socalled illegal emigration to Palestine. The Irgun emissaries had to fight on two fronts.

The negotiations with Schacht and Wohltat did not break up even after the start of World War II. Until America's entrance into the war there was a chance of evacuation. From President Roosevelt's personal file, and from State Department documents, it becomes clear beyond any doubt that one faction of Nazi leaders continued to believe — or pretended to believe — that "the world" might accept Jewish refugees. So, the United States, which still had diplomatic relations with Germany, pursued the talks through Myron Taylor and George Rublee. In fact, in a memorandum "for the president" from Assistant Secretary of State Adolph A. Berle, Jr., dated October 23, 1939, the following picture emerges: Mr. Berle is disappointed. It seems Taylor finally gave up. Berle is informing Mr. Roosevelt that Mr. Taylor is coming to see him because "Taylor committed himself to the British and French thesis before the Inter-Governmental Committee on Refugees meeting." The British and French thesis was to prevent Jews from getting out; they could, God forbid, move on to Palestine! (Berle, 1939)

Says Berle: "After your speech, the French and the British bucked all along the line. They took Myron Taylor into camp completely. Their view was that if they won the war, there would be no refugee problem.

"In committee we stood squarely on the theme of your speech, namely, that we ought to go on studying, surveying, and doing the engineering for resettlement of refugees . . . we are somewhat embarrassed that Taylor committed himself to the British and French.

"If the British and French want to kill the idea, they ought to take the responsibility without hooking you in on it."

II
Leaving Europe:
The Equation of a Rabblerouser

I left Europe for the United States right after Munich, having decided to emigrate as a direct result of an experience as a reporter at the Belgian-French border, in a small village close to the industrial city of Roubaix. My assignment was to describe the reaction of the average French and Belgian worker and farmer to the crisis on the eve of Munich when Chamberlain, Daladier, Mussolini and Hitler met to establish "peace in our time."

It was an experience I shall never forget. Perhaps my reaction to and remembrance of those days are conditioned by the fact that I was a Jew living but a few hundred miles from the German border and, like most Jews on the European continent at the time, I wondered how long I would be able to exist side by side with the Nazis. While all of us Jews cherished the freedom and liberal ambiance we enjoyed in Belgium, France and Holland, we wondered: Will the world allow Hitler to expand, to conquer still more countries and extinguish the lights of freedom in such cities as Paris, Brussels and Amsterdam — even across the channel in London?

Those who did not live in that part of Europe prior to World War II cannot understand what we had, and what we lost. To the young men and women of my generation that time of life became a shattering experience. I remember having nightmares that Hitler would march into Brussels, goose-stepping down the Grand' Place to the entrance of the famous little café where Karl Marx wrote *Das Kapital*.

In those days it was marvelous to walk the streets and boulevards of Brussels. Young students who could not afford to drive cars would promenade for miles through the early hours of the morning, discussing the future of the continent.

We were a generation of dreamers, sensitive and romantic. I remember one friend in particular who, at odd hours, wrote beautiful Hebrew poetry. He and I were the first to "invent" the site-to-site missile, and sending missiles back and forth became one of our most cherished pastimes which amused many habitués at our café table. It was our hope that perhaps someone would design a missile which would take off from the pebbles of the café and hit Adolf Hitler directly in his chancellery in Berlin. That, we said, would be poetic justice: a missile from Karl Marx to Adolf Hitler.

It was not only self-preservation, this fear of Hitler; it was also a profound concern for the people we loved, a deep concern for our fellow men. We did not want anyone to be hurt in the process of eliminating Hitler, not even the Germans around him.

The most enthusiastic supporter of our "missile program" was a young

Catholic lawyer, Gerard, editor of the daily newspaper published by the students at Louvain, the most famous Catholic University in the world. The newspaper, *Avant-Garde,* was liberal and very anti-Nazi. Gerard was a tall, blonde, handsome young man, one of the "planners" of our nonviolent revolution.

After all, the ideal of a European community is not the result of a fantasy. There *is* a Western European community and, in my younger years, Western Europe and England seemed like one big backyard. We moved easily from country to country and, even during the Nazi period, I visited Germany several times, for I wanted to see what was happening there. I vividly recall a conversation with a German to whom I said something I still believe to be true. When he asked why I hated Germany,. my reply was: For the first time in my life you have forced me to hate an entire nation.

* * *

This incident occurred following a tremendous controversy at the Foreign Press Association in the Brussels Press House. Looking back it seemed exactly like a miniature rehearsal of the developments during World War II, at a time when people who should have spoken out remained silent.

The incident was caused by the German Ambassador to Belgium. Each year in Brussels there was a fancy press ball, a highlight of the social calendar. The Foreign Press Association, to which I belonged and of which I was the youngest member, had invited the famous singer, Josef Schmidt, to be the featured attraction at this gala evening.

Frankly, I loved this type of affair because the most beautiful girls vied for tickets and invitations. However, Josef Schmidt, then the Frank Sinatra of Europe, was a Jewish refugee from Vienna. For this reason the German ambassador notified the Foreign Press Association that he would not attend the ball and, in fact, that he had cancelled his reservations. The Committee of the Foreign Press Association was forced to consider two problems: one, the reaction of the Belgian Foreign Offices; and two, the treasury of the Association which depended to a large extent on the income from the ball.

My intervention at that meeting was perhaps the beginning of my career as a rabblerouser in journalism, the start of my continual refusal to accept considered opinions and socalled responsibility when moral issues are at stake. Yet before making my "maiden speech" I was very afraid of losing this battle.

A Polish-Jewish journalist, an elderly gentleman, begged me to forget the whole thing and not create a Jewish issue at the Association. Surprisingly, he was a socialist, but yet I was determined that he would not prevail upon me to keep silent. All I said was, "Are we in Hitler's Berlin or in the free capital of free Belgium? Are we going to adopt Nuremberg laws?" I concluded with a satirical remark that in such a case it would be necessary for me to change my family name, "for I am sure the German ambassador would have preferred a Jew like me not to have been called Nurenberger."

So, in the fall of 1938, while I was covering the situation at the Belgian-French border during the Munich crisis, I thought of that Foreign Press Association meeting and what had happened subsequently.

The house of the Foreign Press Association in Brussels is situated in one of the most picturesque parts of the city — not far from the parliament buildings, across the street from St. Gudule, one of the most beautiful cathedrals in Europe. One day when I was leaving the Press Club, a German colleague, Bayer, the correspondent of the *Voelkischer Beobachter,* pointed to the street lamp and said to me in German, "When Hitler occupies this city, you will hang from this lamp post."

I was flabbergasted, but managed to reply, "I shall try to prevent exactly that — a Hitler occupation of Brussels. What we are doing, those of us who despise your philosophy of hatred, is trying to prevent you from wiping out all the beauty that generations of good people have produced in this part of the world."

I had yet another "battle" with the German government, a more direct one. This occurred at the German Embassy in Brussels. Hjalmar Schacht, then Hitler's financial wizard, had arrived in Belgium, and a press conference was held at the embassy. As a working journalist, I was among those invited. Schacht made a fervent plea that all world governments immediately stop discriminating against Germany. During the question period, I rose from my seat and asked, "Would it be inopportune to ask His Excellency whether a plea for the end of discrimination against Germany would not be more effective if it were followed by a statement that the Government of the Reich has decided to end all its discrimination against its own citizens, including the Jews?"

This again was considered by all "nice" colleagues to be a provocation. After all, Schacht was "not a Nazi." The old fox, ever a diplomat, replied, "This is a political question." Of course I was only a reporter and could not continue the dialogue. What I did was leave the embassy in a manner that indicated I was leaving in protest. This was the *chutzpah* of a young reporter, a chutzpah which has remained with me to this day. I truly identify with my friend, Gerard, who once pointed out to me the old French slogan on his newspaper: "Ne crains *fors* Dieu!" (Don't fear anyone *but* God.)

* * *

In the *Estaminet* of the French village from where I reported the Munich scene, I spent the evenings drinking wine at the village inn and talking to the people, mostly workers, some of them coal miners from the district of Lille. There was no television at that time, only radio. We would all sit at the little wooden tables, fascinated by the voices from the Bavarian capital. We knew that war might break out at any moment. And, while sipping the inexpensive but excellent red wine, we talked of war and the futility of war.

Even then, in this little village café, one could detect the effects of German fifth-column propaganda. Some people said France had no business becoming involved in the war, that it was only a matter between the Jews and the Germans, or between the Communists and the Nazis. What Hitler had succeeded in creating was the fear of war and the feeling among the masses that there could be an accommodation with Nazi Germany. After all, people said, no one could be as bad as Hitler was made out to be. What really shocked me at this border village was the widespread euphoria at the news that the Munich Pact had been signed and there would be no war. At the village inn people were hugging and kissing each other with sheer joy. Feigning a headache, I apologized and went up to my room. I thought, what next?

*   *   *

A few weeks later I left for London, England, where I spent a week at the home of Isaac Nachman Steinberg, having been put in touch with him by the editor of a Belgian newspaper with which I was connected. (Steinberg died in New York several years ago, but in 1938 he was in his prime, full of life and energy.) I was received like a member of the family. What struck me most at his home in Aberdeen Gardens was the religious Jewish atmosphere. Isaac Nachman Steinberg, as students of contemporary Russian history may recall, was one of the leaders of the Democratic Russian Socialist Movement (S.R.) and Lenin's first minister of justice. However, few people knew that he was also a practising, orthodox Jew. How Steinberg managed to be Lenin's Commissar of Justice and *daven* three times a day, I am at a loss to understand. He was probably the only international socialist leader who observed the Sabbath as did his grandfather before him. Once he walked thirty blocks on a Saturday afternoon (from 72nd Street to the Commodore Hotel) in order to give a press conference, refusing to take a car or a streetcar because it was Shabbat. How sad it is to remember such a man in the context of what happened to the Russian revolution and to the Jews of Russia!

Several years after I visited him in London, Steinberg moved to New York and became the leader of the Jewish Territorialists, who sought a Jewish country outside of Palestine; he died a dreamer.

Apparently, it never occurred to anyone during the era of Lenin and Trotsky to harass Steinberg because he was a religious Jew. The conflict between Lenin and Steinberg's political party, the Social Revolutionaries, had nothing to do with Steinberg's Jewishness; the conflict arose from his opposition to dictatorship. (Steinberg was made Commissar of Justice after the October Revolution in Petrograd in 1917. He held this post until 1918.)

When Steinberg left the Soviet Union in 1923 for Berlin, where the majority of anti-Bolshevik Russian exiles were living, his friends told me that he was neither bitter nor angry. Up until the last moment of his life, and despite his daughter's tragic death of cancer, his countenance was benign, friendly and ever-smiling. He was also one of the very few people who look like they truly are: He was tall, had a beautiful Russian-style trimmed beard and the manners of a prince. I don't believe that Isaac Steinberg ever disappointed anyone, or that he ever compromised in matters of ideology or religious belief. During the last months of his life Steinberg was sceptical about Zionism because of the Arab problem. He believed in a democratic version of socialism as the solution to the problems of humanity and in the perpetuation of Judaism, particularly in its ethical expression as the mission of our people. Steinberg lived what he preached. My friend, the Belgian editor and socialist leader, was right when he told me that Steinberg was the last prince of the international socialist movement.

*   *   *

London at that time was not only the capital of the British empire, but was also the most civilized city in the world. The headquarters of many international Jewish organizations were located there. At 77 Great Russell Street, not far from the British Museum, stood the building of the World Zionist Organization. Jewish leaders, especially Zionists, still believed in the moral integrity of England, despite past disappointments. Even the Zionist Revisionists, whose leader, Vladimir Jabotinsky, had consistently warned Jews against relying upon Britain's commitments to Zionism and had preached a militant philosophy for Jewish self-emancipation, had their headquarters in London. The Irgun, the fledgling Hebrew underground army of Palestine, also had an office there.

Jewish leaders who had dealings with the Foreign Office and the Colonial Office, regardless of political conditions, always drew the line between the civilized manner of the individual British official and the ruthless policies which were the legacy of colonialism. Of course very few believed then that British imperialism was tottering. No one could have foreseen the day when Churchill would say, "I did not become His Majesty's prime minister in order to preside over the liquidation of the British Empire," nor that his statement would be received by world public opinion with a benevolent smile.

That England could simultaneously produce the utopian dreams of the Fabian Society and the most hypocritical diplomats such as Neville Henderson, the last Ambassador to Nazi Germany, I believe to be a charm of that country — a charm which has faded forever. It was perhaps this unusual quality of London that lulled Zionist leaders between the wars into believing that one could rely upon Great Britain. The civilized face of the British capital somehow always covered the brutality committed in the colonies.

Chaim Weizmann, who considered himself an Englishman by choice, was not alone in his profound committment to British policies in Palestine. Even Vladimir Jabotinsky never lost his belief in British fair play, despite the colonialist treatment of Jewish emigrants at the hands of the Foreign Office. He, too, thought that a change in British policy was conceivable, but that it would be brought about only by more militant and determined Jewish efforts. Weizmann believed that a change would eventually make it possible for Palestine to absorb Jewish refugees from Europe and that Britain would then discharge her obligations according to the League of Nations' mandate.

From London in the autumn of 1938 one beheld a rapidly disintegrating European continent. Jews were locked within the Fortress Europe, which was ripe for complete takeover by Hitler. In those countries where Jews lived in great numbers, anti-Semitism was rampant. Yet the great democracies indirectly

assisted the Nazis in preparing the Jewish communities for extermination by lock-
ing this Fortress from without and refusing to admit Jews fleeing from the
slaughterhouse. Without exception, the doors of the Free World were closed to
Jewish refugees. One has only to remember the abortive 1938 Evian Conference
and the tragic case of the ship St. Louis. Loaded with Jewish refugees from
Europe, it moved from country to country, including Canada, the United States
and Cuba. But no country accepted them. They were sent back to Hamburg.

*   *   *

Like many young Jews of that period, I was under the influence of those great
orators and political showmen whom many of our people called Jewish leaders.
Like all Jews who love oratory, I used to enjoy hearing the fabulous speeches
at Zionist Congresses in Switzerland, which usually took place at the most ap-
propriate time: summer vacation. We would gather in a picturesque resort like
Lucerne, or in postcard towns and cities such as Basle, Geneva and Zurich, and
endlessly debate Jewish problems. As we listened to the fiery speeches, we believed these congresses were internationally recognized parliaments that could make
decisions on behalf of our people and change the march of history. We were young
and naive and did not realize that among the few hundred Jews who gathered
at these meetings was an elite living upon the misery of the millions in Poland,
Romania, Hungary and other countries where the Jewish people were denied
all human rights.

Resolutions were always passed, and protest statements never failed to impress the delegates. I can still see the British chargé d'affaires at the Zionist Congresses, smiling at those beautifully nonviolent expressions of disappointment
with British policy — the policy that closed the doors of Palestine to the people
whose homeland it was supposed to be, according to the solemnly undertaken
obligations of His Majesty's government.

The Jewish masses in Eastern Europe were the victims of delusions nourished
by these leaders. Were these people charlatans? I doubt it. The more I think about
those years during which the fate of the Six Million was sealed, the more I am
convinced that the Jewish leaders of the time — like those who follow in their
footsteps and are the product of their philosophy — were tragic figures. They
were of a ghetto mentality, a mentality nourished throughout hundreds of years
of living by sufferance rather than by right. Once a man loses his right to be free,
to forge his own destiny, to be equal; once he compromises with human liber-
ties and accepts the status of a pariah, he becomes a slave. The biblical description of the slave who refuses liberation, who says "I love my master" and to whom
the Year of Jubilee is meaningless, is the prototype of certain leaders of the Jewish
people in the diaspora. (Exodus XXI:5)

Before and during the Second World War we were lulled into accepting the
fact that a Jew has to beg for a niche in which to live; that he belongs to a minority
and always has to ask for concessions and handouts. Perhaps the character who
says, "Sir, give me a penny," when the prince is ready to raise him from his status

of an underdog, could best fit the description of certain Jews.

*　　　*　　　*

Now, four decades after World War II, I tend to envy those who can just pass over the years of collective Jewish paralysis. I believe, however, that the Jewish problem still calls for a profound analysis of our past deeds so that a similar tragedy will never be repeated.

In 1933 Vladimir Jabotinsky warned the Zionist Congress in Prague that unless Jews were prepared to fight, the civilized world would accept Hitler's view of Jews as non-persons. I believe that Jewish passivity began with the socalled Transfer Deal in 1933, when cunning Zionist leaders out-maneuvered Jabotinsky and signed an agreement with the Nazis to transfer Jewish capital from the Reich to Palestine.

To this day many speak of the Transfer Deal as a great achievement. Essentially it was an acknowledgement by Jews that Germans of Jewish origin or of the Jewish faith were not equal citizens; that the German government had the right to expel them and legally confiscate most of their holdings. The Transfer Deal of 1933, signed between the Jewish Agency and the German Nazi authorities, allowed wealthy German Jews who emigrated to Palestine to export German goods representing but a small percentage of their property. These goods were then sold throughout the Middle East. Thus the Jewish Agency at that time indirectly became a sales organization promoting Nazi goods in the Middle East.

Although some Jewish capital was saved through this agreement, the Transfer Deal was, in my opinion, the first act of Jewish surrender to Hitler. It created a world image of a Jew who would beg for a penny, a Jew whose moral destruction culminated in the acceptance of the socalled Reparations Deal between German Chancellor Konrad Adenauer and the government of Israel.

Jabotinsky had fought this attitude; he sensed the inherent danger in accepting dollars for the surrender of Jewish dignity. There were many in the Jewish organizations, however, who managed to convince quite a number of Jews that this was a clever move (typical Jewish *chochme*). The war against Jabotinsky, followed by the wars against the Irgun, made a united Jewish resistance impossible and indirectly prepared the ground for the great tragedy of World War II. The mentality of relying upon professional organizations and an elite leadership (most of whom abandoned Europe at the decisive moment) still threatens the entire Jewish way of life and, indeed, our very survival.

Although I did not yet fully appreciate Jabotinsky during those years, I was still offended by the "great achievement" the Transfer Deal was supposed to represent. The Transfer Deal was negotiated by an outstanding Jewish leader, Chaim Arlosoroff, who had lived in Germany before settling in Palestine and was reported to have been a former boyfriend of Goebbels' wife, Magda. I do not know whether this is true, but so it was rumored in the cafés by those who praised the "intelligence" of the Jewish leaders who had saved Jewish capital from Germany through the Transfer Deal. The surrender of dignity was so obvious that it led to an incident which I can never forget; it also led to a certain initiative on the part of David Ben Gurion.

At a press conference at a Zionist Congress in Switzerland I asked Ben Gurion whether it was true that he had sent a cable from Jerusalem to the Nazi government expressing the Jewish Agency's condolences upon the death of Field Marshal Paul von Hindenburg, President of the Reich. The reporters could not believe that Ben Gurion would do such a thing, but I had the document in my pocket. In his usual challenging manner, Ben Gurion, in the tone of a man who is always right, declared: The Jewish Agency is the Jewish government en route. And it is therefore incumbent upon it to try to maintain, as much as possible, normal relations with a foreign state.

This incident led me to publish a very bitter article against Ben Gurion in which I spoke of his betrayal of Jewish youth, of his insult against my generation. I condemned the Transfer Deal as an act of recognition by Jews that the Nazis had the right to discriminate against the Jewish people. I also attacked the attitude of the official Zionist press in Germany, especially the newspaper *Juedische Rundschau,* which headlined the news about the yellow badge in the following words: *Wir tragen mit Stolz den gelben Fleck!* (We carry the yellow badge with pride.) Then and there I decided never to carry the yellow badge with pride. Even though I regarded myself as a man of peace, I swore that I would kill anyone who would force me to live in a ghetto or wear a yellow star.

I profoundly believe that this naive attitude of the official Zionist leadership — vis-à-vis the Nazis — indirectly influenced the passivity of the Jewish people the world over in the oncoming confrontation with Nazism. All the weaknesses, all the foibles of the following years stemmed from the Jews' acceptance of the inferior position thrust upon them.

This surrender to Nazi racial philosophy was the prelude to Jewish laissez-faire during the period of extermination. It also created a psychological ghetto that would result in the disastrous failure of the establishment leaders to rescue their doomed brethren.

If the Jewish revolution in Israel has transformed the Jew from one who passively accepts toleration to one who fights for the right to live, this has come about only because Israel rejects the submissive, ghetto mentality. This mentality was the very essence of the official Zionist policy vis-à-vis Hitler's Germany.

*   *   *

After Munich, when I left London for the United States, I still retained some of the illusions that had nourished the Jews of my generation. I held, for example, the profound belief that liberalism would combat Hitlerism and save humanity from destruction. Like many of my generation, I had confidence in the rest of the world. We believed the world could not possibly be so bad; it could not accept persecution as its daily bread. How wrong we were!

*   *   *

It took several years before I began to doubt the basic humaneness of the world. In 1938 it seemed that only the European leadership had become callous and could not respond to the challenge. But there was hope: The new, growing Jewish community in the United States had imbued us with faith. Thus while I, the young man leaving Europe for North America, was profoundly disappointed in the old Jewish leadership in Europe, I believed all the publicity about the militant American Jewish leadership ready to take up the struggle for the liberation of the Jewish people of Europe in that tragic, post-Munich period. To go to America where Jewish leaders and Jewish organizations were so relatively young was to be obsessed with one thought: how to rescue the Jews of Europe.

By the time I arrived in America I had already met most of the Zionist leaders at meetings in Switzerland and elsewhere. Some of them, such as the late Dr. Stephen S. Wise, were orators fit for the Roman forum. Wise had a lion's voice; he never needed a microphone. He was tall and handsome and wore his hair very long. To European Jews, this clean-shaven rabbi without a *yarmulka* was very different and modern. Because of his English phraseology, beautiful diction and his personal friendship with F.D.R., we believed that he could and would solve problems, impress statesmen, change situations and revolutionize Jewish policies. I think he loved to be called "the Jewish pope," although one of his opponents said of Wise, "As a theologian, he is the blank page between the Old and the New Testament." At the time I was not aware of his intellectual limitations, of his very superficial knowledge of Judaism and Torah.

III
The Malaise:
"Mi Berosh"

On Friday, September 1, 1939, the first day of World War II, while still a cub reporter, I boarded a street car at Sea Gate, then a Jewish writers' summer resort off Coney Island, Brooklyn. The day was beautiful, glorious; the blue skies reflected in the Atlantic as I, a new American, strode nervously through the rush-hour crowd.

The previous night the Germans had invaded Poland; the British and French were about to declare war on Hitler. But on the trolley from Sea Gate to the Coney Island subway, no one else seemed nervous, perturbed or even concerned. There was only the usual laughter and light chatter among the passengers.

                    *   *   *

A woman on the seat in front of me opened her newspaper. The screaming front-page headlines about the European war failed to attract her attention. She turned instead to the lonely hearts column, reading avidly till the end. Intrigued, I wondered: Would the woman ignore the most ominous event of the century? Again she turned the pages, this time to the classified section. Then she switched to a sensational story about some Hollywood scandal. Finally, in typical New York subway fashion, she tossed away the newspaper.

Mustering my most elegant continental manner, I asked whether I might take a look at the paper she had just discarded.

"Go ahead, young man," she said.

I ventured a question: "Did you see that World War II has started?"

"Oh," she laughed, "in Europe there are always wars. Who cares? We are far away . . ."

The woman was an elderly Jewess; the newspaper, printed in Yiddish.

                    *   *   *

Since that day in Coney Island I have never ceased to wonder at the lack of understanding among Americans, Jews and non-Jews alike, of what transpires beyond their continent — a handicap that continues to plague us despite World War II, despite the Korean War, despite Vietnam and despite international terrorism. To me it seems that this peculiar Yankee attitude — the posture of an overly self-confident people — remains fundamental to the political exploitation of the American masses by unscrupulous politicians. Perhaps the contemporary revolt of young Americans signifies the rejection of the isolationist psychology which characterized those who immigrated here, a sentiment they transmitted to their children.

Undoubtedly, on that September day in 1939, the vast majority of American Jews were not involved in the drama which shook Europe. The S.O.S. from across the Atlantic, from the continent with the largest Jewish population in history — and the old home of most of them — was not picked up by the leadership of the American Jewish community. Even today one must question how profoundly American Jewry was moved by the rise of Hitler and his subsequent war of extermination against the Jewish people.

Surely the dictum that environment molds consciousness is true of the American Jew as he awakens from the nightmare of the most tragic years in all Jewish history. Ever since he arrived on this continent, the American Jew has been conditioned to believe that his social duties and community obligations are as divided as the functions of workers on an assembly line: The member of the synagogue pays his dues and shells out his contributions. The rabbi attends to God, the congregant to business. The school is responsible for the education of children. The community leader is left in full charge of the organization, for he knows best how to handle all the problems that, directly or indirectly, constitute a challenge to the Jew as a citizen in general and as a member of the Jewish community in particular. There is also an organization to protect the Jew from antisemitism. Last but not least, there are professionals who secure the future of Israel. Thus the average North American Jew, like the woman on the subway from Coney Island, feels that he or she can easily afford to read the comics or the lonely hearts column in full knowledge that any problem he might face, either as a Jew or as a North American, is being expertly handled by the most efficient professionals.

It would seem, then, that the very possession of an American passport creates contempt toward anyone questioning the self-righteousness cf the Jewish Babbit. The tendency to disassociate oneself from the outside world and its problems has, until recent years, profoundly influenced the Jewish immigrant generation in North America. Even today the involvement of the majority of North American Jews with Israel is conditioned by charitable motives: the Jewish state is for others, for Jews from other continents.

Fleeing oppression and poverty, the Jewish newcomer to these shores was given to believe that once an American, he had nothing to fear. One has only to read the immigrant press — from its very beginnings until 1945 — to understand the New American. He believed that his American passport had solved his problems, ending his insecurity once and for all. But disenchantment followed euphoria when the Depression hit America in 1929. Immigrant communities were more deeply shaken than the old, established American groups, and confidence in the *goldene medina* (golden country) was temporarily undermined.

The Depression gave birth to radicalism and the influence of Union Square upon Jewish masses. Yet, as often happens in Jewish history, euphoria returned as the New Deal immediately transformed the Jewish community. Roosevelt was the new messiah, the God of the Jewish American. He was the liberal who would save the Jew from all evil and give him his daily bread as well. The average American Jew, influenced by "progressive" intellectuals, credulously returned once more to the worship of an invincible United States — a nation, so the creed went, powerful enough to reject and defeat all attempts to change it. The American Jew believed that Roosevelt was the saviour, that he had reestablished the America which symbolized security forever. Even social antisemitism and discrimination against Jews in employment, so widespread until World War II, never created a feeling of revolt. The average American Jew took this "benign" discrimination in stride. He accepted the reality that many businesses were closed to him, that certain hotels would not admit him. While the civil rights movement made American Blacks the most potent revolutionary force this continent has ever seen, no such movement ever stirred American Jews.

Roosevelt was always right, even when he ignored the threat to European Jews. Every politician was right, as long as he put on a *yarmulka* at a Jewish dinner and told the assembled, to their delight, that these manufacturers, real estate operators and garment workers were not ordinary people, but descendants of prophets.

In his autobiography, Bernard Baruch described the naive belief in the politician, the acute psychological dependency of the American Jew upon a leader-savior.

Baruch, probably the most influential Jew in American history, the maker of presidents, was also one of the most lucid observers of the political scene. In this autobiography he relates an amusing story of how Tammany Hall always had the votes of naive Jewish immigrants in its pocket.

One of Baruch's early political acquaintances, he tells us, was William Sulzer, "a flamboyant politician of the old school," later elected governor of New York as Tammany's candidate. Sulzer, who later committed "political suicide" by opposing the Tammany Hall boys, was a master in getting votes the old-fashioned way. Baruch writes: "Herbert Bayard Swope used to tell of the night Sulzer went down to New York's Lower East Side to address an audience of immigrant Jews. He assured these prospective voters that he had personally intervened to bring pressure on the Czar to end the terrible persecutions in Russia.

"To this day," Sulzer declared, trumpeting his alleged success, "Jews go down on their knees in gratitude to pray for William Sulzer."

Swope, then a young reporter, was alarmed by Sulzer's statement. Swope leaned forward and whispered loudly, "Billy, Jews don't pray on their knees."

Sulzer regarded him blandly: "They do when they pray for William Sulzer."

This worship of political idols, I believe, is still characteristic of most Jews. Perhaps the generation gap, from which the Jewish community suffers more than any other group in North America, stems from the fact that the educated youth of today remain unimpressed by the speechmaking and applause at socalled testimonial dinners — which usually end with the dessert of a political address. The young people of North America cannot become excited at the appointment of a "Jewish" judge, or even a "Jewish" cabinet minister, to the same extent as those whose upbringing was influenced for generations by the goy-pleasing ghetto mentality.

Yet in the decisive years of World War II, when the destiny of European Jewry hung in the balance, all Jewish organizational life was conditioned by impressing, or being impressed by, the gentile while ignoring the Damoclean sword hanging over the largest Jewish community in the world.

To better understand the atmosphere which bred this contempt for facts and led masses of people to cling to a mirage, one must realize that those who led the Jewish establishment never thought of altering policies. No matter how acute the problem, they never accepted the necessity for change. Paradoxically, despite their profound belief in the security of the Jewish future in America, they needed Jewish defense organizations, Jewish representative bodies in order to cultivate the illusion of a certain Jewish power which in turn would be recognized by the real power.

In the councils of Jewish organizations nothing is more important than a report of a "secret meeting" with an outstanding political figure or the chief executive of a nation. To this day nothing gives an organization more "power" within the community than being able to include a large number of delegates when the president of the United States or the prime minister of Canada receives a Jewish delegation. When any other ethnic or religious group meets with a head of state, the number of participants is very limited, and usually the meeting is off the record. As an editor of Jewish newspapers, I have always been amused by the photographs submitted for publication after such meetings. The dignitary receiving the delegation is frequently lost in the forest of heads of "leaders" who always have a cheesecake smile for the photographer — even when the issue under discussion is the hanging of the Jews in Iraq.

I have often thought that Philip Roth was wrong to depict Portnoy as a Jewish character as there is nothing particularily Jewish about this unfortunate *schlemiel.* If I had created Portnoy, I would have represented him as living out an act of *political* masturbation. This clinging to illusion, this absolute refusal to face reality, is the source of all the shortcomings in Jewish community life in North America — if reality means a challenge to act and, when necessary, to suffer.

*   *   *

C.F. Ramuz, the French-Swiss Nobel prize-winner, in his novel, *Farinet,* describes a village in Switzerland where all the farmers fall victim to a swindler selling fake gold. Finally the police catch up with the thief and arrest him. Yet the victims are unanimously opposed to prosecution; they refuse to accept the police statement that their gold is not genuine.

Likewise, despite the evidence, most of the "active members" of the North American Jewish organizations refused to face the truth with regard to their erring leaders and community professionals. Let us look at an example:

If the top man is fraudulent, how can he, as a member of the board, impress his son simply because he was appointed to a committee? If the committee is irrelevant, what is the significance of the "member"? And what self-respecting Jew is not a board member, somewhere?

In order to understand this psychology, one has only to ask why the World Zionist Organization and its political parties in the diaspora did not close shop after the establishment of the Jewish state. It did not help that Ben Gurion himself said that a Zionist is one who settles in Israel. Surely raising funds for Israel does not require the costly upkeep of all the political Zionist groups in the diaspora, replete with representatives of political parties relevant to life in Israel, but irrelevant outside the Jewish state.

To some extent, one could say that certain organizations have never recognized the rights of the citizens of Israel to determine their own policies. These groups only acknowledge the *de facto* existence of the Jewish state. Despite all the discussions in Jerusalem, whenever anyone makes a sincere effort to close the offices of such organizations, hue and cry is more intense than at any time of real danger to the Jewish people. And so the measures are postponed *sine die*.

*   *   *

Thus the question: How could six million Jews be exterminated in Europe with the full knowledge of their brethren, their flesh and blood, in the United States? How can one explain that during those years there was never a Jewish Montgomery or Jewish Alabama in the U.S.A.? How can one explain that while so many young Jews sacrificed their lives for Black rights, they were not inspired to fight for the Six Million? How is it possible that to this day very few individuals question reports of "activities" to save the Jews from Hitler's Europe during World War II? Where are the mysterious Jews saved by those who campaigned for their rescue, who inspired the belief that the Jewish organizations were "active," that the professional guardians of Israel neither slumbered nor slept?

*   *   *

Today, in retrospect, all this seems unbelievable. Perhaps it is an act of sub-conscious self-defense when, from time to time, a leader of a Jewish group publishes a statement criticizing Pope Pius XII for his silence or attacks Franklin D. Roosevelt for his lack of action on behalf of Europe's Jews.

Those among us who tried to awaken the conscience of America feel that we owe an explanation to our children. Today, when they read the unforgettable story of what happened in Europe during World War II, they ask: Did you know about it? And what did you do?

When I was with the American army in Germany right after World War II, most Germans, when queried about the Holocaust, would reply: "We did not know." Can the American Jewish leaders who were influential during World War II, who could have acted on behalf of European Jewry, emulate these Germans and say that they did not know?

*   *   *

Behind the exaggerated zeal expended at the anniversaries of ghetto upris-
ings, I detect not only hypocrisy, but the subconscious sabotage of truth. Perhaps
what we really should do is end the emphasis on martyr worship in Jewish history.

Once, during a television debate on the meaning of the Warsaw Ghetto revolt,
I explained my unorthodox position: There is a difference between a martyr and
a hero. The martyr dies beautifully, in despair, saving someone else's honor. The
hero conquers and survives. In most recent Jewish history, the contrast between
these two archetypes has become very sharp. Martyrdom was the lot of those
holy men and women, in Warsaw and other ghettos, who knew that they were
the last survivors of a slaughtered people and that they themselves were doomed
no matter what road they chose. The heroic battle is that of the fighters in Israel
who decided never again to be martyrs, but to be conquerors in order to live.

As a little boy in Europe, I was often told that Jews are cowards. Today we
are told that Jews are aggressors because they refuse to become martyrs in Israel.
Frankly, after two thousand years of martyrdom I like it better when we are called
aggressors. Generations of Jews have been drugged into this martyr worship, a
most dangerous psychological handicap when transmitted to a child through the
teaching of Jewish history.

*   *   *

Perhaps an elderly friend in New York is responsible for my writing this
memoir. We once attended a ghetto memorial assembly where he was deeply
moved by the guest speaker — and even more so by the Prayer for the Dead in-
toned by the cantor. He did not hear himself when he said to me after the
ceremony: "I enjoyed the *El Maleh Rahamim* and the *Kaddish*. The cantor was
magnificent. I enjoyed it so much I cried all the time. A *mechayeh* (That's
living.)"

It may be cynical to relate such a story, but it would be more cynical not to
explain to the younger generation the psychological factors which kept millions
of American Jews from seeing red when they heard that Jewish children in the
millions were being thrown into the crematoria of Auschwitz and Maidanek.

Many of us today believe: "We would know what to do now. Maybe we would
throw a bomb at the Red Cross building to call world attention to this unbelievable
crime." After all, no war crime can be compared to what happened there, because
nowhere in the world were a million-and-a-half children burned alive and their
clothing calmly sorted for the children of the master race. While all this happened, where were those who were dutybound to tell American Jews the horrible truth and arouse them to action?

*   *   *

During the first year of Hitler's rule, I, a young reporter, dared enter Berlin.
I sent a cable through London to the *Jewish Morning Journal* in New York predic-
ting the establishment of concentration camps for Jews in case of war. The story
appeared on the front page on the Eve of Rosh Hashanah, 1933, but who would

take seriously a story filed by a mere boy? Five years later, in 1938, I sent a full report to the same newspaper describing in detail the German plans to exterminate the Jewish people. To the New York editor the article seemed so unbelievable that it was published in the bulldog edition but thrown out of the city edition.

*   *   *

Yet it would be wrong to say that no efforts were made to organize a movement for the rescue of European Jewry; efforts were made by the minority, the dissenters. But they were thwarted by some of the most prominent leaders of American Jewry, a few of whom are still revered within the world Jewish community.

The efforts to save Europe's Jews heralded the beginning of the Jewish revolution which later led to the establishment of Israel. (The beginning of the Jewish revolution is the new era of the hero versus the martyr, which started with the arrival in New York of a few young men, inspired by the teachings of Vladimir Jabotinsky: the Irgun delegation.)

During his lifetime Jabotinsky was the most maligned Jewish leader; today, posthumously, he is among the most revered. Jabotinsky died in 1940 in a youth camp in New York state. His death at sixty of a heart attack was probably brought on by despair due to the utter callousness of the Jewish establishment towards the fate of their fellow Jews across the sea.

The way in which Jabotinsky and, subsequently, the Irgun delegation were received can best be ascribed to a chronic malady from which Jews in the diaspora have been suffering for two thousand years. According to the Talmud, this malaise caused the destruction of both Temples, and it continues to ravage our communities today. During World War II, when our alertness and most articulate efforts were so desperately needed, it caused the paralysis of body and mind.

What is this malady? It can be illustrated by a Talmudic story. In the tractate *Sanhedrin,* in a chapter dealing with those who have a share in the world to come, the rabbis tell us:

Jeroboam (the king who split the Jewish commonwealth into the separate kingdoms of Judah and Israel) has no part in the world to come. Why? The Lord, in his mercy, wanted to save the soul of Jeroboam, the man who imposed himself as king against His will. God seized Jeroboam by the lapel of his garment and said to him, "Repent! Then you and I and the son of Jesse (the Messiah) will take a stroll in paradise."

Jeroboam did not accept this suggestion without conditions. He asked: *Mi Berosh?* Who will be the one to march first (the son of Jesse, the descendant of David, to whom the throne belongs; or myself)? God answered: The Son of David will march first. Then Jeroboam refused; he would not repent.

Since the days of Jeroboam, *Mi Berosh* has been the primary cause of lost opportunities and the greatest tragedies in Jewish history. Who will march at the front? Who will sit on the dais? Who will be Man of the Year? Who will be the leader? Who will deliver the main speech? Who will introduce whom at a meeting? Who will be applauded by the ladies' auxiliary? *Mi Berosh?* How many Jews would have been saved during World War II if it had not been for *Mi Berosh?*

Not for a moment did the Jewish leaders think that all their meetings were worthless in the face of events. The *Mi Berosh* sickness weakened our community to the point where the Allied governments, involved as they were in fighting the war, unfailingly found support among the Jewish leadership for, quite literally, the most destructive policy of all: Postponing the rescue of the Jews held by Hitler.

IV
The Scared and the Doomed
Weizmann vs. Jabotinsky:
The Jewish Civil War

In the summer of 1937, at a World Zionist Congress in Zurich, a young reporter joined the assembly in applauding Chaim Weizmann, then president of the World Zionist Organization, following his "State of the Union" message. To most of us, Weizmann was the "King of the Jews." He lived like a monarch, always surrounded by a coterie of dedicated followers and less sincere professionals. He was tall, slender and regal in appearance, and many who knew Lenin said that Weizmann facially resembled the famous Russian revolutionary. It was also said that he looked a little bit like King Ibn Saud. One of Weizmann's opponents at the Congress jestingly remarked that although the Zionist leader lacked a harem, he had almost as many subordinates as the despot of Saudi Arabia.

A British journalist once observed that in London, from the Prime Minister to the least important cabinet official, they consider him (Weizmann) the uncrowned king of the Jews . . . his influence on Downing Street is immense.

The millions of poor Jews in Central and Eastern Europe believed it; they did not begrudge him his princely standard of living. Years later when I became critical of Weizmann's policies, I often thought of the admiration for this man among the Jews in the ghettos of Europe. I compared him to the Black politicians of Harlem in the forties. They, too, lived like kings amid the misery of the pariahs whose cause they were championing.

At the meeting in Zurich the gathering applauded Weizmann despite his proclamation that only two million — the young, the idealistic — would survive the oncoming flood. The others, he said, because of historical developments, would disappear "like dust."

As I think back at this terrible utterance of a leader of a people, I must confess in his defense that Weizmann was not cynical. He was a ghetto Jew, born and reared in Motele, near Pinsk, a little town in the Russian Pale. Because of his upbringing, to him Zionism was never a *revolutionary* movement as it was to Theodor Herzl, Max Nordau or Vladimir Jabotinsky. Weizmann's views reflected the traditional attitudes of Jews throughout two thousand years of the diaspora: Despite the tragedies that befell them, they maintained a naive trust in an abstract sense of justice which they believed would finally prevail among the nations of the world. Therefore, Weizmann remained steadfast in his conviction that any military action against the British occupation of Palestine was both futile and un-Jewish. In 1947, at a press conference in New York, Weizmann condemned military action on the part of Jews. Jews, he said, should not "play soldier." (By that time Weizmann had been ousted from the leadership of the Zionist Movement by Ben Gurion.) When asked what the alternative was, Weizmann replied, "God will help" — a statement befitting a rabbi, not a political leader. But his charisma was strong and his influence tremendous.

It is pertinent to remark that in Jewish history few political leaders of consequence came from a traditional Jewish milieu. The first liberator of the Jews, Moses, is described in the Bible as an assimilated Jew, a man brought up in the house of Pharoah. Yet when he observed an Egyptian torturing a Hebrew, Moses slew him. Herzl and Jabotinsky both came from non-Orthodox homes. Their attitude towards Zionism was one the world would understand, and they fought to save those whom Weizmann wrote off as "dust."

Jabotinsky was the perennial rebel within the Zionist movement. He was born in Russia but spent most of his formative university years in Western Europe, particularly in Italy, where he was resident correspondent for one of the leading Russian newspapers. He was a typical *fin-de-siècle* liberal with a profoundly innate feeling for human dignity. He respected controversial opinions, and would even bend down to a child when stopped and asked a question. Jabotinsky always listened to others. The paradox was that he was the most *unheard* statesman and writer within what is called the Jewish world. He was a stranger. He was completely free from the ghetto mentality, from fear of the *goy*. On the other hand, eminent Jewish leaders like Weizmann and Nahum Sokolow came from the *shtetl*, from the Yiddish-speaking towns and villages. They never failed to charm Jewish audiences with their Yiddish anecdotes and Yiddish accent.

Jabotinsky was brought up among Russian liberals and Western European intellectuals. His Zionism was intransigent; in this respect he resembled Theodor Herzl, the founder of the Zionist movement. Both men were quite alike in world view, background and manners. Jabotinsky always insisted on proclaiming to the whole world the *true* demands of the Jewish people for the re-establishment of Palestine as a Jewish state. He did not like the compromise formula of building a "national Jewish home" or "spiritual center" which some "wise men" within the Zionist movement produced in order not to shock the "Christian World."

This was why Jabotinsky formed the original Haganah in Jerusalem in the early twenties in reaction to the early Arab pogroms. Jabotinsky was the only Zionist leader to oppose the first partition of Palestine when Britain unilaterally split the mandated territory and Winston Churchill, then Colonial Secretary, turned over Trans-Jordan (today known as Jordan), the larger part of the Palestine, to King Abdullah.

Jabotinsky was the first Jewish leader to be arrested by the British, who imprisoned him at the Acre Fortress. (Twenty years later when his son, Eri, was in the same prison for smuggling "illegal Jewish immigrants" into Palestine, Jabotinsky, then in New York, could not hide his pride that his son had followed in his footsteps.)

The British finally released Jabotinsky and banned him from Palestine. He then travelled all over the world, moving the Jewish masses with his impassioned speeches and his writings. Refusing a British passport, Jabotinsky travelled on a Nansen document as a stateless person. He would accept no passport, he said, but one given him by the government of a free Jewish Palestine.

Jabotinsky was perhaps the only Jewish leader who never doubted that the Land of Israel would become the State of Israel, although he knew that those inheriting the fruits of his labor might liquidate him politically because of his candor and courage. In fact, Jabotinsky wrote in his will that no one was to transport his remains to the Land of Israel unless it was done upon the explicit instruction of the government of a sovereign Jewish state.

During the last few months of Jabotinsky's life (he died in 1940 in a youth camp in New York state) he was under constant attack by the Jewish establishment as an "irresponsible" leader and a pessimist. The campaign against him was so intensive that his last weeks in New York were truly miserable. The entire Jewish press, in the service of the establishment, did not let up in its ridicule. The treatment Jabotinsky received reminds me of Stefan Zweig's description of Herzl's ordeal among the Jews of Vienna at the turn of the century when he first spoke out on the need to establish a Jewish state. Children would run after Herzl in the streets, Zweig writes, and laughingly call him King of the Jews.

I remember accompanying Jabotinsky to a meeting where he was to speak in one of the towns on his American itinerary. Although only ten or fifteen people turned out, Jabotinsky did not cancel the meeting. He said to the assembled, "You are not responsible for those who did not come. You came to hear me." He spoke for two hours, then left without showing any emotion. Such grandeur is characteristic of a true believer.

In 1964, Jabotinsky "returned" to Israel. When Levi Eshkol, then prime minister, brought back his remains to their resting place in the National Cemetery in Jerusalem, the funeral cortège was the most impressive Israel had ever seen. In Tel Aviv alone over half a million people turned out to pay final tribute to a man who died in the diaspora, poor and misunderstood.

*   *   *

Who, then, was Vladimir Jabotinsky? Arthur Koestler, who, during his youth, was an ardent Zionist and went to Israel as a pioneer, tells us the story of this visionary who dared fight the establishment.

In *Arrow in the Blue* Koestler stated his impressions of official Zionism in the 1920's:

" . . . It was a depressing affair. It consisted mainly of appeals for money and money and more money for the Jewish National Fund, money for the Jewish Reconstruction Fund (today the United Israel Appeal), money for the Hadassah Hospital, money for the Hebrew University, for the Bezalel Art School; and money for the salaries of those engaged in collecting money. Zionism was meant as an escape from the ghetto, but the ghetto had caught up with it; it hung like a stale fog over Zionist Congresses and the clubs and offices of the movement. The main duty of its rank and file was to rattle the collection box at a kind of permanent charity bazaar. Hence the old joke: "Zionism means one man persuading another man to give money to a third man to go to Palestine.""

"The great vision of the founders of the movement, Herzl and Nordau, had been whittled down to this dreary, bureaucratized charity. World Jewry had not responded to the historic opportunity offered by the Balfour Declaration; during the ten years which followed it, less than 100,000 Jews had settled in Palestine. The very idea of a Jewish State had been relinquished in favor of the vague term 'National Home' which had no concrete meaning in international law. Immigration was only a small trickle — some ten to twenty thousand people a year. The achievements of the pioneers who drained the marshes and made the stony desert bear fruit again, were admirable, and equally admirable were their communal settlements, where the use of money was abolished and all property down to shirts and handkerchiefs was collectively owned.

"I was saved from disillusionment by a personality whose decisive part in the establishment of the Jewish State has not been sufficiently recognized. His name was Vladimir Jabotinsky."

*   *   *

Because Jabotinsky actually inspired what I call the Jewish Revolution, that is, all activist efforts for the liberation of Palestine from the British — and, indirectly, even the activities of the Irgun in America and Palestine — it is important to understand this unusual personality. I remember a most interesting conversation between Jabotinsky and Chaim Weizmann which took place in 1931 at the Zionist Congress in Basle, scene of the last public confrontation between Weizmann and Jabotinsky. Weizmann approached Jabotinsky and told him, "You made a wonderful speech."

To this Jabotinsky replied, "I am sorry that I cannot repay you with the same compliment."

The conflict between Weizmann and Jabotinsky over what road to take in the struggle for the national emancipation of the Jewish people and the establishment of sovereignty in Palestine has divided the Jewish people to this day. Weizmann was much shrewder than Jabotinsky. He was clever, well-mannered, and personally would never stoop to the level of his supporters' attacks against Jabotinsky. He refused to call Jabotinsky a "fascist." More than this, Weizmann remained Jabotinsky's friend for life. Weizmann's henchmen, however, used the most incredible political trickery to undermine Jabotinsky's position until they made it impossible for him to remain within the Zionist Organization.

Jabotinsky was naive when it came to friends. He was never able to believe that people are as bad as they are, or as conniving as politicians usually are. For example, he respected David Ben Gurion's integrity in the years when Ben Gurion's party machine conspired to liquidate him. When I spoke to Jabotinsky in New York he had only kind words for his political enemies. They knew it, and, therefore, did not hesitate to stab him in the back. Jabotinsky's attacks against his political opponents were frontal and open; those by his opponents were otherwise.

Notwithstanding their personal friendship, Weizmann used his great political talent to undermine Jabotinsky by innuendo and ridicule. In fact, Weizmann had fought Theodor Herzl the same way. In his memoirs Weizmann tells the story of his battles against Herzl. According to him, Herzl was a "Western Zionist" who did not understand the Jewish attitude, the feelings of traditional Jews. Herzl placed political achievement in the forefront of his priorities while Weizmann believed in practical colonization.

This enmity towards Herzl was superseded by Weizmann's fight against Max Nordau and Jabotinsky as well as other political Zionists, including Justice Louis Dembitz Brandeis.

First Herzl and later Jabotinsky fought for the international recognition of the Jewish aspirations in Palestine and for the establishment of a Jewish state. It was imperative, as Herzl formulated it, to find a solution to the *Judennot,* Jewish misery. Weizmann believed in a slow process of colonization in order to build a model center. He never fought for the right of mass immigration into Israel; his was the viewpoint of selective immigration. Because of this attitude, Weizmann won the support of the Jewish establishment in the West where Jewish philanthropists preferred his brand of Zionism to the policies of men such as Herzl, Nordau and Jabotinsky. The latter, lacking the "personal" diplomacy and the "finesse" of Weizmann, made these establishment Jews feel uncomfortable. First Herzl, then Nordau, then Jabotinsky agitated for a mass movement to save the Jews of Europe.

Weizmann had time; he always had time. In his autobiography, he speaks with pride of the fact that in 1948, when the Jewish state was established, there was a nation of 600,000 in Palestine. Six-hundred-thousand Jews — while six million had been exterminated! This was a Jewish state that satisfied Weizmann. He was afraid — and he admitted this himself — of mass settlement.

The high point of the controversy between Jabotinsky and Weizmann came when Weizmann openly attacked mass colonization against his belief in selective immigration. Weizmann describes the first blow against the movement of Polish Jews to settle in Palestine en masse:

In *Trial and Error*, he states, "The controversy had not yet reached, in 1922 and 1923, the fury which was to characterize it later, but it was already very lively. The year 1923 saw the beginnings of a change in the character of our immigration. The early immigrants had been preponderantly of the chalutz pioneer type. In 1923, a new regulation offered settlement visas to anyone who could show possession of twenty-five hundred dollars — this was called the capitalist category — and gave a much-needed opportunity to many Russian Jews stranded in Poland after the war. These new immigrants were permitted over and above those who received 'labor certificates.' And so the immigration figures rose month by month. So, unfortunately, did the unemployment figures, though much more slowly. I was uneasy. True, a considerable amount of capital was being brought into the country by these small capitalists, but openings in industry, trade and commerce were as yet limited, and the numerous small shops which seemed to spring up overnight in Tel Aviv and Haifa caused me no little worry. These people were, as I have indicated, not of the chalutz type, and some of them were little disposed to pull their weight in a new country. A few, in their struggle for existence, showed anti-social tendencies; they seemed never to have been Zionists, and saw no difference between Palestine as a country of immigration and, for instance, the United States. Many of them had no knowledge of Hebrew, and it was soon being said, rather ruefully, that at this rate Tel Aviv would soon be a Yiddish-speaking town. Even to the casual observer, the new immigration carried with it the atmosphere of the ghetto. In the end, I felt that I had to give warning. I had to give it many times, in fact; and its character may be gathered from a speech I made in Jerusalem in October, 1924.

"I said, among other things: 'When one leaves the Emek and comes into the streets of Tel Aviv, the whole picture changes. The rising stream of immigration delights me, and I am delighted, too, that the ships should bring these thousands of people who are prepared to risk their life's savings in the Jewish National Home. Nor do I underrate the importance of this immigration for our work of reconstruction. Our brothers and sisters of Dzika and Nalewki — I was referring to typical ghetto districts of Warsaw — are flesh of our flesh and blood of our blood. But we must see to it that we direct this stream and do not allow it to deflect us from our goal. It is essential to remember that we are not building our National Home on the model of Dzika and Nalewki. The life of the ghetto we have always known to be merely a stage on our road; here we have reached home, and are building for eternity.'

"This speech earned me the hatred of a great many Polish Jews, particularly the Mizrachi (religious Zionists) type — a hatred which I have never lived down. I daresay I might have put it more tactfully, but I felt too strongly to mind. Naturally, such statements got me into hot water; the new immigrants, with their three or four or five thousand dollars each, considered themselves just as good as the men from Daganiah and Nahalal, and I was accused of taking sides, and discriminating between one type of immigration and another. It was not that I did not realize the importance of the small capitalist for Palestine's economy; their industry, diligence and frugality were invaluable assets. But I feared that in the early stages of our growth, a too-high proportion of them might unduly weigh the balance. I feared that too many of them would meet with disappointment in an unfamiliar country, lose their small savings, and be driven to return to Poland or Rumania, and that would have been a catastrophe. In fact, something of the sort did happen, though on a small scale; but small as it was, we were not to escape its dire consequences.

"The most vicious of the forms in which the 'ghetto' influence found expression was land speculation. We had to struggle very hard to suppress this type of activity, which cut at the very root of our land system and hence of our whole work. But the prospect of quick gain was a powerful attraction for many people, and the only way to combat it was to concentrate the acquisition of land in the hands of the Jewish National Fund. This, however, meant much more money than the Jewish National Fund had, or could expect at the time. So we had to stand by and watch the rise in land prices which we knew must inevitably lead to a slump, to failures, to re-emigration, with all the attendant sufferings and difficulties. There were some land speculators who never even came to Palestine. Bogus land companies sprung up, and parcels of Palestine land were hawked on the markets of Warsaw, Lodz and Lemberg, changing hands with bewildering rapidity. We knew that such speculation carried its own nemesis, but it was hard to convince the small man who saw a chance of doubling his life's savings at one stroke. After all, he always knew of someone who had made a fortune that way; why not he?"

*   *   *

If Weizmann had completely won this battle against what he called the ghettoizing of Palestine, there would have been no Tel Aviv in 1948. But there was the "illegal" immigration and there was the "capitalist" immigration. And what the middle class built in those years strengthened the Jewish position when the time came to rebel against the foreign occupation of Palestine.

*   *   *

Because Jabotinsky was so maligned, it is revealing to quote what his political adversary, Weizmann, said about him.

In his book *Trial and Error,* Weizmann speaks of Vladimir Jabotinsky "'. . . a youngster, the youngest of us all . . . a boy wonder." When Jabotinsky was barely twenty he had already achieved a reputation as a Russian journalist and had attracted the attention of Maxim Gorky and Leo Tolstoy. As with all Zionist leaders — beginning with Herzl — who disagreed with him, Weizmann says of Jabotinsky that he was "utterly un-Jewish in manner, approach and deportment." One of the qualities which he considered "un-Jewish" was his "knightliness."

Still Weizmann had to admit that it was Jabotinsky who, thanks to his stubbornness, had established the first Jewish fighting force in two thousand years, the Jewish Legion that fought with Britain against Germany and Turkey during World War I. Weizmann wrote: "It is almost impossible to describe the difficulties and disappointments which Jabotinsky had to face. I know a few people who could have stood up to them, but his pertinacity, which flowed from his devotion, was simply fabulous. He was discouraged and derided on every hand. Joseph Cowen, my wife, who remained his friend until his death, and I were almost alone in our support of him. The Zionist Executive was, of course, against him; the non-Zionist Jews looked on him as a sort of portent. While he was working for the Jewish Legion, we invited him to stay with us in our London house, to the discontent of many Zionists.

"We became very friendly in those days. Some time before I established myself permanently in London, I used to room with him in a little street in Chelsea — 3 Justice Walk — and we had a chance now and again to talk at length, and to indulge in some daydreaming. We had one memorable conversation which opened my eyes. We were beginning our work, and I said: 'You, Jabotinsky, should take over the propaganda of the movement, oral and literary. You are a genius in that field.' He looked at me almost with tears in his eyes. 'Now, Dr. Weizmann,' he said, 'the one thing I am fitted for is political work, and here you are trying to shove me into the entirely wrong path!'

"It startled me beyond words, for political work was precisely what he was unfit for; and above all he was unfit to negotiate with the British. In spite of his fabulous pertinacity, he was impatient in expression. He lacked realism, too. He was immensely optimistic, seeing too much and expecting too much. Nor did all his disappointments in behalf of the Jewish Legion ever cure him of these qualities.

"Jabotinsky succeeded in building up his Jewish regiments and came out with one of them to Palestine when I was there, in 1918. He was promoted to the rank of captain. At the end of that year, when I was leaving the country, he became the political officer of the Zionist Organization. I was, of course, not at all easy in my mind about this appointment, but Dr. Eder was there with him, and I thought the combination would not be too bad."

If Jabotinsky, not Weizmann, had conquered the leadership of the Zionist Organization in the years between World War I and II, there would have been many more Jews in Palestine at the end of the last war and fewer victims in Europe. Probably the streets of Tel Aviv and other cities would have shocked Weizmann, the esthete.

The tragedy of European Jewry, the fact that no mass movement in North America was launched by the Jewish leaders to save them from Hitler's Europe, stems from this conflict within the Zionist Movement: One side, represented by Weizmann, supported his belief that the task of Zionism was to reincarnate the land of prophets and holy men. The other, represented by Jabotinsky, held the philosophy that Zionism's primary task was to save the Jews threatened by extinction. To Jabotinsky, the Jewish state was an instrument to physically rescue Jewish people, not a means towards building a utopian society.

Some say Weizmann was above politics in striving for his goal. Yet one incident he recorded might suggest otherwise. In 1903, as Weizmann tells us in his memoirs, Herzl committed the "crime" of negotiating with the Czar's Minister of the Interior, Wenzel von Plehve, a notorious antisemite whom the Jews accused of complicitcy in the pogroms, including the Kishiniev blood bath. Weizmann speaks very bitterly about Herzl's meeting with von Plehve. Herzl believed that he had to negotiate with the man because (as Weizmann concedes) he wanted a quick solution, the evacuation of Jews from that hell. Herzl had hoped for Russian and Turkish support in an opportunity to colonize Palestine, but Weizmann criticized him by saying: "Antisemites are incapable of aiding in the creation of a Jewish Homeland." Weizmann said this of von Plehve in 1903. However, in 1933, Weizmann supported the Transfer Deal between Hitler's Germany and the World Zionist Organization. Had he forgotten by then that "antisemites are incapable of aiding in the creation of a Jewish Homeland"? Or was von Plehve, a little antisemite from Russia, more dangerous than Hitler? Perhaps the answer is that in 1933 Weizmann belonged to the establishment.

*   *   *

Hundreds of thousands of European Jews, if not millions, were victims of the politics that rocked the ship of rescue. This ideological storm and conflict among Zionist parties started as early as 1933, when Hitler became the chancellor of Germany. Unexpectedly, however, the year began with a serious split within the World Zionist Movement, and this split lasted until 1948.

In the early thirties the World Zionist Movement was ideologically divided between the socialist Zionist groups and the Nationalist "Revisionist" militant organization led by Vladimir Jabotinsky. In retrospect it seems that both wings of the Zionist Movement — the socialist and the "revisionist" — became much too involved in the ideological debate on the future of Palestine. Histadrut (the Palestinian Labor Unions' Federation) then started its march towards power within the Jewish community in Palestine and the World Zionist Movement. David Ben Gurion, its Secretary General, aspiring for leadership of greater scope, had already defined the ambition of the labour movement when he coined the slogan: "Mikita Leam" (from class to nation). It was an overt battle against Jabotinsky, who did not recognize the historic role of the Histadrut.

I believe Jabotinsky was wrong in this respect. Had he not given his Revisionist Movement the image of being anti-Histadrut, "anti-labor," the political battle and split within the Jewish people perhaps might not have reached the point of actual enmity. Of course, Jabotinsky had been provoked, but at one decisive moment he lost his self-control. On the other hand, Ben Gurion was a cool, calculating and very clever politician, always interested in winning the next election. Although uncompromising in climbing the ladder of power, Ben Gurion was a political pragmatist. He surrounded himself with middle-of-the-road, bourgeois Zionists who opposed Jabotinsky's "extremist" aim to ship masses of Jews into Palestine.

In 1933, Chaim Weizmann, later the first President of Israel, supported the "moderate faction" within the Zionist Movement, as did most of the German and British Zionists. Despite the emergency in Europe, they believed in "selective emigration" to Palestine, a slow process, although they officially opposed the British policy which had already begun to reduce Jewish immigration into Palestine according to the "absorptive capacity of the country." Their opposition, however, was not a matter of principle, but was based on the number of immigration "certificates" to be allocated. Thus Weizmann became the ally of Ben-Gurion and like-minded Labor Zionist leaders who wanted control of immigration for their political party, and were determined to apply the system of selective *aliyah*.

The Labor Zionist Movement had already begun to absorb industries. By aligning itself with the moderate "general Zionists" — and certain factions within the Orthodox establishment — the Labor Zionists were moving towards gaining control of the World Zionist Organization and its fundraising apparatus.

An additional factor was the strange alliance between labor and wealthy Jews throughout the world who wanted Zionism *in moderation*. These rich Jews hoped to see a vaguely defined Jewish spiritual center in Zion; they greatly feared the radical policies of Jabotinsky and his followers. That, too, was the period when many leftist Zionists still flirted with Marxism. The extreme-left Hashomer Hatzair group (now a part of the Marxist Mapam Party) was pro-Soviet, despite the fact that Zionism was oppressed in the Soviet Union. Yet it was still difficult for Jabotinsky to rally Jews against communism, although the persecution of Zionists and Jewish religious practice in Russia was then far more severe than it is today. However, it suited the leaders of the Histadrut to ally themselves with all these groups, the extreme left and the bourgeois, moderate, non-militant Zionist parties, in order to gain control of the Jewish Agency Executive, the body internationally recognized as representing the Jews with regard to Palestine.

So the Labor Zionist Movement, which, in Poland, a country with the greatest concentration of Jews in Europe, was the smallest political party among Jews (it never succeeded in electing even one member to the Polish Parliament) became, thanks to its strange bedfellows — especially the Weizmann "general Zionists" — the power controlling the Zionist purse strings and the distribution of "certificates," the emigration permits to Palestine. The control of these emigration permits became an effective instrument of patronage which provided the Labor Zionist Party with additional influence within Jewish communities. The largest Jewish political parties in Poland at that time were, among the non-socialists, the Zionist Revisionists and the Orthodox Agudat Israel; among the socialist Jews, the anti-Zionist "Bund" which controlled the Jewish trade unions.

* * *

Jabotinsky declared political war against the Labor Zionists because he had detected their ambition to dictate policy to the entire Jewish people. This basic power structure — sharing patronage with "coalition parties" — has remained to this day the "democratic" foundation of the World Zionist Movement. Because of this, the government of Israel, for almost three decades, was virtually the private property of one political party which controlled Israeli political and economic life — and Jewish communities throughout the world. The "Labor Alliance" with groups having vested interests in the fundraising apparatus and in the Palestinian economy formed an international class of professional Jews always at the service of the ruling party, which controlled fundraising and fund disbursement.

To this day the Labor Histadrut in Israel has remained the only trade union organization in the free world which is simultaneously a workers' organization and the largest employer in the country — a company that controls big business. This political power remained solid until the Begin victory of 1977. The question is not whether it was good for the organized Jewish people or for Israel, but the fact remains that until 1977, the opposition was always broken — by hook and by economic crook. This political factor determined Jewish politics during the challenging, decisive years from 1933 to 1945.

In 1933, the Zionist Revisionist movement, then a tremendously influential group throughout Europe, was provoked into leaving the World Zionist Organization by this coalition of anti-revolutionary Zionists and all the Socialist parties. Due to the doctoring of the history books, young people today are ignorant of the campaign, unparalleled in Jewish history, launched against the Zionist Revisionists and Vladimir Jabotinsky, the most outstanding Zionist leader since Theodor Herzl.

Also in 1933, the Arlosoroff murder split the Zionist movement to the point of civil war (a war not yet over despite many armistices). In the summer of 1973, the Israeli press finally revealed all the facts about this cause célèbre.

It happened accidentally. Tuvia, the brother of Yehuda Arazy (Tennenbaum), who, under the British administration had been the police inspector in charge of the Arlosoroff case, suddenly appeared at a cemetery where Menachem Begin, Leader of the Opposition, was addressing a memorial gathering for Abba Ahimeir. According to the British and the then Labor Zionist Establishment, Ahimeir was one of the alleged "murderers" of Arlosoroff.

Tuvia Arazy made a graveside statement that he had come to ask for forgiveness of Abba Ahimeir (who had died eleven years earlier). He was now ready to publish all the documents pertaining to the Arlosoroff case which his brother, Yehuda, had left with their late father, Abraham Tennenbaum, and which were now in his possession.

It must be noted that Tuvia Arazy was not your average Israeli. Before retirement, he had been a senior official in Israel's Foreign Ministry, and had served as Israel's ambassador to Peru and Cyprus. He had been a loyal Labor party member, and an opponent of the Revisionists and the Herut (the party led by Begin). Arazy must have suffered some pangs of conscience when he appeared at the Ahimeir memorial service in Tel Aviv and approached Begin to inform him about the secret police file pertaining to the Revisionist "plot" in the murder of Arlosoroff.

Chaim Arlosoroff was murdered in the spring of 1933, while out on a stroll. The assassination took place on the beach of Tel Aviv, on the spot where the Dan Hotel stands today. Although to the general population the killers were obviously Arabs, it served the political interests of the Labor Party to accuse the Revisionists of the murder. This also served the policy of the British Administration. Three Revisionists were arrested and tried for killing the popular, 34-year-old head of the Jewish Agency. The three were Dr. Abba Ahimeir, an editor of the Revisionist newspaper who was accused of planning the assassination; Abrasha Stawsky and Tsvi Rosenblatt, who were tried and found guilty of murder. The latter two received death sentences but were released after five years in jail. The only survivor of this tragedy was Tsvi Rosenblatt, who was present when Tuvia Arazy appeared at the cemetery to ask forgiveness for hiding the documents for so many years.

In 1955, however, Yehuda Arazy caused a sensation in Tel Aviv. While addressing a B'nai B'rith Lodge, he stated, "I believed for only forty-eight hours that Jews had assassinated Chaim Arlosoroff." Arazy, who had been the inspector in charge of criminal investigation of the Mandatory Police, was deeply involved in the affair. As early as March 28, 1933, several days after the murder, Yehuda Arazy told his British superiors in a written statement that he did not believe the three Revisionists were guilty. Arazy, however, was a loyal party member and was secretly connected with the Haganah. He was told to keep quiet. All the then leaders of the Jewish Agency who had exploited the Arlosoroff affair wished to rid Palestine of the Revisionist influence. Yehuda Arazy had appeased his conscience by mailing his report to the British authorities. Yet all he had accomplished was to be taken off the Arlosoroff case. For twenty-two years Arazy had kept silent. Although he made his statement in 1955, the documentation was not published until June 1973, when it caused a sensation in Israel.

Following Tuvia Arazy's appearance at the cemetery and the subsequent publishing of the secret Yehuda Arazy report, members of the Israeli government influenced Menahem Begin to let bygones be bygones and not use this case in the the approaching election campaign. Actually, forty years later, few Israelis remembered the case; fewer cared. This was half a year before the Yom Kippur War, when Israelis were busy enjoying life in the security of their fool's paradise.

Prominent, conscientious Israeli journalists tried to revive the case, stressing that it was pertinent to the present, as many of those responsible for the libel and slander against the Revisionists were still among the leaders of the State of Israel, some in the highest government posts.

One of Israel's most brilliant young journalists, Dan Margalit, wrote in *Haaretz:*

" . . . we, the offspring of the Halutzim (pioneers) of the second and third Aliyah — the sons of the leaders of the Histadrut, and the grandsons of the founders of national institutions, second and third generations of Nahalal and Dagania — we who were born into the Labor movement and knew about it before we learned to read and write — we had always been told that the world was divided between the beautiful Left and the ugly Right . . . the Right was always in the eyes of the Left . . . ugly, fascists, brown shirts, a cult of dictatorship and . . . Arlosoroff murderers."

Margalit then describes how the Israeli schoolchildren of his generation were brainwashed regarding the role of the Irgun. He remembers as a child having once asked his grandfather why he alone, out of a large circle of family and friends, refused to become involved in political activities.

Margalit's grandfather told him that a short time after Arlosoroff's murder he was talking to Arab merchants who proposed to point out to him the Arabs who had murdered Arlosoroff. The grandfather went immediately to Dov Hoz, then the head of the Haganah, and told him that there were Arabs ready to deliver the real murderers, that there was a chance suspicion would be lifted from Jews. Hoz listened but refused to meet with those Arabs. "Forget it!" he told Margalit's grandfather. "Don't become involved in this. We know how to conduct this case."

Dan Margalit's concluding observation is extremely moving:

". . . my grandfather remained a loyal party member until his last days."

This darkness-at-noon atmosphere has not yet found an Arthur Koestler to properly describe it. There is no one to psychoanalyze Jews who refuse to "speak evil" of those of whom evil should be spoken, those who prefer the perversion of justice to "insulting" such sinister plotters. Of course, the Yom Kippur War and its aftermath completely relegated this tragic episode in Israeli and Jewish history to the background.

I was a mere boy at the time of the Arlosoroff murder and lived far away from the great Jewish centres. I must confess that the campaign of vilification in the anti-Jabotinsky press for a while led me to believe that Stawsky had murdered Arlosoroff. I was a great admirer of Chaim Arlosoroff. Today we know that Arlosoroff did not agree with Ben Gurion and Weizmann that there could be an accommodation with British imperialist policy in Palestine. A man of barely thirty, he had risen to the leadership of the Jewish Agency as head of its political department. As long as Arlosoroff was alive, Ben Gurion had no chance to ascend to the leadership of the Jewish Agency.

I interviewed Arlosoroff in Brussels two weeks before he was killed. I remember to this day his analysis of the eventual — and unavoidable — conflict between Britain and the Jewish people over Palestine. Had he lived, the Jewish Civil War would never have reached its tragic proportions.

I read recently that it was Arlosoroff, perhaps not less than Jabotinsky, who was convinced that only a Jewish revolution in Palestine would return the land to our people. I had known it since that interview; the revelations did not surprise me. But Arlosoroff was a careful, extremely dexterous politician who did not proclaim his convictions publicly. Perhaps a British hand was responsible for his tragic death at such a young age — perhaps. But one thing is certain: Dividing the Jews in Palestine into two opposing camps suited the British perfectly.

The activities of the Irgun delegation in the United States were launched through the American Friends of a Jewish Palestine, which supported the "illegal emigration" to the Holy Land. Then another American front organization established the Committee for a Jewish Army. The aim of this group was to mobilize public opinion for a Jewish military force that would fight with the Allies against Hitler. This, of course, was Jabotinsky's idea.

At the very beginning of this campaign in New York, the Irgun representatives were fortunate in finding a supporter in an outstanding political writer. He was Pierre Van Paasen, the son of a Dutch-Protestant clergyman, who became interested in Jews at a very early age. Van Paassen had a profound knowledge of Hebrew and of Jewish classical letters. He was not one of those non-Jewish politicians who nonchantly speak of their admiration "for the Jewish people," but was truly a friend of the Jews and remained one to the end of his life.

Van Paassen became the active head of the Committee for a Jewish Army.

He was not just a Zionist, but a revolutionary Zionist. Because he was a dissenter who joined the unpopular Irgun "boys," the establishment machine maligned him and his motives. But he carried on and did a lot to popularize the ideas of Jabotinsky and the Irgun in North America.

In 1942 Hillel Kook and Samuel Merlin almost succeeded in convincing the War Department to support the idea of establishing a Jewish army — almost. The Committee for a Jewish Army of Palestinian and Stateless Jews then numbered among its members Chief Justice Harlan Stone and other notables respected throughout the United States. However, a historian of the establishment admitted, this activity perturbed "the Zionists of a more conventional stripe." Rabbi Stephen S. Wise led the delegation of the Zionist Organization of America to Washington to protest against the Committee for a Jewish Army. Congressman Sol Bloom, always at the service of the State Department, obliged Wise by helping him cancel a deal with the War Department. "Wise explained that the proposed Jewish army seemed imprudent and objectionable to the majority of American Jews." He won the battle. The Jewish army was not to be.

The way in which the American Jewish establishment prevented concrete action on behalf of Europe's Jews was in accordance with International Zionist establishment policy. In 1940, Vladimir Jabotinsky, a few months before his death, succeeded in enlisting the support of the then British Ambassador to the United States, Lord Lothian, for his plan to create a Jewish army. Britain had just been through the tragedy of Dunkirk, and the nation was under siege. Lord Lothian wrote to Jabotinsky in June, 1940 to show sincere appreciation of the Jews' desire to help at this crisis.

According to the same source "the project" frightened the American Zionist establishment, which wanted no part of the flamboyant Jabotinsky. A few days before a well-publicized Zionist rally, four Zionist leaders — Louis Lipsky, Rabbi Wise, Eliezer Kaplan (then treasurer of the Jewish Agency in Jerusalem), and Solomon Goldman — called on Lord Lothian in Washington and announced that "responsible Zionist quarters disassociated themselves from Jabotinsky's adventurous scheme." Lord Lothian found it prudent not to be represented at the rally. In the June 21 issue of *New Palestine,* the official organ of the Zionist Organization of America, support was given to the Jewish Agency's plan for a Jewish army, which, it was said, would consist merely of "four divisions of Jewish soldiers in Palestine for the defense of Palestine and the Near East, plus eventual recruits from neutral lands who are living as refugees in those lands . . . Jabotinsky's plan for an army . . . miscarried."

One of the most interesting documents of this period was made public by the British Foreign Office and published in London. In one of these documents it tells that in 1940 Jabotinsky proposed to establish a Jewish Army that would join the Allies in the war against Hitler. This proposal was rejected by the British cabinet under the pressure of Jewish opponents of Jabotinsky. At the British War Cabinet meeting, it was reported (the documents published in London show) that the acceptance of Jabotinsky's plan would have strengthened his position among

Jews against Chaim Weizmann, who, in the eyes of the British Colonial Office and Foreign Office, was a much easier man to deal with than the intransigent Jewish revolutionary leader.

The document reveals that when Neville Chamberlain resigned as Prime Minister to make way for Winston Churchill, Vladimir Jabotinsky, then in New York, cabled Churchill his congratulations and his wishes for success "in your colossal mission." Jabotinsky then said, "I will speak for the movement which identifies essentially with the Hebrew military tradition that has come to life again . . . I suggest to you a program for common effort. I am cabling you this plan because I believe that you realize the necessity of altering, in every direction, the previous government's policy that almost extinguished the magnetism of those abroad who strove to become your allies. We have been forced to become anti-German and we are ready to fight . . .

"I suggest to mobilize and to establish in all units of Allied Armies, Jewish units on condition that such units are similar to the Polish Army in exile and another condition: that your Government finally put an end to the policies of Malcolm MacDonald and that the destiny of the Land of Israel not be proclaimed officially before the Peace Conference.

"I can assure you that 130,000 Jews can now be mobilized for such units even on the Continent . . . Jews dispose of certain organizational instruments in several countries."

Churchill knew Jabotinsky and respected him very much. He knew that he was a friend of Great Britain. Yet when the contents of this letter became known to the Foreign Office, the bureaucrats began to shiver. They knew of Churchill's open-mindedness and were afraid of his decision. They also remembered that when Churchill was the First Lord of the Admiralty, he had already spoken of mobilizing Jews for service.

Memos were exchanged among various officials of the Foreign Office in order to prevent Churchill from supporting Jabotinsky. Also, the then Colonial Secretary, Lord Lloyd, made the following remark: "No matter what we are doing in the area of mobilizing a Jewish Army, it is absolutely wrong to support Jabotinsky because he is the political opponent of Dr. Weizmann. Also, it should be understood that whatever we are doing, we must refrain from any suggestion that the mobilization of such an army is related to our policy on Palestine as defined in the White Paper." Lloyd then warned Churchill that Jabotinsky's real plan was to establish a Jewish state in Palestine on both sides of the Jordan, and that he would eventually use such an army for that purpose.

Another British statesman who supported the group opposed to Jabotinsky was Foreign Secretary Lord Halifax, one of Chamberlain's appeasement clique.

Here it should be mentioned that one of the British friends of the Irgun who helped Jabotinsky, Colonel Patterson, came to America to support the Committee for a Jewish army. (Patterson was the non-Jewish Commander of the Jewish Legion established by Jabotinsky during World War I.) In connection with Jabotinsky's plan, Patterson suggested the immediate establishment of a Jewish army of 100,000. He had discussed this plan with the Canadian government and reported to Churchill that Canada was sympathetic to the plan. Also, said Patterson, he was ready to go to Canada to begin the training of this Jewish army. Yet the Whitehall bureaucracy, the cabinet ministers, made every effort to dissuade Churchill from helping this plan to materialize.

One official of the Foreign Office was an exception to the rule. He told the Cabinet that if the Germans were to occupy Palestine, the Jews would not be armed and would fall victim to the German extermination policy. Yet Lord Lloyd was absolutely opposed to this plan. Churchill was overwhelmed by this opposition and replied to Jabotinsky in a diplomatically worded letter, probably prepared by the Foreign Office, that the Jews would be welcome to serve individually, but not as a distinct army.

One should not forget that this was the period when England was threatened as never before. France had fallen, and Churchill's only consideration was to save the British Isles from invasion. When told that a Jewish army would undermine the position of Britain in many areas of the world, he gave in.

This episode certainly is relevant to what happened later and is an illustration of how the Jewish establishment fought any serious effort to organize world Jewry against Hitler.

Their actions were dictated by the fear that Jabotinsky could become a real challenge to Weizmann and go on to become the leader of the Jewish people. *This has remained the preoccupation of the establishment.*

*   *   *

In 1948, Israel had to face the tragedy of the Altalena. The provisional government of the State of Israel ordered that an arms shipment brought in on the ship by the Irgun for the conquest of Jerusalem be surrendered immediately to the Haganah, contrary to a previous agreement. The secret deal had been made between Ben Gurion and Menachem Begin, the Commander of the Irgun, on the understanding that these arms, at that time tremendously important for Israel, would be used to liberate Jerusalem.

There are different opinions concerning the cause of the tragedy. The Altalena arrived on the shores of Israel immediately after a United Nations-imposed armistice, and Ben Gurion officially stated later that there should have been no importation of arms at that time. On board the Altalena, which was carrying cannon, aerial bombs, guns, tanks and anti-tank guns, as well as medical supplies, were potential Irgun soldiers, volunteers from America. Abraham Stavsky, the man who had helped procure these arms in France, was on the boat. He was met by Peter Bergson (Hillel Kook) and Samuel Merlin, then Herut members of the Knesset. Menachem Begin, Commander of the Irgun, came to greet his friends arriving from the United States.

One should remember that at that time there was still no unified Israeli army: There was the Haganah; there was the Irgun, the Palmach, and the Stern group (Fighters for the Freedom of Israel — "Lechi"). They were all under the supreme authority of the government of Israel, but had separate commanders who coordinated activities among themselves.

When the Altalena arrived in Israel, it is possible that Ben Gurion had second thoughts about allowing the Irgun to become too powerful and perhaps conquering the Old City of Jerusalem — Begin's avowed aim when he brought in the Altalena. Ben Gurion's opponents say that he was determined to liquidate the Irgun, his old political enemies — an operation he preferred to the liberation of Jerusalem. Those who defend Ben Gurion maintain that the attack on the Irgun ship, (during which Merlin was wounded and Stavsky killed), was necessary in order to end the rivalries among armies and establish a unified Israeli Defence Force. The Altalena incident, Ben Gurion's friends claim, provided the excuse for liquidating all separate armies. A member of the Israeli General Staff at the time stated recently that although Ben Gurion ordered the Altalena to surrender unconditionally, he did not authorize the command to open fire. The commander who actually ordered the attack was a member of the Leftist Marxist party who wanted to liquidate his "fascist class enemies" on the boat.

That day the newborn nation was on the verge of civil war. Some members of the government, including the revered Rabbi Yehuda Leib Maimon, called for Ben Gurion's resignation. Many were afraid that the Irgun, which had a strong base among the people of Tel Aviv, would respond by counter-attacking the Palmach or the Haganah and would, with the support of the Stern group, capture the government. This was prevented thanks to Menachem Begin. Begin, despite the tragedy, saw that a counter-attack by the Irgun would destroy the Jewish state in its infancy. He preferred to demonstrate strength by surrendering to the official government. Begin went on radio and, for the first time since he had emerged from the underground, wept as he said, "We did not become the Irgun to shoot at Jews but at our enemies. We surrender in order that the Jewish state may live."

Many of Begin's friends accused him of cowardice. Some who criticized him were members of the Israeli government. In his memoirs Begin says of this difficult decision not to shoot back: "To avoid bloody civil war at all costs — this principle, tempered in the sufferings of the 'season,' we observed years later in the test of blood and fire of the Altalena."

*   *   *

In 1933 the civil war among Zionists was only beginning. The Revisionists were accused of killing Arlosoroff, and it was said that Stavsky and another Betari, Rosenblatt, were guilty of the murder. It came to a point where the then Chief Rabbi of Palestine, Abraham Isaac Kook, approached the Holy Ark in Jerusalem's Central Synagogue on the Sabbath, appealing to Jews to end the campaign against Stavsky: "I swear that he is innocent!" And the revered rabbi put his hand on the Holy Scroll.

Yet the split did not heal; political factionalism did not cease. The leftist Zionist politicians, especially the Marxists, were ready to destroy the "fascist"

Revisionists. They needed a Jewish "fascist" party in order to continue their climb to power. And, of course, it suited the British to encourage this fratricide. Stavsky was freed. But Jewish unity was broken and was not reestablished until 1964 when Levi Eshkol, then Prime Minister of Israel — against the advice of Ben Gurion — brought back the bones of Vladimir Jabotinsky to the Land of Israel.

Helped along by the British, the campaign against Jabotinsky consolidated the power of the leftist Zionists within the Jewish Agency and the World Zionist Movement. In August of 1933, at the World Zionist Congress in Prague, the World Zionist Organization split. The Revisionists soon left the organization and established the New Zionist Organization at a congress in Vienna. I believe this was Jabotinsky's greatest tactical error. A friend of mine who opposed Jabotinsky's policies once joked about the Revisionists leaving the World Zionist Organization: "Jabotinsky's leaving the World Zionist Organization reminds me of the anecdote about the man who caught his wife in the act of adultery with his business partner. So he walked out of the store and out of his house. He abandoned not only the adulteress — his wife — but also his business."

Thus the Labor Zionists who had forged the alliance with the timid, frightened pro-British wing of General Zionists gained final control of the entire World Zionist Movement and its fundraising apparatus. There was no opposition except from breakaway factions — a situation that prevails to this day in the Jewish state.

Yet the issues dividing the official Zionist Movement and Jabotinsky were of historic importance, involving cooperation with the Germans and the mass exodus to Palestine.

There was the problem of selective emigration to Palestine, of slowly building a model country with socialist experimental stations, a country that would be an example to the world (according to some of the socialist dreamers) versus a homeland that would immediately take in as many hundreds of thousands as could force the gates open.

At the last World Zionist Congress in which he participated, Jabotinsky defined the purpose of Zionism not as a movement to establish a spiritual homeland for the Jews, but as a haven for the rescue of *all* those threatened by Hitler. Then he again proclaimed the urgent need for unconventional evacuation methods to settle Jewish masses in Palestine. The absorptive capacity of that little country was greater than all the experts predicted, and Jabotinsky thought that millions could be settled there, not tens of thousands, as the British and some of their frightened Zionist supporters believed. Today, of course, history has proved Jabotinsky right. There is no end to the absorptive capacity of a motherland that embraces and harbors her children.

The basic point of contention between these two Jewish armed camps was the issue of the so-called illegal emigration to Palestine. The more the British curtailed immigration to appease the Arabs, the more convinced were the disciples of Jabotinsky and the members of the fledgling Irgun (which then began its counter-terror against Arab terrorism) that Jews must be brought into Palestine despite the occupying power. In the eyes of the Irgun, Britain was no more the mandatory power that had undertaken to help establish a Jewish homeland in Palestine, but a colonial regime at war with the aspirations of European Jews to settle in the only country where they would be welcome and where they could rebuild their lives.

So the Irgun inaugurated the most glorious chapter in recent Jewish history, the so-called Aliyah Bet, the illegal emigration. Poor, destitute, yet imbued with the faith that theirs was the right to populate Palestine with Jews and bring the day of Hebrew sovereignty closer, they started operating.

In Poland, Vladimir Jabotinsky established a special department to handle the emigration. But the Irgun had to fight two battles: The first was waged against the official Zionist organization which, fearing it might lose control over the would-be immigrants, complied with the policy of selective absorption. The other, of course, was against British rule in Palestine.

The extent of the success of the Irgun in bringing Jews to Palestine can be measured in terms of the sheer numbers — tens of thousands — who immigrated through the Aliyah Bet. Today in Israel there are several hundred thousand Jews who, with their children and grandchildren, form the community of "illegal" olim.

I remember my last talk with Abraham Stavsky, or Abrasha, as we called him, in Paris, two weeks before he boarded the Altalena. It was three o'clock in the morning and we were walking up and down Boulevard Hausmann, near my hotel. I asked Abrasha, "Are you still bitter about the accusation against you, the libel that you murdered Arlosoroff?"

Abrasha was tall and heavily built. He looked like a bully but had a heart of gold. He said, "Don't you know that I am going to Israel to see thousands of those whom I helped bring to Palestine through the Illegal Aliyah? We wanted a Jewish state, and now we have it. It does not matter who is in the government. But the remnant of our people is saved."

Abrasha started crying. These were tears of joy, for he had confided in me that this time he was helping to procure, as he said in Yiddish, "di richtige schoire" (the real merchandise), arms needed for Israel's defence. He wiped the tears from his face and turned around towards the Avenue de L'Opera. I walked with him a few more minutes until we reached the Comedie Française and then left him. Neither of us said good night or goodbye; we just separated. Two weeks later I read that he had been killed by a *Jewish* gun on the Altalena while trying to unload arms vital for the defence of the *Jewish* state.

By 1939 Jews knew they should try every possible route to leave Europe, and the illegal immigration to Palestine was well under way. But the Irgun had no money. The outbreak of war had closed off all sources of financing the illegal emigration to Palestine, a very costly operation when one considers that the Irgun had to buy many second-rate boats to ship would-be immigrants through the Mediterranean. British embassies throughout Europe were alerted to prevent precisely this, and the official Zionist leadership also opposed the influx of refugees on the grounds that they were ill-prepared to be pioneers in the new land.

In the face of this opposition, the Irgun decided to send a few emissaries to America. One of them was Yitzhaq Ben Ami, then a student at the Hebrew University, who had inherited some money and was a young man of independent means. He also had previous Aliyah Bet experience. Raziel, then the commander of the Irgun told "Mike" (Ben Ami) that he should go to America at his own expense and organize a committee for the support of an uninterrupted "illegal" rescue operation to Palestine.

At that time Mike had behind him three years of experience in this field as head of the Irgun Aliyah Bet organization in Europe. He had successfully shipped "illegal" Jews from Czechoslovakia, Poland, Hungary and Austria to Israel. He had even negotiated with the Gestapo and Adolph Eichmann, and wrung some concessions from the Germans when he convinced them that he would take out Jews from German-occupied countries.

One must remember that during this period German government policy allowed Jews to leave territory under German occupation. The extermination program was decided upon later when the Germans became convinced, in the words of Rabbi Michael Dov Weissmandl, that "there are those who want to sell Jews but there is no government who wants to take them."

Mike arrived in the United States to work with two Irgun emissaries who had preceded him. Immediately, however, he encountered the enmity of the organized Jewish establishment.

A professional Jew by the name of Henry Montor, then the executive vice-chairman of the United Jewish Appeal in America, circulated thousands of copies of a "personal and confidential" letter asking Jews not to support the illegal emigration to Palestine. Suffice it to say that in that infamous letter, dated February 1, 1940, a time of extreme emergency for Jews in Europe, when it was imperative to evacuate the maximum number of Jews through all possible means, Montor's five-page letter (and I stress "in the name of the United Jewish Appeal") concluded with the following evaluation of Palestine as a haven for Jews:

"Palestine can provide for only a segment of those who need its freedom and security that is due to a combination of political hindrances and financial handicaps. Until the resources of Palestine are adequately developed, immigration from 30,000 to 60,000 a year may be possible, until a larger number might be consistently and continuously reached. Under these circumstances," Montor continued, "therefore is it not essential for responsible leaders to concern themselves with the necessity of selective immigration, particularly under the arduous conditions that surround unregistered immigration at the present time?"

This circular was mailed on the stationery of the United Jewish Appeal "on behalf of American Jewish Joint Distribution Committee, United Palestine Appeal and National Coordinating Committee Fund." The names on the stationery were those of the most prominent Jews of the time, including Albert Einstein, who had signed on to help the United Jewish Appeal but probably never saw the letter. Its purpose was to urge Jews not to give money to facilitate the illegal emigration. Meanwhile, boats filled with refugees from Hitler's Europe were stranded at the Danube. Montor, on this letterhead, dared state the following:

"In public discussion, it is considered inadmissible for a Jew even to conceive of the possibility of criminals in Jewish ranks, but inasmuch as this is a confidential letter, I think it is fair to you and to the interest with which you are concerned to point out that many of those who have been brought into Palestine by the Revisionists . . . have been prostitutes and criminals — certainly not an element which can contribute to the upbuilding of a Jewish national home in which Jews everywhere might take pride. The increased incidence of crime in Palestine in the past year is (sic) the most tragic reflection of the haphazard and irresponsible guidance of unregistered immigration by certain groups."

Other *bons mots* from Montor follow:

" . . .The United Palestine Appeal is a fund-raising instrument of the Jewish Agency for Palestine, as well as the Jewish National Fund. Whatever may be the attitude of the Jewish Agency toward unregistered migration to Palestine, it cannot, as a legally constituted body, publicly emphasize any interest in or sympathy to such immigration as it may and does have . . . At the present time, the Jewish Agency for Palestine is engaged in conversations with the British Government for an issuance of a new labor immigration schedule for the six-month period beginning April 1st . . . As you know, even provisions of the White Paper provide for an annual immigration schedule of 10,000 a year, aside from such certificates as may be made available to refugees from the total number of 25,000 separate certificates which the Government promised to place at the disposal of refugees. Public emphasis on unregistered immigration and acknowledgement by such a body as the Jewish Agency that it not only endorses, but finances such unregistered immigration, can only strike a disastrous blow at the possibility of facilitating the entry of legal properly qualified immigrants into Palestine.

"The American Friends of Jewish Palestine was created by a group of Revisionists, headed by Rabbi Louis I. Newman, who declared that their major purpose was to raise funds in the United States for unregistered emigration to Palestine. It may be assumed, therefore, that the American Friends of Jewish Palestine, which it claims, might, nevertheless, have turned to such Jews in America as were sympathetic to unregistered immigration into Palestine to ask for support of this project. The American Friends of Jewish Palestine declared publicly that the regularly constituted bodies would not and *could not, even if they wanted to, because of their legal character,* finance unregistered immigration into Palestine. That was supposed to be the excuse for the creation of such a separate organization.

" . . . For many years, Revisionists in every country, including the United States, have denounced and sabotaged the fund-raising bodies included in the United Palestine Appeal, that is the Jewish National Fund and the Palestine Foundation Fund. Even in Palestine itself, the Revisionists, with their tactics of violence, made raids upon the central headquarters of these national funds. But when it became involved in a difficulty of its own making, the American Friends of Jewish Palestine sought public sympathy by denouncing the United Palestine Appeal for not giving funds to it when it had claimed all along that the United Palestine Appeal was unworthy and should not be supported.

"The facilitation of unregistered immigration to Palestine is one of the most serious tasks that face the Jewish people now and in the future. Two elements must be kept in mind: First, the needs of refugees escaping from certain destruction in Europe and, secondly, the requirements of Palestine for immigrants who can contribute to the constructive growth of the country in order that room may be made for additional immigrants. Whatever interest in unregistered immigration may have been exhibited by individuals associated with the Jewish Agency for Palestine was based on a recognition of the fact that 'selectivity' is an inescapable factor in dealing with the problem of immigration to Palestine. By 'selectivity' is meant the choice of young men and women who are trained in Europe for productive purposes either in agriculture or industry and who are in other ways trained for life in Palestine, which involves difficulties and hardships for which they must be prepared physically and psychologically. Sentimental considerations are, of course, vital and everyone would wish to save every single Jew who could be rescued out of the cauldron of Europe.

"But when one is dealing with so delicate a program as unregistered immigration, it is obviously essential that those people sent to Palestine should be able to endure harsh conditions under which they must live for weeks and months on the Mediterranean and difficulties which await them when they land on the shores of Palestine. It is tragically true that scores of some of the unregistered immigrants who have been undernourished and underclothed on the unseaworthy boats that cross the Mediterranean died in the hulks of those ships.

"Certain responsible and experienced persons have been facilitating the immigration of Jews to Palestine on an unregistered basis. During the past four weeks, for example, some 2,200 of such young men and women from Germany, Poland and elsewhere have been brought together on the Danube for transport to Palestine. Seven hundred and fifty were shipped on one boat. You will not have seen in any of your newspapers reference to this activity, because these responsible individuals are not concerned with making prestige for a party or a political enterprise, but are profoundly desirous of assuring the safe arrival of these productive young men and women into Palestine. They recognize that the greater the publicity that surrounds such activities, the less possible it is to carry on with the entry of Jews into Palestine on this basis.

"You will recall that one of the sad aspects of the case of the St. Louis was the sensational publicity that reached every front page of the country's press and thus made it difficult for the Cuban Government (sic) to retreat from the original and unwise decision that it had originally made for the exclusion of the 900 passengers on the St. Louis.

"When the Revisionist-sponsored transport on the Danube became a public issue two weeks ago, a responsible individual indicated to the American Friends of Jewish Palestine that this particular affair could be satisfactorily liquidated if the American Friends of Jewish Palestine would cease its separate fund-raising activities, at which it had already proven unsuccessful, and if it were to agree to "selectivity" in immigration and also if it would give public accountings of the funds which had been taken from individuals for their transport to Palestine. The American Friends of Jewish Palestine declined to meet these conditions because, apparently, they were more concerned with utilizing the incident for buiding up of prestige for their organization than they were in settling the fate of 2,000 Jews. They preferred instead to continue hurling charges at responsible Jewish leaders upon whom the brunt was being placed for a situation which they had not created and for which they could not be held accountable, by any stretch of the imagination.

"It is important for a leader like yourself to have before him the facts with regard to the nature of immigration sponsored by the Revisionists. The leaders of these 'tours,' most of them concerned with the private profit to be derived from the enterprise, have gone through various communities in Europe and have announced to whoever would listen that their transport to Palestine could be assured on the payment of a certain sum, always far in excess of the $100 which is required for the passage of an individual from the Danube to Palestine. In some cases the amounts taken were $500 or even more. In any event, the sums were always in excess of what would have to be paid by that individual to a regular shipping company. Thus, even the 2,000 people who were assembled by the Revisionists on the Danube brought together a total of approximately $200,000 of their own funds. A great many of the passengers were old men and women, whose fate must be the sincerest concern of every Jew, but who were, obviously, not fitted for the hazardous journey across the Mediterranean in boats whose captains consented to this traffic only because of the exorbitant amounts they could command. In other words, the Revisionists were not conducting a public enterprise but were engaged in collecting dollars from human beings whose anxious desire led them to pay any amount demanded of them in the frenzied hope of reaching the haven of Palestine.

"Those who have concerned themselves throughout their lifetime with the building of a Jewish National Home in Palestine have been directing their aspirations toward two objectives: The first is to make possible the entry into Palestine of Jews who need homes, and the second has been to create in Palestine a center where Jewish ideals might be translated into reality.

"The whole structure of the Jewish National Home, resting on delicate political, geographical, economic and social foundations, must ultimately topple if its underpinnings are weak and unsound. What Palestine needs today are young people who have an understanding of what the Jewish National Home is meant to be and whose energies and resources of talent are such as to create the possibilities for additional large immigration.

"There could be no more deadly ammunition provided to the enemies of Zionism, whether they be in the ranks of the British government or the Arabs, or even in the ranks of the Jewish people, if Palestine were to be flooded with very old people or with undesirables who would make impossible the conditions of life in Palestine and destroy the prospect of creating such economic circumstances as would insure a continuity of immigration.

"I have gone at length into these fundamentals, because I believe that a great many unfair and unfounded accusations have been made because of the political differences between the Revisionists and the official agencies.

"No reasonable person has ever said that Palestine could hold all the millions of Jews who need its shelter, even if legal and unregistered immigration combined were to make feasible the entry of all these millions of Jews. We start then with the assumption that Palestine can provide for only a segment of those who need its freedom and security."

Montor later became the head of the State of Israel Bonds organization in America. Of course, he will never be tried by a Jewish tribunal because he belongs to the "right" Zionist party, but at that time Ben Ami and his friends of the Irgun delegation had to fight not only the British and not only the Germans, but also the establishment.

Opposition of this nature by the establishment against the Irgun continued throughout the war. No matter how dangerous the Jewish situation in Europe became, no matter how urgent it was to save lives, politics prevailed. Why, when it was possible to save human lives by "illegal emigration," did the establishment fight it? When it became impossible to send Jews to Palestine during the war and temporary havens for Jews who could be rescued were needed, all these fund-raisers suddenly became "political Zionists," demanding from the British and American governments verbal statements about the Jewish future in Palestine *after the war.* Why, instead, did they not raise the purely humanitarian aspect of saving human lives?

First Yom Kippur in New York

Right after Yom Kippur, immediately following the fast, all the Yiddish theaters opened on Second Avenue. In 1939 Yiddish culture was still very much alive in New York, and the traditional première in the many theaters marked the beginning of the season.

This was the first Yom Kippur of World War II, yet on Second Avenue that evening no one seemed disturbed by the impending tragedy. Thousands strolled happily between First and Fourteenth Streets. No one would think that while the Yiddish language, alive with laughter and gaiety, echoed down this New York boulevard, Nazi armies were overrunning the Polish cities and towns where Yiddish culture was born.

It was a wonderful evening, the traditional evening to go out. All the Yiddish writers and journalists were there for the opening of the shows. At the famous Yiddish Art Theater, Morris Schwartz was still king. He received us, his friends from the Jewish press, with his friendly smile and warm, baritone voice. Ludwig Satz reigned at another theater on Houston Street. Menasha Skulnik still sang with all his power, "I don't know how they do it but they do it." (I believe

Skulnik was the greatest of all the Jewish comedians. His later Broadway career in English never reduced his popularity or the *schmaltz* of his humor, and in Yiddish he was the epitome of the Chaplinesque *schlemiel.*)

After the theater it was customary to finish off the evening with a visit to the Café Royale, located across the street from the Yiddish Art Theatre. I remember Morris Schwartz being as happy as ever, his towering figure dominating the café. Schwartz was not only a great actor, but certainly the most talented promoter and PR man the Yiddish theater ever had. As he and I talked, I thought of the Europe I had left behind and of the Jews who had been left to their destiny. That night who would have believed that a war had started which would wipe out the glorious Jewish communities of Europe. Schwartz was in a good mood; he asked me, "Well, what do you think about the future of the Yiddish theater?"

I told him, "You are finished." That day I had attended one of New York's "modern" synagogues, and on my first Yom Kippur in America I was shocked by the typically American, commercialized staging of the services. I said to Schwartz, "You are finished because show business in America has been taken over by the modern rabbis. In the future, Jews will enjoy the acting of their 'spiritual leaders,' the greatest showmen of them all." When I tried to turn the conversation of our party to the problem of European Jewry, pointing out the headlines in the morning editions of the dailies, everyone brushed it aside as irrelevant to this beautiful evening. The people at the Royale were interested only in dissecting each show produced on the Avenue.

Later that night another friend and I left the café deeply perturbed. We took a long stroll, from 12th Street to 125th Street in Harlem. When we reached the Black area it was morning, and we were still talking. Neither he nor I could understand how all these eminent writers and Jewish leaders with whom we had sat at the café had not once uttered the word "war." We were at war; we were Jews. We had been singled out for extermination by Hitler. And, although the United States was still not officially at war with Germany, we Jews had been declared enemies of the Reich. Our brethren overseas were under attack, but in America few seemed to take seriously the Nazi statements that one of the primary aims was to exterminate the Jewish people.

Jabotinsky's name came up. To me, reared in the liberal milieu of Western Europe, his name was still associated with certain Jewish elements of the extreme right. Yet I did not agree with some of my friends who maligned Jabotinsky, for I had been very impressed by his warning, issued at the very beginning of the Nazi era, that Hitler's words were to be heeded, that the dictator was speaking in earnest.

The friend who accompanied me on this nocturnal stroll was very close to the playwright and storyteller Ben Hecht. Hecht, who was inspired by Jabotinsky, was destined to play a tremendous role in the work of the Irgun delegation in the United States during World War II.

What Shmulik (Samuel B. Rose) told me was a revelation. He spoke about the difficulties Jabotinsky was encountering within the leadership of the Zionist movement in America, and said that certain "leaders" were openly fighting his proposal to establish a Jewish army which would serve with the Allies. I asked how they dared ridicule the founder of the Jewish Legion, the original Haganah. Yet while I asked the question I knew the answer: By then I understood the Jews in the United States. I saw how they had behaved that Yom Kippur night, the first Yom Kippur of World War II, and I knew what Jabotinsky meant when he spoke about underestimating the danger to Jews in Europe.

(I once asked Jabotinsky, who came to New York from London in 1939, whether the Jews in England were Zionists. He chuckled, "They are exactly like the Jews here in the garment center; they produce pants — the best ones!")

That night Shmulik and I talked for a long time about a few of Jabotinsky's disciples who had arrived in the United States to organize active resistance to Hitler's war against the Jews in Europe.

V
Paralysis of the Jewish Mind;
The Guardians of Public Funds

These pages are a postscript to the most decisive years in the history of the diaspora, 1933-1945, when the Holocaust led us directly into a new age in the annals of the Jewish people: the era of the Jewish revolution. The reader may be shocked by accusations against men who have been worshipped by Jews the world over and who, on account of extreme adroitness and dexterity in handling public relations, are still considered fighters for Jewish freedom.

During Hitler's war against the Jews, these men, representing the "new class", the "leaders" and professional Jews, lost courage; they passively watched the destruction of European Jewry. Not all of them were villains; some were merely naive. Others were simply defending their vested interests, their "class" and their organizations against the beginning of the Jewish revolution led by the Irgun both in Palestine and the United States. These socalled leaders lived in an atmosphere of isolationism and introversion. Then, just as today, there were too many organizations.

The more I think of what happened during World War II, the more I am convinced that the essential factor contributing to the catastrophe was Jewish fatalism. A complete mental paralysis seized our people from 1933 to 1945. This paralysis of the collective Jewish mind stemmed from a business-as-usual attitude which prevailed. Today many wonder why the Jews of Europe did not resist. Yet more important is this question: Why was there no active resistance, no militancy on their behalf in the free countries of the West, especially in Palestine and North America?

*   *   *

During World War II many of our leaders placed their hopes in different personalities or governments, believing that such terror, such murder, would not be tolerated by "world conscience." Naively they believed that the leaders of the anti-Hitler coalition were truly concerned about those caught in the Nazi squeeze.

The Saint from Neutra

In September 1942, I attended an unusual meeting at the offices of the World Jewish Congress, then located at West 42nd Street. Because of my intimate friendship with Rabbi Benjamin W. Hendles, I was invited to this gathering of historic significance. At the time Hendles was executive vice-president of the Orthodox Agudat Israel. He was a refugee in the United States, caught in the maelstrom of the war. In his native Warsaw Rabbi Hendles had been one of the democratically elected leaders of the Jewish Community Council. In 1939 he came to America on an educational mission, leaving his wife and children in Poland. He was unable to return due to the outbreak of hostilities in Europe, and his entire family perished in the Holocaust. In the United States Rabbi Hendles worked closely with the Irgun delegation and was cochairman of its National Jewish Council. Thus our close friendship developed from a working relationship.

At the meeting all attention was focused on a cable from Isaac Sternbuch, the Vaad Hatzalah representative in Montreux, Switzerland. Because of wartime censorship the message had been transmitted in code through the Polish Consulate General in New York City. A former Torontonian, Dr. Julius Kuhl, who during World War II served as attaché at the Polish embassy in Berne, sent the message to the Polish Consul General who in turn transmitted the cable to Dr. Isaac Lewin with a request that it be conveyed to Mr. Rosenheim.

The wire submitted by the Polish Consulate General dated September 3, 1942, read as follows:

"From Sternbuch to Jacob Rosenheim:

According to the last authentic and repeated information, the German authorities recently evacuated completely the population of the Warsaw ghetto. One hundred thousand Jews were murdered in the most bestial manner. The mass murders still continue. From the corpses the Germans make soap and artificial chemical fertilizers. Those deported from other occupied countries meet the same end. One must assume that only energetic action on the part of the United States could put a stop to these horrors. Do immediately whatever is possible in order to provoke reaction; move statesmen, the press and the public."

Sternbuch demanded that Stephen Wise, Rabbi Eliezer Silver, philosopher Jacob Klatzkin, Dr. Nahum Goldmann, Nobel Prize winners Thomas Mann and Albert Einstein, the Lubavitcher Rebbe and others be informed. Sternbuch asked that receipt of the cable be confirmed.

In his books historian Isaac Lewin correctly states that this was the first reliable information confirming the massacres in Eastern Europe. Allegations in some writings that it was Gerhard Riegner of the World Jewish Congress who transmitted the first reports are erroneous. Riegner spoke of plans for annihilation, while Sternbuch already had all the facts.

It is noteworthy that Sidney Silverman, a British Labor Leader who had wired Stephen Wise about Riegner's information, added a postscript: "The (British) Foreign Office has no information and cannot confirm this message." In fact, Wise admitted he had never heard these details before.

Wise promised to discuss the cable with the American Secretary of State, which he did. The Secretary told him that this kind of information was merely "war propaganda." (Such rationalizations from the State Department and the British Foreign Office were a good excuse to explain their passivity. This contemptible attitude continued until mid-1944, when the War Refugee Board was established.)

When Hendles informed me a few days later about this report from Dr. Wise, he added, "I am sorry that I did not transmit this information to Ben Hecht (the writer who at that time headed a front organization of the Irgun). Now the matter is not being given publicity because Rosenheim promised to keep it strictly secret in exchange for the assurance that the United States government would take some action immediately."

How did this information reach the United States?

It is here that the Saint from Neutra makes his appearance.

During the war years Neutra, a town in Slovakia, had two rabbis who were also the heads of a local yeshiva: Samuel David Ungar and his son-in-law, Michael Dov Weissmandl. It is remarkable that as early as 1940 these two small-town rabbis detected the corruption within the German war machine and dared suggest to some Nazi leaders that money be exchanged for lives. The bribes were accepted; human lives were saved.

Thus Weissmandl emerges from the war as perhaps the only *statesman* who saw the writing on the Teutonic wall before Churchill and Roosevelt.

*   *   *

Several years ago in Washington I met a remarkable man, Josef Lettrich, who played an important wartime role in his native Czechoslovakia. During World War II Dr. Lettrich was a leader of the Czechoslovak underground fighting the Nazis. A Slovak jurist and political leader, he was involved in the Slovak national uprising against the Germans in 1944. Following World War II he became president of the Slovak National Council, the parliament of his country. When the communists overthrew the government, Lettrich left for the United States.

In his book on the history of modern Slovakia, Lettrich devotes a chapter to the tragic end of Slovakian Jewry; his writings aptly explain Weissmandl's understanding of the problem.

"Although the Jews represented an insignificant minority in Slovakia" — there were only about one hundred and fifty thousand of them in 1938 — antisemitism there was more ferocious than in Hitler's Germany itself.

When Czechoslovakia split up following the Munich crisis, the Slovak fascists established the Nazi-controlled "independent" Slovakia and immediately began to persecute the Jews.

A Slovak cabinet minister, Ferdinand Durcansky, had promised Nazi Field Marshal Hermann Goehring that "the Jewish question will be settled in the same way as in Germany" and the Slovak rulers became most enthusiastic persecutors of the Jews. As early as October 1938 they issued a government decree placing the Jews outside the law. Although the Slovak fascist leaders were Catholics, in their anti-Jewish legislation they declared as "Jews" converts who had become Christians after 1918, or those who had one Jewish parent, or had married a Jew, or had been living with a Jew in an "illegal union."

In many respects this Slovak version of anti-Jewish legislation went beyond the laws of the Third Reich.

At the beginning of 1942, a Slovakian cabinet minister, Vojtech Tuka, entered into an agreement with the notorious chief of the German Police Forces, Reichsfuhrer Heinrich Himmler, "to help solve the problem of the Jews." The

Slovak Jews were to be deported to Poland, and the agreement was later confirmed by the Slovak "parliament."

At the Nuremberg Trials it was reported that by the spring of 1942 "about seventeen thousand Jews were taken from Slovakia to Poland and that later about thirty-five thousand Jews were deported to Poland."

While the official leaders of the Slovak Jewish community initially believed that the Germans were only deporting them to labor camps, Weissmandl immediately realized that they were destined for death.

By 1940 Weissmandl had established a network of underground couriers who smuggled his alarming reports to Switzerland. The representative of the American Orthodox Rescue Committee in Zurich, Hayim Israel Eiss and, upon his demise, Isaac Sternbuch, in turn found ways to transmit these messages through the Polish embassy in Berne to the United States.

With his perceptive mind and unusual intelligence, Weissmandl completely understood the internal moral collapse engendered by the German war machine. From his small study in the yeshiva he observed the doings of the Germans and decided that no matter how brutal some of these gangsters were, a few of them, in very sensitive positions, were ready to take out some kind of insurance policy in case Germany lost the war. There were, of course, those fanatics who were determined to go down with Hitler if he failed, but there were all the others, at the very beginning of the Nazi war adventure, seeking a means to save their hides in case of debâcle. What many observers in high diplomatic posts did not see, this "old-fashioned" rabbi, with his unusual sense of human psychology, had learned about the Nazis.

Weissmandl, who died a sick and broken man in Mount Kisco, New York (he lost his wife and children in the Holocaust), never forgot and never forgave the Jewish leaders of the Free World for their neglect — crime, he called it — in failing to save their brethren locked within Hitler's Europe.

Weissmandl, as I remember him, had an innate knowledge of human behavior. When this Jew with a long beard and sidelocks, clad in hassidic garb, was negotiating with high-ranking German officials about the rescue of Jews, he was ever aware of one very pertinent fact: Jews could be bought; to the Nazis Jews were business. The contact with Jews abroad would be important if Hitler lost the war; for them it would be an alibi that they were not really killers, but humanitarians who had helped save people from the gas chambers. This, Weissmandl understood, might help save the Jewish hostages. He was also well aware of the Nazis' cupidity and avarice — characteristic of all gangsters.

The longer the war dragged on, and especially after the fall of Stalingrad, the more it became evident that the Germans were losing. The Nazis who were dealing with Jewish lives — who had undertaken to liquidate all Jews in countries under Nazi control — were divided among themselves. One group was ready to die with Hitler; the other, determined to save their own skins. Hence, as Weissmandl rightly noticed, there was an opportunity to stop the slaughter, at least in Slovakia and Hungary. The problem was to find money in the Jewish communities abroad to buy off the murderers. More than anything else, it was vital to convince these butchers that Jews overseas would remember them after the war. At one point the Archangel of Death, Reichsfuhrer Heinrich Himmler, the most powerful man next to Hitler, was invloved in these negotiations.

I will never forget Weissmandl's testimony before the Nuremberg War Tribunal. He and others confirmed that the appeal to foreign Jews and the American government to buy off the Nazis could have resulted in the saving of lives. But until late 1944 the State Department — and certain Jewish leaders — were unwilling to risk money for blood. Whenever Weissmandl met men who had been in a position to raise money for the rescue operations and failed to do so, he would angrily declare, "I should not talk to you because you knew, you were told, you had the chance, but you criminally neglected the opportunity to save lives. You stood idly by the blood of your brethren."

A Toronto businessman, Herman Landau, who was involved with his late brother Henri in the Montreux, Switzerland activities of the Vaad Hatzalah as a representative of the American Orthodox rabbinate, vividly recalls the day Weissmandl arrived in Switzerland, burst into his office and hysterically cursed everybody. He said, as Landau remembers, that there was no use talking to any of those Jews abroad because they were criminals; they refused to save people from killers. Instead of secretly negotiating for the release of hostages, they made public statements and sought publicity as "leaders of their people." Weissmandl, at that moment, did not know that men such as the Sternbuchs, the Landaus and Dr. Julius Kuhl, who represented the Vaad Hatzalah of the American Orthodox Rabbis in Switzerland, or Dr. Reuben Hecht, a Swiss Jew who represented the American Irgun delegation in that country, were almost helpless. (In 1977 Dr. Hecht became advisor to Israeli Prime Minister Menachem Begin.) After the war, when Weissmandl's memoirs of that period appeared, he understood that most of the Orthodox rabbis in America and the Irgun delegation there were not only foiled in their efforts to arouse the Americans to "buy Jews" — this was Ben Hecht's overt slogan — but were maligned by those in the Jewish establishment who feared "competition" in the field of fundraising within the Jewish community.

Yet in 1942 the first message from Weissmandl, under his pseudonym, Ungar, concerning the total annihilation of Jews, was transmitted from Switzerland to Jacob Rosenheim in New York. That old man, a true patriarch with the elegant manners of a Frankfurt Jewish patrician, in his determination to obtain united support for such an action, somehow committed the error of seeking the help of the establishment generally and of Stephen S. Wise personally. When Rosenheim received the message confirming the ongoing extermination of Jews, a meeting was called by the Orthodox rabbis and Agudat Israel. Subsequently Rosenheim met with Stephen S. Wise.

Of course, as we know now, the State Department's attitude was consistent with Jewish policy:

(1) that any effort to save the Jews must be postponed until the Allied vic-

tory; (2) that the American government was opposed to buying the goodwill of the Nazis; (3) that everything possible was being done and nothing else could be done.

Still, the alarming cables from Weissmandl and others persisted.

In New York a nonsectarian organization created by the emissaries of the Irgun, the Emergency Committee to Save the Jewish People of Europe, tried to impress upon the government of the United States that there was an emergency, that Jews were being killed. Full-page advertisements in the newspapers accused the Roosevelt administration of neglecting an opportunity to save human lives and failing to recognize that there was an all-out Nazi war against the Jews, a war of extermination. The Orthodox Vaad Hatzalah was poor, had practically no funds and did what it could to dispatch some money through underground channels to Switzerland. Led by a dedicated couple, Isaac and Recha Sternbuch, the Vaad Hatzalah continued to alarm America via the Polish Embassy. The Sternbuchs and their friends could not understand the weak response of the American Jewish leaders. In one cable, Sternbuch asked Rosenheim to inform Dr. Stephen S. Wise and other Jewish leaders about the situation. He was sure they would help.

*   *   *

In the late fifties Rabbi Weissmandl, then a refugee from Slovakia in New York, published a volume in Hebrew titled *Min Hamaytzar* (From Distress). It includes all his correspondence during the war years, but remains largely unknown to the public due to its archaic, Responsa language.

Around the time his book appeared, Weissmandl met Peter H. Bergson (Hillel Kook) who, during the war years, had headed the Irgun delegation in America. Upon meeting Bergson, the old rabbi (whose yeshiva in Mount Kisco, N.Y. was sponsored by Billy Rose) said, "I came to see you because I just found out that you were the only one during World War II to fight for us . . . Unfortunately you, like me in Slovakia, had to defend yourself not only against the enemy, but also against the misunderstanding of many Jews."

Weissmandl's book is perhaps one of the most moving documents by a survivor. Its very theme — a quotation from a verse in Deuteronomy (29,6:8), "You will be put up for sale, but there will be no one to buy you!" — exactly describes the position of European Jews during World War II.

Weissmandl, who had been involved in wartime negotiations with the Nazis and pro-Nazi Slovaks, was disappointed with both the Jewish leaders in the Free World and with the Catholic Church. He later revealed that the representatives of the American Jewish Joint Distribution Committee in Switzerland had had a chance to save great numbers of Jews from Slovakia and Hungary, but refused to "gamble" money.

By 1943 many Nazis had already realized that they would have to save their skins, so Dieter von Wisliczeny, Eichmann's second-in-command, suggested several deals to the secret committee in Bratislava of which Weissmandl was a member. In fact, negotiations had started as early as 1941, when the Eichmann organization still believed that Jews overseas and Allied governments were interested in "buying" Jewish lives. Wisliczeny believed that there was enough money and enough Jewish influence in the United States to find some deserted country in the Americas where European Jews could be accepted, even temporarily. Of course, he demanded to be paid for this service. Every day, Weissmandl tells us, Wisliczeny would ask Gross, Weissmandl's representative, "Well, what is world Jewry doing?"

Weissmandl established contact with the representatives of the American Jewish Joint Distribution Committee in Switzerland. As he tells it in Min Hamaytzar:

"Many times I have written letters in Hebrew in the name of the Orthodox community in Slovakia and Hungary — letters dispatched by a special messenger from Budapest — and the reply has always been negative. It was impossible to tell Wisliczeny what we have achieved because we have achieved nothing."

These negotiations continued until the fall of 1942. Wisliczeny then told Gross, "Don't make a mistake. International Jewry is opposed to any deal to save you. Your night is black. It begins now and there is no morrow for you."

Wisliczeny then became incensed and started reciting the usual Nazi slogans against Jews: that the Jews in America were busy boycotting the Nazis; that they were involved in the war against Germany; that they had pushed the United States into war; and, therefore, that the negotiations were over. Wisliczeny, during one of these conversations, told the delegation of the Orthodox Jewish Community Council in Slovakia that the German Consul General in New York had reported that Stephen S. Wise, the leader of the American Jews, was not interested in the European Jews, only in a war against Germany. Wisliczeny even produced a photostat of an American Jewish newspaper to prove his point.

It is evident that by ignoring the corrupt Eichmann machine, the Jews in a position to help made these mad dogs even more ferocious. Weissmandl was not taken seriously. In one of his acrimonious letters to American Jewish leaders, the rabbi wrote: "You are dealing with Nazis. You are afraid to risk money for lives. You are insane!"

Weissmandl made the intensely practical suggestion, smuggled abroad in memos, that Allies bomb the bridges and railroads leading to Auschwitz; this would effectively slow down the process of extermination. In itself, this was one of the Irgun delegation's demands in America. *After* the war it was proved that such bombardment would have saved lives.

When one of Weissmandl's memos was intercepted by the Germans, they were relieved to learn that their transportation system to Auschwitz would remain intact. They need not have worried: The British High Command opposed destruction of the routes to the death camps.

Guardians of Public Funds

In one of his most caustic dispatches from Bratislava during the years of the Holocaust, Weissmandl characterized the leaders of the Jewish philanthropic organizations in the United States as the "most conscientious guardians of public funds."

These people, he writes to his contacts in Switzerland, have been entrusted with funds to do exactly what we here, embattled in a struggle for survival, are asking them do do: to use their money to save lives, to buy lives if necessary. But they would not take such "risks." They would like to deal with the Nazi murderers in the way one deals with businessmen. They want Wall Street securities. They demand all kinds of guarantees while each moment that passes means more lives lost . . . The Germans with whom we negotiated and with whom we entered into this money-for-life deal are now complaining that some publicity is being given these secret negotiations. "All of us have warned against publicizing such news as we know that among the German authorities there is a division of opinion about this issue: The crooks with whom we deal like money, so we have a means of saving lives; the fanatics want to exterminate us all."

Weissmandl emerges from this study as the *only* leader of European Jews during World War II. He alone understood that the Germans could not have "achieved" in open cities such as Prague, Budapest, Bratislava and Cracow what they did in off-limits camps. The map that Weissmandl sent abroad by special courier, a detailed map of Auschwitz with a request that the crematoria be put out of order (and which would require at least a year to repair), wound up in the wastebasket of some bureaucrat in a New York Jewish office.

The information from Bratislava was transmitted to all Jewish leaders, including Stephen S. Wise, whose supporters bragged that he alone had the "key to the White House." Today there remains no doubt that a strong démarche on the part of Jewish leaders of influence would have forced Allied Headquarters to consider these requests and thus save human lives.

However, these demands came from "irresponsible groups" who knew nothing, while the Jewish establishment knew everything. Therefore, the "unimportant groups" advocating such steps were publicly maligned, and the bickering among Jewish organizations continued while millions of lives were on the scales.

It is understandable why those responsible for this policy have seen to it that the story of our generation is not communicated factually to children in the Israeli public schools. If they ever become acquainted with these facts and begin to ask questions, God knows what would happen to some of the street signs in the Israeli cities named in honor of certain "prominent" Jewish leaders!

It is perhaps relevant to mention here that the Germans who were determined to exterminate us sensed that these non-modern Orthodox Jews with beards and sidelocks were somehow more dangerous to them than those who spoke the contemporary language of politics. Weissmandl began his rescue operations and formulated realistic policies in 1940 while others, as we can see from the records, still believed that the war would soon be over and there was no physical danger to the Jews.

A pertinent example of the German attitude can be found in a secret circular to the German occupation authorities issued by the *Reichssicherheitshauptamt*, dated November 25th, 1940:

"In the case of emigration of Jews from the territory of the General-Gouvernement (German name for occupied Poland) . . . I have to insist that the following be observed: The continuous emigration of Eastern (European) Jews signifies a continuous spiritual regeneration of World Jewry. For the Eastern European Jews, because of their religious Orthodox tradition, with their rabbis, Talmudic scholars and so on, sought after especially by American Jewry . . . constitute the most important blood infusion giving more power to Jews. Such an emigration would mean a spiritual renewal of Jews in the United States and a better organiztion and concentration of their activities . . . they would then become strong in their battle against Germany."

This circular was signed by Hans Frank, Hitler's governor of Poland.

Weissmandl, in cooperation with Gizi Fleischmann, the representative of the Jewish Agency in Bratislava, occasionally succeeded in transmitting through underground channels almost one hundred communications to Switzerland — to the Sternbuchs — in which it was clearly indicated how rescue efforts might best be undertaken.

Today we know that because of his unusual diplomacy in dealing with the German gangsters, Weissmandl succeeded in saving a substantial number of Jews in Slovakia. Unfortunately he failed in the most important undertaking of all: the plan to stop *all* deportations in exchange for money. The money did not arrive. However, at the very beginning of the war, Weissmandl did succeed in having many children smuggled out of Poland to Hungary.

The most important messages from him and Gizi were the ones in which he announced he had made a deal that would postpone deportations indefinitely. Weissmandl candidly advised his friends abroad that if it were within his power to deliver money to the Nazi gansters who were ready to accept bribes, *all deportations* could virtually be brought to a halt until the end of the war. This was confirmed by Gizi Fleischmann!

The rabbi described in detail the types of officials with whom he was dealing. When Wisliczeny, the German bureaucrat in charge of exterminating the Jews, received his first payment, he kept his word and stopped the deportations. Eichmann's deputy was greedy, an easy man to buy off. Weissmandl informed his friends abroad that there was no danger that any funds would land in the German war treasury. Those who were bribed put their money into their own pockets; they were saving up for defeat.

Weissmandl, who was very well-informed about the world situation, cautioned the Jews in the Free World against the "explanation" that there was a danger in aiding the enemy. "This is pure nonsense," he declared. In one letter Weissmandl cited the example of sending Allied food shipments to Greece (this was actually a breach of the blockade of enemy territory). He wanted to know whether Jewish leaders abroad were less interested in the lives of their brethren than were the Greeks in America or the friends of Greece in the food program for starving men and women.

It must be repeated again and again that the most serious crime on the part of the Jewish leadership abroad was committed in 1943. By then they all knew the facts. Ever since the fall of 1942 the leaders of the Jewish Agency in Jerusalem had been receiving up-to-date information about the German Final Solution. Gizi Fleischmann and her friends, the Zionist representatives in Bratislava, stated in an underground appeal to their leaders in Jerusalem that unless funds were forthcoming to cover the obligations undertaken by Weissmandl, the shipment of Jews to the extermination camps would be resumed. Gizi alerted Sally Mayer, the representative of the American Jewish Joint Distribution Committee in Switzerland, to the situation. She confirmed that the Weissmandl initiative had given the Jews of Slovakia a respite of several months, and that unless the greedy Nazi gangsters received the money promised them, the deportations to the death camps would resume in the spring.

Gizi Fleischmann had always been a dedicated Zionist. In her native Bratislava she represented the most important and powerful world Jewish organization, and secretly remained in constant touch with the headquarters of the World Zionist Movement in Jerusalem. Gizi informed her superiors that the deportations could be stopped quickly — if certain terms were met.

Toward the end of 1942 when the German killers received the first blood money, they became very business-like. Historian Isaac Lewin quotes documents proving that Dieter von Wisliczeny, after receiving his first payment, became so enamored of the plan that he brought an offer to exchange lives for cash from Himmler himself. Wisliczeny's plan also had the approval of his superior, Adolf Eichmann.

(Here I would like to remind the reader that this offer was made in December 1942, almost a year after the decision to implement the Final Solution was made at the infamous Wannsee Conference.)

Wisliczeny arrived in Bratislava on December 8, 1942 and reminded Weissmandl's committee and the other Jews with whom he had been in contact that he and Eichmann had kept their word in 1941 in halting the deportations upon receiving payment.

Wisliczeny then proposed a new scheme for which his super-boss and others would want to be paid if its provisions were met. They asked that a substantial sum in American dollars be deposited in a Swiss bank in return for which they, the murderers, would take it upon themselves to halt *all deportations of Jews* (except in Germany proper and Bohemia where they had no authority). Also, says Lewin, who kept all the relevant documents, these Nazis declared that they would find ways to relieve the situation of the Jews in Poland through a special agency to be established in Berlin. Through this agency the Jewish hostages would be able to communicate with their friends abroad once a month and receive food packages and clothing. They pledged themselves to completely suspend the socalled "second" deportation in Poland, and stated that they would guarantee replies from the people involved to be delivered to the senders.

By this time these Nazis had already received, through Weissmandl, sixty-two thousand dollars in American funds and one million, three thousand crowns in Slovakian money.

On November 15, 1942 the murderers were due to receive another twenty-five thousand dollars and seven-hundred-thousand crowns. Weissmandl and Fleischmann could not raise the money in Bratislava, so they sent out an alarm to Jews living abroad. Eichmann and Wisliczeny waited for the money until July, 1943. Then Eichmann threatened the Jews that he would resume more extensive deportations if the ransom money was not delivered.

*   *   *

In Switzerland, Sternbuch, who had received these appeals, dispatched the documents to New York. Dr. Lewin then went to see several outstanding, influential American Jewish leaders. By May, 1943 in New York, Lewin had in his possession the original letter from Slovakia, including information concerning the plan to halt all deportations. In the presence of a witness he showed a photostat to these leaders. Their reply: This was a black market operation which would have to be approved by the American Department of State!

Lewin reports: "In the month of May, 1943, all efforts to obtain a substantial amount of money in order to slow the tempo of the Nazi murder machine met with no success. As long as there was no approval from the Department of State, the Jewish leaders in America were afraid to undertake anything upon their own responsibility."

Lewin also notes that in their communications Weissmandl and those with him observed that Himmler and his gang did not intend to deliver this money to the German government, but were determined to keep it for themselves for *after* the war. While some funds Weissmandl received from the Sternbuch committee relieved the situation for a time, large amounts could not be raised because of the opposition of the establishment. Therefore, the Wisliczeny plan to halt all deportations never materialized. Only a year later, after the War Refugee Board was established, did something begin to happen, but by then it was too little and too late.

During 1943, the time of greatest opportunity for rescue, the establishment leaders in America were busy fighting every move by the nonsectarian Emergency Committee. This committee was fighting to save the Jewish people of Europe by bringing about the establishment of an American government agency that would assume the responsibility for rescuing the Jewish hostages from Hitler. If there had been such an agency, there would have been no problem finding funds to buy off German gangsters. The very existence of such an agency would have impressed these pragmatic Nazi gangsters and might have induced them to desist.

Yet Weissmandl, assisted by Fleischmann, did not relax for a moment. He continued to send out his appeals.

Gizi Fleischmann was an idealist who could not understand why all her appeals to Jerusalem were ignored. It was the leaders of the establishment there who decided what they would or would not do about the ransom money and about saving Jews from Nazis. It was they who believed themselves to be the divinely-appointed representatives of all Jews, including those in Hitler's camps.

Why did the Zionist leaders in America act the way they did? Did they not know that the man who made all the decisions concerning European Jews at the State Department was Assistant Secretary of State Breckenridge Long who, according to his own memos and diary, was an antisemite?

Professor Henry L. Feingold, an outstanding historian who wrote an important book indicting the Roosevelt administration, documented Breckenridge Long's enmity towards the people he was supposed to rescue. Long openly derived pleasure from the attitude of certain American Jewish leaders. He said, "There is no cohesion nor any sympathetic cooperation — rather rivalry and jealousy — among the Jewish organizations."

Jewish people looked up to the Jewish Agency in Palestine which, in the words of one of its leaders, knew "how to handle the affairs of the Jewish people." They did not need Weissmandl's information. Certainly those involved, like Gizi Fleischmann, must have believed it and transmitted to them all the facts.

* * *

The main problem facing the would-be rescuers was the deadline in this macabre money-for-blood deal.

The New York Orthodox Vaad Hatzalah decided to meet it, to pay the ransom on time, no matter how difficult it might be to raise the funds, because such an appeal could not be made public. They wired their committee in Switzerland (among whom was Reuben Hecht, the representative of the Irgun's Emergency Committee to save the Jewish People of Europe) that Weissmandl should go ahead, that the money would be deposited. The cable never reached Switzerland; it was stopped by the censor. Who was the censor? When it came to Jewish affairs in the United States, the censor was the American Jewish Joint Distribution Committee. Moe Levitt, then its executive director, absolutely refused to allow the cable to go through. The American government had appointed the JDC as the clearing house for all such messages. Levitt later admitted to Irving M. Bunim, the Young Israel and Orthodox Vaad Hatzalah leader (after the committee discovered that their cable had been intercepted), that American Jewish leadership could not afford to become involved in "illegal transactions."

The Weissmandl appeals from 1940 onward at first were not directed exclusively to Orthodox groups in Switzerland and the United States. As he told me later in New York, Weissmandl first sent all his information and suggestions to the Zionist organization, the Jewish Agency, the Joint Distribution Committee and other establishment offices in the belief that these influential groups, and men such as Dr. Stephen S. Wise, would move heaven and earth to rescue the Jews who could be saved.

When Weissmandl negotiated this biggest blood-for-money deal, one of his agents (who had dealings with Eichmann himself) pointed out to him the value of contact with influential American Jews. Eichmann was told, in the name of Weissmandl, that he should realize that the American Jewish Joint Distribution

Committee, which collected millions on behalf of European Jewry, certainly would not hesitate to place a million dollars in a Swiss bank at the disposal of Himmler, the man who controlled the death machinery, if human lives could be saved.

"Who would have believed," Weissmandl says in his memoirs, "that the attitude of the Joint would be different?" After the murder of so many, "did we need a permit from the Allied governments to bribe Nazi officials in order to save lives?" (Later on, in 1944, Eichmann dispatched Joel Brand, a Budapest Jew, to Chaim Weizmann, for Eichmann had lost his belief in the Joint. He wanted contact with influential Jews. These Germans knew that the official Jewish organizations in America would not budge.)

*   *   *

One evening in the fall of 1972 Bunim and I had a conversation in his apartment on Central Park West. We tried to reconstruct what had occurred during the latter period of the Holocaust when two million of the Six Million were still alive, when certain members of the Nazi government knew that Germany was losing the war and were therefore interested in an outside contact.

In this connection it is important to study the cables and letters addressed to Dr. Isaac Lewin. The cables were transmitted by Sylwain Strakacz, Polish Minister in New York. In late summer, 1944, an underground message reached the Polish Embassy in Washington with reliable information that there was an immediate possibility of saving the Jews in Auschwitz. For one million Swiss francs, according to Isaac Sternbuch, there was an opportunity to "buy" fifteen thousand Jews immediately. The deal suggested by Sternbuch was clear: No money would be given to the Germans before the people reached the outside world and, even in that case, it would be deposited in a Swiss bank so they could withdraw it only after the war. In that cable Sternbuch warned that "even the slightest indiscretion in this particular case might endanger the entire plan as well as the lives of the people we are trying to save."

The Polish government cautioned Lewin not to forget that Sternbuch's words should be taken very seriously because he had already "scored many successes in saving the lives of countless individuals."

This was the basic point made by Weissmandl: A continuous flow of money, even small amounts, along with uninterpreted negotiations, could have prevented murder. Yet those in control of the funds of the Jewish Agency in Jerusalem and the Joint Distribution Committee in New York would not "gamble" ransom money. They gambled with the lives of their fellow Jews.

In a communication to the Jewish Agency in Jerusalem in March 1943, at the very beginning of the "Final Solution," Gizi wrote, "One becomes overwhelmed by despair that our activities have been ineffective for months. Therefore I am forced to inform you that if we miss an opportunity, who knows if there will be another one." And in another message, "I am still alive. Why, I don't know."

Gizi went to incredible lengths to impress upon the leaders of the Jewish Agency in Jerusalem that they must take seriously the possibility of rescue, but to no avail. The *leaders* sat in their offices and discussed the post-war aims of the Jewish people. Documents also prove that these leaders tried to withhold information concerning the extermination from the Jewish community in Palestine and from the press.

"Are You All Insane?"

The more one delves into the documents relating to the Jewish tragedy within Hitler's Fortress Europe and its echo throughout Jewish communities in free lands, a question imposes itself:

Should the story be told? Should one reconstruct from documents now available — and from one's personal experience during World War II — the march of events, the moral decline that made Jews in the Free World passively accept the extermination of the Six Million?

There is no question that we are dealing here with the story of our generation. But again one asks: How can we live with the facts as they emerge stubbornly from the evidence now available; that men, glorified as leaders of a Jewish renaissance, actually appear as villains in the most tragic chapter of the entire history of our people?

Yet this same gnawing conscience that persists with the query as to the advisability of such revelations says clearly: Has the establishment that carries such a burden of guilt given up, relegated itself to the shadow of history? Has it made room for others less guilty to continue in the effort to redeem what is redeemable, to revive what could be made to live and flourish again? Or has this new class of professional and semi-professional Jewish leaders entrenched itself with such power that the facts of history will remain hidden till the end of time? If so, then our children and children's children will never know how many among the Six Million were betrayed.

As I travelled throughout the world, digging deeply into documents and observing the universal Jewish picture as it looks today, I asked myself whether one has the right to hide from posterity the true story of our generation. There were no questions asked during World War II. Asking questions was *chutzpah*; so was demanding an accounting.

I believe these revelations are necessary. It is imperative to analyze events leading to the closing of the avenues of rescue of the Jewish hostages of the Nazis during World War II.

Is it possible that recognized "world Zionist leaders" refused, during World War II, to deal with the problem of rescue? Yet, again the facts persist; they cannot be eliminated. I wish I could simply bypass them as irrelevant to our present existence. Yet the Six Million, their souls, flutter over the country which was promised them as a national home. The souls of the Six Million and those who would have been born from them look down upon us whenever we walk the streets of Jerusalem or bask on the beaches of Tel Aviv.

I am here, but where are they? It was for them, for their survival, that the

Jewish extablishment created a powerful, expensive organization. And if, during World War II, this organization completely ignored the cry of distress so movingly described by the most articulate of Auschwitz survivors, a saintly, revered rabbi, who am I to decide that the story of the generation should not be told?

As in a Talmudic tale of the martyrs, the obsession remains: The skins, the parchments have been burnt in Auschwitz and Maidanek; the letters inscribed on the parchment, the souls, have moved in here, under these blue skies, and their reflection in the azure of the Mediterranean is clear. They say: "We are here, and we want to know why we have been abandoned. We want to know why the then chairman of the Jewish Agency's 'Rescue Committee' in Palestine during World War II dared tell his committee that the Zionist movement would *not* spend a penny of United Jewish Appeal funds to save the Jews from Europe, but would continue to build the Jewish nation in Palestine.

"The Jewish nation? Which Jewish nation — without us — and why without us? Why was an emissary of the Jewish community in Budapest turned over to the British when he brought the message from Hungary that the Nazis would continue to burn us alive unless you consented to buy us, to ransom us?

"Why is it that when the only man who understood our situation, a saintly rabbi in Slovakia, warned you that 'you have become insane' if you contemplated dealing with the Nazi murderers as you would with normal politicians, this appeal, too, was ignored?

"For whom were you building the renascent Jewish nation if not for us, the Six Million? Or did you, even during the years of our martyrdom, continue to believe in the cliché of 'selective immigration', of admitting to Palestine only those whom you considered worthy of being saved?"

*　　　*　　　*

These thoughts are not fantasy. No matter how painful, the facts portraying the explicit relationship between those who considered themselves the saviors and leaders of the Jewish people and those who were left behind to perish must be told.

For example, is it possible to eliminate from the records the charge, the accusation by Irving Bunim, leader of the Young Israel movement in America, that during World War II executives of the American Jewish Joint Distribution Committee intercepted and stopped a cable to Switzerland stating that the Orthodox Vaad Hatzalah would pay ransom money to Nazis for Jews "up for sale?" Is it possible to deny that by this action the Joint contributed to the liquidation of innumerable thousands of hostages?

Today, in the hijacking era, millions of dollars are sacrificed to save a few people, or even one person. Yet in the most crucial years of World War II, our bureaucrats and the "new class" with vested interests in fundraising, who never ceased collecting money in America for "Jewish survival," dared state they would do nothing "illegal" to rescue Jews from Slovakia or Hungary . . . They would not jeopardize their standing with the American government, the British government, or the Russians — three governments that refused to lift a finger on behalf of Europe's Jews.

*   *   *

In the face of Nazi crimes, the *laissez-faire* attitude in New York among the philanthropists who collected money for the victims of Nazism in Europe was similar to that of the Zionist establishment in Palestine. The latter, despite the incessant British war against the remnant of the Jewish people in Europe and the harassment of Jewish escapees on the seven seas, had continued to maintain the best possible relations with the British administration in Palestine.

Possibilities for rescue were also confirmed by the official representatives of the Jewish Agency in Budapest and Bratislava who urged the Palestinian Jewish leaders to take seriously the offers of corrupt Nazi bureaucrats. No action. Finally the Nazi gangsters became convinced that the Jewish leaders in the Free World would *not* ransom Europe's Jews. This conviction on their part that the American and Palestinian Jewish leaders, including Chaim Weizmann, did not really care sealed the death warrant. Even the suggestion that ransom would be deposited in Swiss banks and not be released before the end of the war did not move the Jewish leaders to rescue their brethren. (In fact, even for those few who were eventually shipped out of Germany, no money was ever paid. There was no one to collect it after the war.)

The "big organizations" ignored all these possibilities for rescue while the "little organizations," such as the Irgun delegation in America and the Orthodox Vaad Hatzalah in New York, endeavored to raise the funds. These groups were maligned and the personal integrity of their members was attacked. The activists were branded as irresponsibles who would undermine the Allied war effort because they were willing to "deal" with the Nazis.

"The Account With Ourselves"

As we unfold the pages from the story of the Holocaust generation, the history of the battle for Jewish survival in Europe, there is one area which had been relegated to the background — what one historian calls "the account with ourselves." While we elaborate on the sins of others — and naturally the accounting with those who actively pursued the policy of genocide must take precedence over any other guilt by association or by silence — we minimize our own responsibility. Yet when we strike the balance of the role of those Jewish leaders who failed to act, we cannot simply dismiss the facts, as did Nahum Goldmann, by saying, "We made a mistake."

From personal observations and direct involvement in certain rescue efforts, I am profoundly convinced that this era of cynical disregard for human life — liquidating political opponents in the name of an ideal — our acceptance of the right to kill political enemies is a natural sequence of the events in Europe during World War II. Auschwitz and Maidanek have conditioned the world to tolerate political crimes of a kind never before recorded in history. Indirectly, we all suffer today because we refused to act during the war when we discovered the crimes being perpetrated in the extermination camps.

The marriage of cynicism and murder in the forties gave birth to the present state of mind where people accept murder and violence against innocents with incredible tolerance.

So when we review our own Jewish role in this tragic period in man's history, "the account with ourselves" must be honest and candid.

Bunim and the Rabbis Confront Morgenthau

As Irving Bunim recalled in his conversation with me, in negotiations with the Joint Distribution Committee and other American Jewish leaders, the expression "ransom" always came up. "A dirty word." In this connection Bunim never forgot the words of the late Rabbi Aaron Kotler, one of the sages of Israel, who became incensed when Moe Levitt of the JDC began speaking about "ransom": "Of course it was ransom, and had the Jews paid ransom, we know the situation would have looked different today!"

Irving Bunim sarcastically described the treatment given him by some of these "guardians of Jewish public funds." Once when he visited the office of the American Jewish Joint Distribution Committee, Joseph Schwartz, then the JDC executive head, told him in Yiddish:

"Ihr zucht a naya kremel." (You want to start a new racket.) In other words, all these religious leaders, the American rabbinate, the sages of Israel, such men as America's most respected rabbis — Aaron Kotler, Eliezer Silver, Dov Leventhal and Israel Rosenberg — were interested in becoming involved in a "new racket," while the well-paid officials of the Jewish organizations were pure idealists!

This attitude, Bunim remembered, did not manifest itself only during World War II. It began as early as 1938 when the first Irgun delegation arrived in the United States to promote the socalled "illegal aliyah" from Eastern Europe to Palestine. The head of the delegation was a British officer, Colonel Patterson (a friend of Jabotinsky), who declared at a dinner in New York, launching a campaign supported by Bunim and Young Israel, that "nothing is illegal when one can save human beings kept illegally in Europe by the British."

In response to this call, Stephen S. Wise publicly attacked the Irgun. He stated "on behalf of the World Zionist movement" that Palestine "will not be liberated by force of arms . . . This is a game of the Revisionists," he said. "Jews will be liberated by the conscience of the world, by the progressive world." Yet the leader of the Religious Zionists, Rabbi Meir Berlin (Bar Ilan), who happened to be visiting the United States, told Bunim to just go ahead and support "these boys" because what we are interested in at this moment is to fulfill the commandment of "V'Shavu Banim L'Gvulam" (and the sons will return within their borders).

Recalling those days, Bunim told this writer the frightful story of how the American Jewish establishment thwarted rescue attempts:

"We had received a message from Isaac Sternbuch, our representative in Switzerland. Sternbuch was then negotiating indirectly with a most influential hangman of the German gangster empire, Heinrich Himmler, through the Swiss pro-fascist statesman, Jean-Marie Musy. The first deal with Hitler had been one-hundred-and-seventy dollars a head; then they went down to seventeen dollars a head for liberating Jews from camps. This information came in code through the Polish Embassy in Berne, Switzerland, in a wire from Dr. Julius Kuhl, then an embassy attaché, to Dr. Isaac Lewin, now Professor of History at Yeshiva University.

"The cable was unequivocally clear: The deal had to be accepted within twenty-four hours; otherwise it was off. The money was supposed to be deposited in Switzerland, in a trust account controlled by Musy.

"This occurred on the Eve of Yom Kippur. We responded immediately by cabling our unconditional acceptance and our readiness to raise the funds.

"A few days later we went to Washington to obtain some help for the transfer of the money, which as I said, was to be held in Switzerland until the end of the war. In Washington we discovered that the cable with our reply had never reached our contact in Switzerland. It had been held back upon the decision of the Joint!

"Thus we had to start anew. We went to the Joint and, after some haggling, the Joint bureaucrats permitted the cable to go through. Thus four days were lost.

"This is only one example of the actions of the American Jewish Joint Distribution Committee during World War II."

Bunim recounted another incident involving the JDC:" At a certain point in its rescue efforts the Vaad Hatzalah in Switzerland was in immediate need of two million dollars to prove to the gangsters in Berlin that we meant business. In a very short time we managed to raise over one million; I don't know how. So we went to the JDC and showed them a clipping from *The New York Times* with the news that the first group of Jewish refugees had arrived in Switzerland, thanks to the Vaad Hatzalah.

"Moe Levitt, the executive head of the JDC, again began to raise objections. 'This is ransom,' he said. 'The American government will never permit paying ransom. The Russian government will disapprove because you are helping the enemy . . . the British will veto it for the same reason. This is dangerous.'

"I became desperate," Bunim recalled. "Here we are trying the impossible to save people and the official of the largest Jewish philanthropic organization in the world is afraid of what the Russians might say.

"We said to Levitt: The Germans took away billions of dollars from Jews the world over. Who objected against that? Did not these billions help the Nazis?

"Rabbi Aaron Kotler, the late revered Talmudic scholar who was a member of our delegation and a leader of the Vaad Hatzalah, said to Levitt:

"'Let us imagine a situation in which an enemy surrounds ten soldiers who are standing behind a cannon. So when you tell the soldiers to run away, you are giving the cannon to the enemy. You, because of your opposition to help ransom these people, are turning over all the ammunition to our enemy . . . all we want to do is to save the Jews . . . Suppose we give the Nazis one or two million dollars, will that change the war situation?'

"Eventually, under the pressure of important UJA contributers, the JDC agreed to lend the million dollars to the Vaad Hatzalah, but then the problems of obtaining a licence to send money to Europe from Washington arose. The man to grant it was Secretary of the Treasury Henry Morgenthau, Jr., who until that time had not been active in Jewish affairs. It seems that the issue of the licence had turned Morgenthau into a most dedicated activist in the field of rescue.

"It happened," Bunim relates, "when the Vaad Hatzalah delegation went to see the Secretary of the Treasury. We were told not to invite Moe Levitt to join us. But when we arrived in Morgenthau's office, the first word we heard from the Secretary was the expression 'ransom' almost in the same tone as we had heard it before from the JDC leader . . . There must have been some contact between the JDC and this Department. It could not have been just an accident.

"When Rabbi Kotler heard from Morganthau's own lips that he was hesitant to issue the licence because of the law against trading with the enemy, the old rabbi became so infuriated that he exclaimed, in Yiddish: 'Tell him that if he is afraid of his position as Secretary of the Treasury of the United States, one human life is worth more than his job.'

"Morgenthau looked up at Rabbi Kotler, at his fiery black eyes, at his nervous hands; he was shaking. So Morgenthau asked, 'What did the rabbi say?'

"I tried not to offend Morgenthau, so I translated Rabbi Kotler's remark freely. I said, Mr. Secretary, the rabbi thinks that perhaps because of your high position in government you cannot force the issue but he wants you to remember that saving one life is worth more than all government positions.

"For the first time, it appears, Morgenthau was moved to tears. He remembered his Jewishness. He got up from his chair, looked straight into Rabbi Kotler's eyes, and told me, 'Tell the rabbi I am a Jew. I am willing to give up not only my position but my life as well to help my brethren. You are getting your licence.' Of course, in this particular case, the deadlines had passed; it was too late . . ."

This incident, according to Bunim, had a tremendous influence upon Morgenthau. Later, when Roosevelt appointed him to the War Refugee Board, he showed more courage than any other Jewish official.

One should not forget that even after the creation of the War Refugee Board, a watered-down compromise version of what the Emergency Committee had demanded, the State Department never acquiesced to unusual "illegal" ransom translations. Morgenthau accused Breckenridge Long of antisemitism in the presence of President Roosevelt. He said that he was particularly antisemitic.

Morgenthau also suggested that the "pattern of the Administration's policy was set according to the President's wariness rather than his moral indignation." One of his associates is reported to have remarked that by its attitude the U.S. government was acquiescing "in the murder of Jews."

Morgenthau had become convinced that rescue was possible through Romania, France, Hungary, Switzerland, Turkey, Spain, but, as he told Secretary of State Stettinus, "In plain words . . . I am convinced that Breckenridge

Long . . . is deliberately obstructing the execution of any plan."

On January 16, 1944, Morgenthau told Roosevelt, "Your subordinates (Breckenridge Long) . . . are taking steps to prevent the rescue of Jews."

Bunim, who lives with the nightmare of the lost opportunities, described to me another influential Jew and his attitude toward rescue:

"At one point it was possible to bring more Jews to Switzerland on condition that more food be made available to the Swiss. That was the time when the Swiss government had ceased fearing the Germans. Bunim was told to see Governor Herbert H. Lehman, then head of UNRRA (United Nations Relief and Rehabilitation Administration).

Bunim went on to say that "the president of Switzerland told the American Rabbinical Vaad Hatzalah at that time, that he was willing to admit as many Jews as possible, but 'we must get more food.' So we went to Lehman. We told him the whole story about Musy and Himmler, and the Sternbuchs, that there were another 1,730 people en route . . . he seemed very moved . . . his cheeks twitching but he was adamant — and afraid. 'What can I do? he said. The Swiss government is not a member of the United Nations and UNRRA cannot be of any help.'

"Just like that he turned us down; it was tragic. But we did not give up. We went to see his associate, a young Brooklyn man by the name of Abraham Feller, a lawyer. I was very friendly with his parents. So I went to him and said: The bridge is burning. In Manhattan they say it's the Brooklyn bridge; in Brooklyn they say it's the Manhattan bridge. He helped us. The International Red Cross undertook, through his intervention, to supply the food."

*   *   *

In his uninterrupted flow of messages Weissmandl did not cease to explain; he thought that people did not understand him. And in a handwritten message, sent through a diplomat, he said: "In the name of all saints here, I am using the Halachic "Shevua d'Oraita" (the severest oath according to the Torah), with a full knowledge of all its implications according to rabbinic law, that you must bring together people of all factions and read to them the letters I dispatched through diplomatic channels. Remember that I wrote to Sally Mayer (the leader of Swiss Jewry and representative of the JDC) and to the others in America. Not one second can you lose. Again I am swearing a Shevua d'Oraita; don't wait one second!"

The "big organizations" ignored it; the "little organizations," the Irgun delegation in America, the Orthodox Vaad Hatzalah, were accused of undermining the Allied war effort because they were ready "to deal with the Nazis."

Weissmandl said, "We have the right and the duty to give you orders, because your most holy duty is to save the Jews from the Nazis. Is this not enough, or have you become insane?"

In another communication Weissmandl says, "I am sending you this message through a Catholic priest, in Hebrew; he will explain to you the situation here;

and he is waiting for an answer. There is nothing else I can say."

Continuously, Weissmandl urges action, always finding new ways for rescue, including buying false passports and identification cards, but only the least influential Jews and the least financially established are responding. Today we all know that Eichmann's right hand man, Wisliczeny, corroborated these facts when he testified at Nuremberg; and later, in Slovakia, when he was on trial for his miserable life.

"Suppose," Rabbi Aaron Kotler said once during his meetings, "we lose two million dollars, we get less Jews out of German-controlled territories than we're promised; would this be considered a failure?"

                    *   *   *

From the correspondence now available it becomes evident that the figure of Weissmandl towers over all Jewish leaders in Nazi occupied Europe. It is nonpareil, peerless. From the beginning of the war almost until its very end Weissmandl repeatedly informed Jewish organizations abroad not only of the nature of the tragedy, but of the opportunities for rescuing people who became a nation of hostages. But in retrospect it seems that he, too, committed a grave error when he believed that the leading Jews in the West would become as active as he was and unite in an unequalled effort to save those singled out for destruction. While he knew the doomed, he did not know the scared — the politicians among his own people in the Free World. To him it was so simple: The graft-ridden German occupation officials could be bought. Even when there was a doubt as to the effectiveness of this enterprise, he followed the age-old dictum of his religious tradition: The saving of one human being is more important than breaking all rules. At the beginning, he believed naively, despite his profound intelligence, that Jewish leaders abroad were the same defenders of their people of whom he had read in Jewish history books. He could not have believed that in the West those who controlled Jewish community funds collected for such an emergency would refuse to "gamble" money in exchange for human lives.

Whenever Weissmandl sent his alarming messages to the West, he made sure they were corroborated by outstanding local community leaders who did not share his religious or political views but were known to Jewish leaders abroad. Also, Gizi, his colleague, communicated independently with Jewish leaders in Palestine and Switzerland asking them to heed Weissmandl's admonitions and requests. She warned that unless funds were transmitted to buy off German officials, the deportations to the death camps would be resumed.

In Jerusalem, Yitzhak Greenbaum, the head of the Jewish Agency's "Rescue Committee," stated he would not spend a penny on rescue. "Jews must wait until the Allied victory."

Gizi Fleischmann did not live to see the day of Allied victory. She perished in Auschwitz. When the Germans finally lost faith in the delivery of money, they resumed the deportations and Gizi was one of the first to be cremated alive. If she had survived the war, we might have had another prosecutor to support

Weissmandl in his accusations against the war criminals among her own people.

Weissmandl and the Church

A controversy is still raging concerning the role of the Vatican during the Holocaust. It became especially bitter following the presentation of Rolf Hochhut's play, *The Deputy*, in which the German writer accuses Pope Pius XII of silently acquiescing in the slaughter of the Six Million.

Weissmandl had dealings with the Catholic clergy in Slovakia during that period, and his experience was one of total disappointment in the princes of the church. The communications he sent by underground courier to the pope himself had no effect, Weissmandl says. In order to make sure they reached the pontiff, he wrote them in Hebrew. All the messages were received by the Vatican. But the replies, according to Weissmandl, were such that the Catholic dictator of Slovakia and his clique understood them to be *consent* to the crime.

Weissmandl tells the story of his visit with one bishop to whom he appealed for help. The bishop was cynical; he said there were no innocent Jews. When the rabbi asked him about the innocence of the little children, the reply was the same: There are no innocent Jewish children.

However, Josef Lettrich, the former democratic leader of Slovakia, disagrees with Weissmandl. This bishop was not the rule, but the exception. Lettrich apologized for the Vatican and blames the Slovak Catholic-fascist regime and its fanatical, medieval hatred of Jews for the situation in Slovakia. The fascist Slovak government was interested in more than eliminating the Jews physically: A special agency was created to take over "Jewish property," Lettrich says. Thus hatred was combined with greed.

According to Lettrich, "The Vatican repeatedly and energetically intervened with the Bratislava government against the application of the 'Jewish Code,' the racial legislation that included rules contrary to Catholic principles." Lettrich also maintains that the Vatican was "unable to presume that in a country which purports to be governed by Catholic principles, such grave measures could be put into effect." But Lettrich did not have the experience of Weissmandl. The Vatican, of course, had all the information.

The late Dr. Aryeh Leon Kubovy (Kubowitzki), World Jewish Congress secretary general, in an essay published in Volume VI of *Yad Vashem Studies,* defended Pius XII against certain accusations of complicity. Kubovy says that we have more than "one single account to settle:" First, with Germany, and not with Nazi Germany alone; then with the Allies who knew and who "did not allow our tragedy to affect the strategy of the war"; with the International Red Cross; and, "last but not least with ourselves, for our shortness of vision."

Kubovy, who, after the war, was received by the pope, was a diplomat. He thanked the pope for the help extended to the Jews in Italy during World War II. But Kubovy maintains that it was the silence of the churches the world over more than that of the pope that hurt the Jews in Europe. The princes of the church were determined not to get involved.

From my own studies on the subject it seems that assistance to the victims of the Nazis on the part of the church depended on the situation and the atmosphere of the respective country in which it operated. It is true that in liberal countries such as Italy, France and Belgium, Catholic clergy helped hide Jews from the Nazis. Yet in countries where antisemitism was traditional, such as Poland and Slovakia, the Catholic clergy certainly deserved the bitter censure of Rabbi Weissmandl. Concerning Slovakia one must remember that its ruling Catholic party took over the reins of government with the help of the Germans. It was overtly antisemitic. And while the pópe kept his silence during the war years (Hitler, the "Catholic," was never excommunicated), the official Vatican newspaper *L'Osservatore Romano* on March 14, 1939 celebrated the takeover of Slovakia by the Catholic fascists.

Livia Rothkirchen, the historian of Slovak Jewry, says that the socalled independent Slovakia was "very near Hitler's heart." However Rothkirchen maintains that the Vatican mildly "expresses regret" at the racial policy of the Slovak government. Although there was a series of interventions, the apostolic delegate in Bratislava did not protest to President Tiso against the deportations. It is difficult to believe Lettrich that Rome was fooled by having been given incorrect information. On the other hand, Weissmandl was not impressed by verbal statements and protests. He was dealing *very concretely* with saving lives, and the pope had certainly failed him and the other Jews trapped by the Nazis. In his book, *Min Hamaytzar,* Weissmandl says:

" . . . The message to the pope was based on the assumption that Tiso, the President of Slovakia, as a Catholic priest, is subject to the pope and therefore must obey him. The pope has the power to threaten him even with excommunication should he refuse to listen . . . The fact is that it was the Slovak rulers who asked the Germans to "remove" the Jews from the country. For each deported Jew the Germans paid the Slovaks five hundred marks.

" . . . The memorandum to the pope which I wrote in the name of the rabbis in Hebrew was composed carefully. I described the situation exactly."

Lettrich says that Sidor, Tiso's ambassador to the Vatican, misled the pope. Weissmandl's letter to the pope was delivered to Rome by this same Sidor, who received thirty thousand marks for the "errand!" This episode, the buying of Sidor, again proves Weissmandl's contention that if his committee had had sufficient funds, many a tragedy could have been averted.

Weissmandl's letter to the pope provoked a pastoral letter to Tiso. At a meeting of the clergy, Father Tiso read this papal message, which he interpreted in the following manner, according to Weissmandl: The pope asks us not to deport converted Jews which means that the authentic Jews should be deported; the pope says we should not divide families which means that when we deport Jews, we should also deport their children.

A Bishop Peceni then asked Tiso: "What will happen to us if the Allies win the war and the Jews return from Poland?"

To this Tiso replied, "I assure you they will not return."

Rabbi Weissmandl's father-in-law, Rabbi Samuel David Ungar, once undertook a personal mission to intervene with his "friend," Archbishop Kmetko of Turnau. He asked the archbishop to help stop the cruel deportations. The elderly archbishop (he was 82 at the time) told Rabbi Ungar, "Don't be afraid that your people there will starve; they won't; they will all be exterminated, the young and the old."

Concerning the role of the apostolic delegate, about whom others say he delivered "protests" from the pope, Weissmandl relates: He said, "There is no innocent Jewish blood."

Thus, when one considers the apologetics of certain Jewish and Catholic historians and public statements by the Slovak clergy, Weissmandl's personal experience must weigh very heavily against them. No wonder Weissmandl was incensed when he heard in New York that Kubovy had visited the pope.

Weissmandl never trusted the Germans and those who collaborated with them. When the Germans finally caught him and shipped him on a train to Auschwitz, he again showed his indomitable courage by jumping off the train. Not only did Weissmandl survive, but a true story of what happened to the Jews of Slovakia was not lost to posterity; nor was the Jewish establishment's record of timidy, fear and surrender.

*   *   *

VI
Official Zionism vs.
The Jewish Revolution

*. . . Si «Dreyfus» n'avait pas été Dreyfus, aurait-il
même été «Dreyfusard»?...*

In 1961, when Ben Hecht published *Perfidy,* a book which contains serious accusations against the Jewish establishment during World War II, many were
shocked by its tenor. The Jewish Agency, instead of refuting the arguments, fought
back with a brochure attacking Hecht.

Some of the facts still need to be explained; others which Hecht did not mention must be told. Hecht wrote *Perfidy* following the famous Kastner trial.

During the war years Kastner represented the World Zionist Organization,
the Jewish Agency and the American Jewish Joint Distribution Committee in
Budapest. Ultimately he was convicted for cooperating with the Nazis in mass
murder.

In 1954 Malkiel Greenwald, a Chaplinesque character, an elderly Hungarian
Jew who immigrated to Israel in 1938 and had lost a son in the Irgun revolt, was
dragged into court for having "maligned an official of the Israeli government."
The plaintiff was the State of Israel because the "insulted party," Dr. Rudolph
Kastner, was a leading member of the governing Labor Party and editor of *Uj
Kelet,* the Hungarian-language daily controlled by his political party.

In a widely circulated pamphlet Greenwald, who lost eighteen members of
his family during the German occupation, accused Kastner of having cooperated
with Eichmann himself in the extermination of Hungarian Jewry. Kastner was
also accused of having defended, at the Nuremberg War Crimes Tribunal, Nazi
monster Kurt Becher, collaborator of the notorious Gestapo bureaucrat Kaltenbrunner. Allegedly Kastner had defended him because Becher was his partner
in crime.

At that time Moshe Sharett was prime minister of Israel. Sharett must have
felt that he himself was under attack because until this day his role in another
rescue effort has remained a puzzle, to say the least. This questionable role of
Sharett was often mentioned in connection with the failure of Joel Brand, who
was sent by Eichmann to meet with Weizmann and Sharett to suggest the infamous
money-for-blood deal. (The Nazi was ready to sell a million Jews to the World
Zionist leaders.) Yet when Sharett met Brand at Aleppo, Syria, British secret
agents were there; they arrested him and took him to Cairo where he remained
until the end of the war.

Brand, who lived in Israel after the war, published a book in which he accused Sharett of having delivered him to the British instead of listening to his
story. However, Brand was never jailed by Israeli officials for defaming a former
prime minister.

So when Greenwald published his pamphlet against Kastner and the establishment, disseminating these allegations, the Government of Israel sued him for libel.

A former Irgun commander and brilliant young lawyer, Shmuel Tamir, took up the defense of poor Malkiel and succeeded in turning the case into a *cause célèbre* against Kastner and those who backed him. (Tamir was Minister of Justice in the second Begin government.) It was the most sensational trial in the history of the Jewish state. At the beginning the government attorney bragged that he would close the case within a week and put Greenwald in jail for maligning a leader of the ruling Labor Party. As it turned out, the deliberations of the court continued for four years.— from 1953 until 1957 — and Tamir, like a lion, stood by Greenwald until the presiding judge stated, "Kastner sold his soul to the devil."

All the facts mentioned by Greenwald were substantiated. Not only did Kastner cooperate with the Germans by "drugging" the Jews whose leader he was, by making them believe that the trains to Auschwitz were actually taking them to some ideal town where they would be better fed and obtain better living quarters; Kastner was the only Jew in German-occupied Budapest who lived in luxury until the end of the war. He had a villa, a car, private telephone, secretaries, a mistress, and was wined and dined by the Nazi killers. He was also the only Jew allowed to leave German-occupied Hungary and return there when he went on a mission to Switzerland together with a Nazi official.

*   *   *

For his services Kastner received a gift: exit visas to Switzerland for 1,300 "prominent" Jews, his friends and relatives, while, directly and indirectly, he encouraged close to 600,000 Jews to travel to the Shangri-la in Auschwitz.

So, after the war — a service for a service — Kastner appeared in Nuremberg and in a written document absolved Kurt Becher, who would have been executed, of any guilt in the extermination policies of the Germans. It was also established during the Kastner trial that he performed this mission on behalf of Becher with the concurrence and approval of some officials of the Jewish establishment in Palestine, and had travelled to Germany at the expense of the Jewish Agency!

This case illustrates a part of history which answers why the collective will of American Jewry was paralyzed during World War II; why many thousands of Jews who could have been saved by the socalled illegal aliyah were left to die in Hitler's dungeons; and why we failed to save those who could have been saved from Auschwitz and Maidanek.

The first Irgun emissaries who arrived in the United States two years before the outbreak of World War II had a single mission. In 1938, when Polish Jewry felt the noose around its neck, these Irgun revolutionaries knew that those facing extermination would not be saved unless they were moved by any possible means to Palestine. So they activated the Aliyah Beth to Palestine, organizing the smuggling of European Jews into the Jewish homeland, which British imperialist considerations had arbitrarily closed to those who needed it most.

An outstanding historian of this period, Haim Lazar-Litai, in his story of Aliyah Beth ("illegal" emigration), relates in detail this unusual and courageous fight against the closed doors of Palestine — a battle against the most powerful empire on earth. The "smugglers" were the sons of middle-class families, mostly students who had left the universities in free lands, including the academies of Israel, to become underground workers. They faced harassment on two fronts: first from British Intelligence, then from the Zionist Establishment which believed in *selective emigration* to Israel.

Is it not unbelievable, as Lazar-Litai records in his book, that the first British official to limit Jewish immigration into Palestine was a Jew many admired? He was Viscount Herbert Samuel, an observant Jew whose appointment as the first High Commissioner of Great Britain in Palestine in 1920 created euphoria among Jews.

When Samuel was called to the Torah on the *Shabbat* following his arrival in Jerusalem, he wept when he recited the verse, "And on His throne there shall sit no stranger." Samuel's appointment generated the same type of enthusiasm which generally occurs when someone of Jewish descent becomes a high official in any country. When this happens Jews illogically feel they have attained full emancipation. In the case of Herbert Samuel, Jews believed: We have reached a new height; a Jew rules Palestine!

*   *   *

Herbert Samuel's philosophy (and he was, besides being a politician, an outstanding liberal thinker) was similar to that of Leon Blum who had become the first "Jewish premier" of France. Blum's "liberalism," so dangerous in the years when the world had to face Hitler led him to speak out *against* the inevitability of war. Very close to the outbreak of World War II he spoke — as if from another planet — about hope for peace and the need to lay the intellectual foundations for a new social order. Despite Hitler — and in cooperation with Hitler — he believed in the possibility of a permanent peace and the abolition of poverty. Leon Blum became the prime minister of France, Jews were moved to talk of messianic days in Europe. Blum, in my opinion, was a "good Jew," better than many others who had attained high positions. In his memoirs, when he speaks of the Dreyfus affair, he says something that could be applied to many frightened Jews. Describing the atmosphere of fear among the French-Jewish elite during the Dreyfus crisis, when that class of prominent Jews to which Dreyfus himself belonged wanted to hush up the entire case "in order not to provoke antisemitism," Blum writes: "Were Dreyfus not Dreyfus he would have been against publicizing the Dreyfus case."

Blum was an excellent polemicist, an important political theoretician. Perhaps more than anything else, however, he was a typical French *homme de lettres* who loved the best wines and the finest poetry. But in my opinion he was one of the worst prime ministers France ever had. He had no contact with the people he claimed to represent. The son of a wealthy family, he was catapulted by some accident of history into presiding over the first government of the Popular Front, an alliance of communists and socialists. I doubt that ordinary French dock workers really understood his sophisticated, literary French.

It is not surprising that in two decisive crises he failed France, Europe and the rest of the world. He failed to save the Spanish Republic during the Axis-provoked Franco revolt because he was afraid to act. And, as many remember, he instituted his infamous *non-intervention* policy while the Spanish falangists were murdering people.

Blum's failure was even greater with regard to Germany. Historians now agree that the German General Staff would have liquidated Hitler if the French had acted when Hitler crossed into the demilitarized zone. In fact, Hitler gambled and defied his military advisers when he claimed that no one would dare move if he broke the German committment not to let the Reichswehr reenter the border provinces on the Rhine. In this, too, Blum was an appeaser, although he was not directly responsible for the non-intervention in the Rhineland. What is more, in a signed editorial in the official Socialist daily, *Le Populaire,* of September 27, 1938, Leon Blum admonished his friends to trust Hitler. In his editorial Blum drew the following conclusions:

". . . After and before the address of the Fuehrer-Chancellor, it is still true that the part of the litigation that remains between the Reich and Czechoslovakia can and should be regulated through an honorable and equitable agreement."

About the Munich agreement he said: "Will the Munich Agreement become the point of departure for wider negotiations in order to attain a general settle-ment of European problems both in the economic sphere and in the political arena, thus bringing about the solid peace, the equitable peace, the indivisible peace, the disarmament peace?"

I wonder what Leon Blum thought when, as a Nazi prisoner in Buchenwald, he had a great deal of time to think, of the "indivisible peace"with Hitler. Did he think back to the months when he was prime minister of a powerful France, when he, and he alone, could have stopped Hitler without the risk of a world conflagration?

I believe that the tragic example of Leon Blum compares to that of similarly idealistic Jewish statesmen who are convinced that their personal elevation to high office is of benefit to Jews. Herbert Samuel probably thought so. The British Colonial office must have been responsible for this Machiavellian appointment, knowing full well that Herbert Samuel was a "Zionist" of a certain stripe, one who could be duped into becoming an instrument of their policy to destroy the Jewish national home.

Upon his appointment in 1920, Herbert Samuel immediately limited Jewish immigration to 16,500 per year. A year later, after the first Arab pogroms, he gave the Arab terrorists an additional bonus: He proclaimed a temporary halt to Jewish immigration altogether. Then he formulated the policy of immigration according to the "absorptive capacity" of the country. Samuel, a Jew and a "Zionist," was the first to activate the British policy of breaking its committment to help develop the Jewish National Home. If he were alive today, he would have been surprised to see how many Jews Israel can absorb.

*   *   *

Samuel also instituted the policy of issuing "certificates," immigration permits for Jews. Later on the Jewish Agency used these certificates as patronage by distributing them mainly among those supporters of the political factions which in turn supported its regime. It was this curtailment of Jewish immigration that created the illegal aliyah.

Despite all the difficulties, the British interception and cruel sinking of boats, the Aliyah brought tens of thousands of Jews into Palestine from 1937 to 1940.

*   *   *

Several years prior to World War II, Jabotinsky published an essay in the *Jewish Morning Journal* in New York, in which he defined the ideal of "adventure." He told the youth, over whom he had considerable influence, that they should regard it as their personal challenge to bring Jews into Palestine. He knew, he said, how difficult it would be, but the alternative was to abandon the ideal of national salvation. He wrote: "Whistle when they say there are laws and that it is forbidden . . . Great Britain has lost the right to be considered with respect from an ethical point of view . . . Everything Great Britain is doing in the Land of Israel is against elementary ethics and justice . . . Just as we fought Czarist Russia we have to fight Britain in our own land. Britain is still powerful and she can do what she pleases in Eretz Israel; but she lost the moral justification for her presence there . . . The British regime in Eretz Israel now is just evil."

And to those who were afraid of being imprisoned, he said that to a freedom fighter prison "is not a tragedy at all . . . This is the way it will be in Palestine," Jabotinsky concluded, "if it is true that we are still a people alive."

Those whom Jabotinsky inspired to sacrifice their youth in order to save Jews in Europe had to fight the official Zionist establishment which wanted to control immigration. These idealist young people were not frightened, but the effectiveness of their work was reduced. If their efforts had been supported from Jewish public funds, they could have saved ten times as many as they did, and Hitler would have had fewer Jews for the crematoria.

*   *   *

Before discussing the activities of the Irgun delegation in America in the battle for help in effectuating illegal immigration, it is important to analyze the background of two mainstreams within the Zionist Movement. The two were philosophies in conflict; rather, there was the dogmatism of the conservative Zionists whose leader was Weizmann and the pragmatic approach of revolutionary Zionists symbolized by Jabotinsky. At first sight it may seem that Weizmann, who used to tell Jews that "there is no short road to Jewish emancipation," was the practical man, the one who lived without illusions. He pleaded for patience.

(This was a program for Jews who could wait . . .) Weizmann knew that those who supported him would think about how to talk to the English, how to talk to Jews, how to inspire confidence. "You cannot rush," he said.

Weizmann is described by most historians of the Zionist movement as a pragmatic Zionist, a careful Jew who would not antagonize non-Jews but would always negotiate patiently, wring from them one concession after the other, and build not only the Jewish homeland, but a homeland of Jews worthy to be the sons of prophets: There would be social justice, no exploitation of labor, a model society, according to the old Hebrew expression, "a light unto the nations." To Weizmann, as to Ahad Haam, the philosopher who dreamed of a cultural Jewish centre in Palestine, the most important achievement of Zionism would be this model society, no matter how small, how numerically insignificant, where Hebrew culture could flourish: a kind of Jewish vatican.

It was no accident that Weizmann fought any attempt to support the "illegal immigration" when the doors of Palestine were closed, and that he resented anyone who contradicted his views. For example, at the beginning of World War II, in London, where he lived, when asked by one of the Rothschilds to help the Irgun's Jeremiah Halperin bring a boat of the Aliyah Beth to Palestine, Weizmann said that he "would not sit down with a satan." This was already at a time when no other avenue of Jewish rescue from Europe existed.

Weizmann was still the unhurried diplomat, puffing his long cigarettes at meetings in the Foreign Office and opposing any financial aid to the Irgun "illegal immigration" movement. Herbert Samuel, who, during World War II, was chairman of the British Committee for German Jewry, also refused to allocate funds (which the Committee had in abundance) with which ships could have been bought and Jews transported to Israel. Even British Chief Rabbi Joseph Hertz could not change the opinion of Samuel and Weizmann; they would not budge.

It was inevitable that this philosophy came into conflict with a more activist policy. The philosophy of Zionism supported by Weizmann and Samuel in England, and by Stephen Wise and Nahum Goldmann in America, was a Zionism which could never solve the problem of Jewish homelessness. It appealed to Jews prominent in finance, to philanthropists to whom it was a matter of pride, of social standing, to be able to point out to non-Jewish friends that not only have the Jews given the world the Bible and the prophets and Christianity, but in this day and age they have succeeded in creating a Jewish spiritual center in Palestine. This kind of Zionism never would have created the enmity of Arab chauvinists — or British colonial officials. However, as often happens in history, the British and Arab chauvinists — including the notorious Mufti of Jerusalem, who later collaborated with Hitler on the Final Solution (he had been appointed by Herbert Samuel to the leadership of the Palestinian Arabs) — did not buy even this watered-down version of Zionism. They did not believe Weizmann. It seemed illogical to them that Jews would satisfy themselves with colonizing 20,000 or 30,000 immigrants each year at a time when millions needed a homeland. Both the British and the Arabs suspected Weizmann and his friends of subterfuge, of actually cooperating with the extremists while playing the role of moderates. For they knew that Jews could not, in the years 1933 to 1945, cling to selective Jewish immigration and an experimental type of Zionism when the question of emigration from Europe was a matter of life and death for the Jewish people.

The British did not accept even the minimal demands of the Zionist establishment, but harassed even this selective immigration movement. It was this extreme attitude on the part of the British (starting with England's first socialist prime minister, Ramsay MacDonald, and ending with Foreign Secretary Ernest Bevin) that undermined Weizmann's pro-British Zionism. If Bevin had agreed to President Truman's appeal in 1945 to allow 100,000 displaced persons to enter Palestine legally, many Zionists would have been opposed to the establishment of a Jewish State as something that could wait.

One should not forget that as late as the beginning of 1948, Goldmann and Sharett (Shertok), two typical Weizmann Zionists, urged Ben Gurion not to declare a Jewish state because they had been warned by the then United States Secretary of State, George Marshall, that a Jewish State would not be able to endure an Arab attack.

Sharett and Goldmann voted against the establishment of a Jewish state. So did other moderate "Zionists." But Ben Gurion, who, in 1946, was instrumental in toppling Weizmann from the leadership, knew that the revolt in Israel, the terror, the conviction of the Jews that there could be no cooperation with England, might culminate in the proclamation of a Jewish state by the "terrorists." (Menachem Begin actually warned Ben Gurion that if he did not declare a Jewish state, the Irgun, then in its heyday, would establish a Jewish government.)

Begin was then about to join the Hebrew Committee of National Liberation in Washington, headed by Kook and Merlin, in proclaiming a government in exile. Ben Gurion knew that this could happen, and he also knew that he would have no other opportunity if he missed this one. Of course Ben Gurion understood that Russian support for the idea of a Jewish state at that time, as expressed by Andrei Gromyko, the representative of the U.S.S.R. at the United Nations, was the result of the anti-British revolt by the Irgun and the Fighters for the Freedom of Israel (Sternists). In fact, the Soviet Union, which recognized the Jewish State a few minutes before the United States, believed that Israel would adopt an anti-British position in the Middle East.

*   *   *

All these developments came later. During the years when the lives of the Six Million were in the balance, the official Zionist Movement in the Free World was influenced by Weizmann's cautious policy of not wanting to antagonize the British. As early as 1933, the Jewish Agency, in the wake of the Transfer Deal with Germany, continued to import German products into the Middle East as partial reparations for the Jewish capital confiscated by Hitler. At the same time it continued to harass the Irgun-sponsored Aliyah Beth.

Lazar-Litai tells the story of Norman Bentwich, also a Weizmann Zionist, who came to Vienna during a critical moment and threatened the Irgun delegates with exposure if they did not stop taking Jews out through "illegal" means. As it was, they were denounced to the British, and the entire British Diplomatic Corps was alerted in all the countries from which the "illegal emigration" had been organized. The Zionist establishment never protested this cruelty towards those who were running from the Nazis.

It is remarkable that the Irgun managed to smuggle so many thousands into Israel. Each time Jabotinsky's group obtained transit visas, the British discovered through informers what routes the refugees planned to take and pressured the governments of Greece, Turkey, and Yugoslavia to cancel the visas when the refugees were already en route. There were instances in Palestine, after refugees did land safely, when establishment representatives arrested them and kept them incommunicado in kibbutzim. This, after all their suffering, was the reward that awaited them in the Promised Land.

*   *   *

The establishment Zionists attacked the revolutionary Zionists as dogmatic, yet the old-line Zionists were themselves obsessed with theories and dogmas. Many of them were Marxists and applied all kinds of dialectics to justify their persecution of the Irgun people, whom they called fascists. Yet these socalled fascists who responded to the call of Jabotinsky were the only pragmatic Zionists. They understood that the Hitler era was not a period in which Jews had the luxury to develop slowly a new society such as could have evolved in the quiet years of nineteenth century Enlightenment.

In the years preceding World War II, as well as during the war, there was no time to be concerned with whether the American government or the British government would accept the principle of the establishment of a Jewish state in Palestine. The revolutionary Zionists knew that in Eastern Europe the pervasive antisemitism would result in cooperation with Hitler, even by people who were anti-German. They also knew that the Nazis had declared war on the Jews and that if the Jews remained in Europe, they would be exterminated.

In their pragmatism the revolutionary Zionists told whoever would listen that this was no time to plan a society. This was not the time to agree with Weizmann who had the *chutzpah* to say that he would not want to transplant the Nalewki, the Jewish ghetto of Warsaw, to Palestine; he aspired to a model colony. The revolutionaries refused to accept the implicit assumption that Europe's Jews should become the guinea pigs for an experimental Jewish spiritual center in Palestine. To them, as to Herzl, Nordau and Jabotinsky, Zionism was a political movement, a national liberation movement whose primary aim was to save the Jews from extinction. They were not influenced in their calculations by economic experts and desk strategists, but by the urgency of the problem. They knew that hundreds of thousands had to be relocated and that only pressure and more pressure would force Britain, prodded by other countries, to honor its pledge to open the doors of Palestine.

Now we know that the Irgunists were right, that Jabotinsky was right. To-day's Jewish population in Israel clearly refutes the theory that the country could absorb only a limited number of people. Jews have demonstrated that immigration, even in a poor country like Palestine, can be made to work.

The paradox is that the Irgun people, who were the political Zionists and whose mentor was Jabotinsky, refused to talk about the establishment of the Jewish state during the emergency (1942-45); they were concerned only with the rescue of their brethren. In fact, later, during the war years in America, the Emergency Committee demanded only one thing: that Jews be moved from the danger areas, if need be, in refugee camps in friendly and neutral countries, and that their political future be determined after the war.

If this is not pragmatism, what is? The Irgun people and those who supported them knew that during World War II, when Britain stood alone against the Nazis, no promises by America, no committments on Palestine, would be relayed to Churchill at the time of Hitler's most spectacular victories. The issue was to win the war. And in order to win the *Jewish* war against Hitler, the Jewish revolutionaries realized the futility of discussing post-war aims when the only problem was saving the lives of those trapped by Hitler. Up until 1942 the Germans were ready to release all Jews if any haven, any place on the map, even a new Egypt, could be found for them.

On the other hand, those Zionists who wanted to appease their consciences and continue enjoying ideological debates, public dinners and oratory, refused to sacrifice personal rapport with non-Jewish politicians. Instead of supporting the Irgun's campaign, they financed PR offices from Jewish public funds in order to discredit the Irgun and its rescue activities. They did not understand that genuine political Zionism was the prerogative of the Jewish revolutionaries. For if tens of thousands of Jews had started moving from the lands of oppression and extermination, Britain could no longer have kept the doors of Palestine physically closed.

Before America entered the war, it was still possible to arouse the world by literally marching from the countries under Nazi rule toward freedom, as Jabotinsky has suggested. Self-emancipation, he said, is an adventure. He called upon hundreds of thousands to rise and walk, despite possible physical attacks. If Jews had listened most of them would not have been exterminated because what the Germans did in the slaughterhouses, they did under cover of night. I doubt whether the German army, even then, would have dared shoot hundreds of thousands of Jews walking out of the Reich. Yet, because of Jewish politicking, not only was this movement discredited (as was the movement to establish a Jewish army which would have helped European Jewry escape Hitler), but the Jewish revolution was postponed. Most of those for whom Zionism was something real disappeared forever from the face of the earth.

I remember the official Zionists harassing the Irgun front organizations in America for "betraying" the Zionist ideal because the Irgunists stated unequivocally that both politically and legally the Hebrew nation, the potential nation that would settle in Palestine, consisted of the stateless Jews of Europe and the Jews of Palestine. Today, years after the establishment of the State of Israel, how many Jews from America, England, France, have settled in Israel? How many Zionists and Zionist leaders have settled there?

(It is interesting to note that all the Irgun emissaries refused American passports and settled in Israel — despite the establishment Zionists, who certainly did not want them there.)

This determination to live in Israel was also part of the philosophy which stemmed from the belief that no one needed a new official American statement confirming the Jewish right to Palestine. Such a right had been established by the Balfour Declaration, by the League of Nations' Mandate, by American endorsement and by Jewish blood, sweat and tears.

The pragmatic program of the Jewish revolutionaries completely failed to win over the majority of American Jews. This was true in the issue of "illegal" immigration, in the campaign to establish a Jewish Army, and when it came to the Emergency Committee's demands for Allied intervention against the extermination of Jews. The Committee had hoped that such intervention — by threatening reprisals against the Nazis through such means as declaring the Jews prisoners of war, by appealing to the Red Cross and by creating areas of Jewish concentration in countries close to the German borders with the American guarantee that such areas would be evacuated after the war — would have saved countless lives. The plan failed because each Irgun initiative was destroyed by the counter-propaganda of those who feared that the success of the Irgun would mean the end of the Jewish establishment.

*   *   *

Establishment Zionism has no meaning today, unless it is to lend financial support to political parties in Israel. Such support serves only to entrench even more deeply the political fighting among the close to twenty parties and factions in that country. This suits the establishment, for the in-fighting deflects attention from the basic question: Why do American Zionists stay in America when the doors of Israel are open to them?

However, today the people who dwell in Zion are beginning to resent their exploitation by the clever fundraisers of the affluent Free World. Eventually they will refuse to wear pants with the inscription "donated by the United Jewish Appeal." They will demand to live as normal people. After all, what is Zionism if not the movement to normalize the existence of those who consider themselves the Jewish nation?

VII
Battle for Leadership

It would be incorrect to assume that despite Dr. Stephen Wise's hold upon American Jewish life during World War II, despite his support of Roosevelt and his artful use of oratory, no one ever challenged his position as the "Jewish pope." In fact, Stephen Wise was dethroned following a personality clash which developed from an ideological feud with a "greater man."

The man who "dethroned" Wise from the Zionist movement during World War II became the most popular and idealized orator and political leader of American Zionism. He was Dr. Abba Hillel Silver, spiritual leader of the temple in Cleveland, Ohio.

Silver was not the average Reform Rabbi with a superficial seminary knowledge of Judaism and Hebrew. He was a Jewish scholar, and was interested in one issue only: securing American political support for establishing a Jewish Commonwealth in Palestine *after the war*.

Ben Gurion did not like Stephen Wise's endorsement of Roosevelt's meandering policies on Palestine. Wise's heresy consisted of giving lip service to Brandeis Zionism, which Weizmann detested, and to the person of Brandeis himself. Weizmann probably never forgot the Brandeis insult at the London Conference in 1920, when the Justice insisted on a financial statement covering the Zionist budget and expenses. According to historian Frank E. Manuel, this strict persistence on the part of Brandeis was also considered an insult "by others in Weizmann's circle who controlled the purse, including Mr. Menachem Ussischkin, who was in charge of the Jewish National Fund."

Yet Weizmann did not figure out that Ben Gurion would eventually use Silver not only to get rid of Wise, who consistently defended Roosevelt's policy vis-à-vis the Jews and accepted the president's political statements about his platonic love for Jews as political documents, but also to remove Weizmann himself.

This bickering within the leadership of the Zionist establishment has some comical aspects. I attended the Zionist Congress in Basle in December, 1946, when Weizmann was ousted from the presidency. He was practically crying at that congress, he was so deeply hurt. The Weizmann people, including my personal friends Louis Lipsky and Jacob Fishman, were shocked. I remember how angry they were when they took me for lunch to the Messe Restaurant in the congress building.

Fishman, a Weizmann follower to the end, died at this congress of a heart attack. Some spread the rumor that he died because he could not stand the conspiracy against Weizmann. I knew that Fishmann suffered from a serious heart condition. A few days before the start of the congress, when we had to walk up the stairs in a Paris hotel, he had suffered his first mild attack. However, despite his anger, I do not believe the Weizmann episode killed him.

Weizmann was eliminated from the leadership because the time had come to show the survivors in the D.P. camps that Zionism had entered an era of active opposition to Britain. Ben Gurion, perhaps the cleverest Jewish politician of all, kept Weizmann out of the active leadership and brought him from Switzerland to Israel after the proclamation of the Jewish state, making him president in the full knowledge that Weizmann would forgive everything after his coronation as king without crown.

Later on, after Ben Gurion had used Silver, B.G. helped certain Zionist politicians in America, especially those around Goldmann, Silver's number-one political enemy, to get rid of him. This was after Silver, with rarely matched eloquence, had expounded the Jewish case in the political struggle at the United Nations. The partition resolution demanding establishment of a Jewish state was, of course, the culmination of this struggle.

Ben Gurion discarded Silver when he felt Silver was no longer useful. This attitude was even more marked among Ben Gurion's Labor Party friends who agreed with the moderate Zionists and could never forgive Silver for his militant stance. After the establishment of Israel, they gained control of the government and in that euphoric period it was easy to dictate policy to foreign Jewish organizations whose influence on the Jewish masses was dependent on their rapport with the regime in the Holy Land.

For a short period during the war years, Silver managed to rally American Jews under the banner of Zionism. Here again we find a discrepancy between what was needed in the war years for Jewish survival — rescuing living Jews from the Holocaust — and the formulation of Zionist policy for the post-war years. If the issue had been to create a political climate whereby Zionism would become the policy of the United States government, then Abba Hillel Silver certainly would have deserved an outstanding place in Jewish history. But, unfortunately, he, too, was overwhelmed by Zionist political activity at a time when Jewish efforts should have been concentrated in a humanitarian direction, towards saving the lives of those who needed Zionism.

By May 1944, Silver still did not realize where he had failed. It is true that Silver, unique among the international Zionist leaders of that period, was not involved, at least publicly, in witch-hunting against the Irgun delegation. In a speech to the leaders of the American Jewish community, he even publicly acknowledged the activities of the Irgun-organized Committee for a Jewish Army, and said that both the official action of the establishment in arming Jews and the Irgun activities had failed. It seems Silver was drugged by his belief that the most important thing was to unite American Jews to demand the establishment of a Jewish Commonwealth in Palestine.

There is no question that Silver had a profound understanding of the Irgun. He understood that it was the Irgun in Palestine and the Irgun delegation in America who had raised the banner of Jewish revolt in Palestine; that it was the

Irgun who had fought to save the people in Europe who needed the Jewish homeland. Indeed, Menachem Begin, Commander of the Irgun during the war years, paid tribute to Silver for his understanding of the beginnings of the Jewish revolution. He was probably unaware of Silver's double-talk and his fight against the Irgun delegation in America.

The Jewish politicians in Palestine tried everything to erase the fame of the Irgun. Like their American counterparts, they saw in the Irgun a competitor for Jewish leadership. But, according to Begin, this was not the case with Silver. In his memoirs, Begin says about Silver, "The impression Dr. Silver made on me lasted a long time . . . he is a personality, I told my colleagues. Dr. Silver was the first Zionist leader from whom I heard words of encouragement for our struggle instead of the usual denunciations of the 'dissidents.' He expressed the hope that the fighting unity achieved in the resistance movement would continue. He felt it had to continue. American public opinion was sympathetic to the fighters for," he told Begin, "they, too, had to fight the British by extralegal means."

Begin also says that when he visited the United States, there was pressure on Silver to issue a statement denouncing the "dissidents" on behalf of the Zionist Emergency Council. Silver refused. He told one of the leaders who pressed him to declare his opposition to the Irgun, "The Irgun will go down in history as a factor without which the State of Israel would not have come into being."

But this change of heart with regard to the Irgun came late, too late for the Jews of Europe.

Addressing a national conference in Cleveland on May 17, 1944, Silver, whom many considered an outstanding statesman of Jewry, delivered an address which today seems naive and irrelevant to the emergency. Even then time remained to save Jews. Of the Six Million, two to three million were still alive. But in this address, later published in a selection of his speeches, Silver said, "The American Jewish community faces the problems which the war forced upon it in a creditable manner. We have no reason to condemn or disparage ourselves. We have not, of course, responded as fully as we might have or as we should have to the challenge of the great testing time. But what group has?"

It must be stressed again that this goodbye to the last Jews of Europe was made when there was still an opportunity to save lives. But Silver, then leader of the Zionist movement, was busy extracting a commitment from the American government that it would support — after the war — the Jewish demands for an independent commonwealth in Palestine. He had to compete with Wise. He seemed to regard European Jewry as something of the past when he said:

"A disaster for which even our long tormented history can offer no parallel, swept over our people in Europe — left them broken, decimated and doomed." He continued to describe in the same beautiful English prose, of which he was a master, the travail of European Jewry. And he dared say, "though we cannot help them fully, we did not fail them utterly . . . we were not unwilling, but inept. We permitted precious months and years to slip by while the Nazi scythe swung wider and ever wider swaths and mowed down the Jewish communities of conquered Europe one after another in a bloody harvest of death."

He repeated here the same reproach levelled at Stephen Wise, who always accepted Roosevelt's assurances without criticism, "Governments, friendly governments, beguiled and misled us with vague promises and ineffectual rescue agencies and conferences."

He concluded, "We did not know how to focus the attention of what remained of the free and decent world, so absorbed in its own problems, upon the appalling tragedy of our people, nor how to induce action. And so many perished who might have been saved."

Ben Hecht still urged action. And in London, a great friend of the Jews, Lord Wedgewood, was still calling upon parliament that Britain, even at this late hour, should open its doors to Jewish refugees. Yet the Zionist movement had written off the Jews and the War Refugee Board, eventually established by the president following two years of agitation by the Irgun delegation, was organized so that the failure of its rescue mission in Istanbul would be inevitable.

The Irgun delegation, refusing to plead with organizations to recognize the right of Jews to enter Palestine, established the Hebrew Committee of National Liberation, with an embassy-in-exile in Washington. The embassy declared that Britain was in Palestine illegally because it had broken its pledge to the League of Nations, and that Jews should start moving in rather than wasting time on speeches and dialectics.

Again the Irgun delegation in America demanded that the surviving Jews in Europe be declared prisoners of war, and the International Red Cross be given the task of contacting and saving them. The delegation also demanded recognition of the Hebrew nation as a member of the United Nations. The Irgun was always ahead of the game, and the Jewish leaders, including Silver, the most militant among the Zionist leaders, were not ready for the challenge.

To me, Abba Hillel Silver will always remain an enigma. No one else among the Zionist leaders had such influence upon the Jewish masses during the crucial war years. But he used his influence for political ends. To a certain degree he understood, as he said, that to avoid the Jewish issue during the war because "of military expedience" was wrong. Yet he clung to Britain's legalistic White Paper even when it was time to act. It is paradoxical that he was profoundly touched by the tragedy, but could not liberate himself from the futile, rhetorical exercises at Zionist conclaves and meetings. His analysis was right up to a certain point. This is why many saw in him the new Jabotinsky. But they did not realize that there is a time for political Zionism and a time for humanitarian Zionism. At the time when it was vital to implement humanitarian emergency measures, Silver personified political Zionism, the expedient of internationally legalizing the Jewish claim to Palestine.

On May 2nd, 1943, when Silver's militant Zionist policy was adopted by the Zionist movement in America at a conference in Philadelphia, he was in seventh heaven. To this day I do not know why he did not sense the irrelevance of such a conference at a time when at least four million of the Six Million were still alive. North Africa had already been occupied by the Allies, and there was a possibility of moving Jews there temporarily, leaving the political situation until after the war, after the rescue. Yet Silver was concerned that the president of the United States refused to mention the political issue of Palestine in a message sent that year to the United Jewish Appeal. Silver did not sense the irrelevance of his observation that in 1942 the president spoke of Palestine in a message to the United Jewish Appeal meeting, while in 1943 he did not mention it. Silver could not understand what the young, amateur politicians of the Irgun realized: The president of the United States would not enter into a conflict with England on postwar policies at a time when England was in the forefront of a war against Hitler.

Despite his Zionist militancy, Silver did not understand that those in the State Department and the British Colonial Office who were not interested in rescue work or in bombarding the crematoria in Auschwitz must have cynically appreciated that the Jewish leaders were demanding solutions to postwar problems, solutions that could be postponed with a good conscience.

I often wonder what would have happened if Silver had been sympathetic to the Irgun struggle for Palestine and supported the American "dissidents" in their battle for the surviving European Jews. I think the balance sheet would have been very different. Silver, and others, did not seem to embrace the philosophy of Ahad Haam: "When a country is destroyed the people can return and rebuild it. But when a people is destroyed, who will rebuild it?"

This, essentially, is the tragedy which I call our paralysis during World War II. Somehow our collective Jewish brain did not function. We saw issues, political challenges and solutions on a grand scale, but were blind when it came to seeing those in the extermination camps who had a right to expect from us "extra-legal" activity to save their lives.

VIII
Wise and Goldmann

What was the attitude of the "recognized" leaders of American Jewry during World War II? Here I would like to discuss the characteristics of the two men who were "the most important leaders of American Jewry" during that period. The best public relations people were available to them through the two organizations they controlled, the World Jewish Congress and the American Jewish Congress. One of the two, Nahum Goldmann, the controversial former president of the World Jewish Congress, employed an incredibly large public relations staff the world over. Some working editors and writers in Jewish newspapers were also on his payroll. There was a time when Nahum Goldmann controlled the socalled Jewish Telegraphic Agency, subsidized from Jewish public funds. This came to an end after the matter was raised at a Senate hearing in Washington, where it was proved beyond a doubt that the Jewish Telegraphic Agency was nothing more than a publicity outfit feeding newspapers PR concoctions.

Of these two leaders, both very much in the public eye during the years of the European Jewish tragedy, I must say that Stephen Wise seemed the more sincere. Although he had all the foibles of a showman, his limited knowledge of Judaism and of the Jewish people made him believe, I am convinced, that whatever he did was right. In contrast to Wise, Goldmann was extremely shrewd, cunning and conniving — a clever politician if ever there was one. Goldmann never resigned his "leadership," not even when Israeli Premier Golda Meir attacked him for his much publicized "plan" to see Nasser and settle the Israeli-Arab problem with him. Many of us remember the publicity stunt of promoting this pie-in-the-sky meeting that never came about. However, it gave Goldmann the opportunity to attack the Israeli government because he had never forgiven those in power in Jerusalem for not appointing him foreign minister.

Goldmann always considered himself, next to Wise, the divinely-appointed diplomat of the Jewish people. With his innate immodesty, Goldmann, in his autobiography, attacks the lack of action on the part of Jewish leaders during World War II, but does so with his usual cleverness. As long as he was still "a leader of the Jewish people," he believed that *he* was the spokesman for Israel. (Goldmann was the "Zionist" par excellence who recognized the State of Israel only *de facto*.)

Goldmann says, "I lived through this era and all its day-to-day events. I do not pretend that either my close friends, like Stephen Wise, or I, foresaw the full extent of the slaughter. It would take someone with the character of a Nazi to foresee such a catastrophe." Goldmann then proceeds to say that he "issued warnings in every speech he made at World Jewish conferences." He says that Dr.

Wise did the same, "with greater authority."

We should wonder why Hitler did not tremble when he read the rhetoric of Dr. Wise or Dr. Goldmann at meetings and press conferences.

These remarks and similar ones with Goldmann's camouflaged *mea culpa* have been incorporated here only to inform future generations of his tremendous diplomatic *achievements*. When he speaks of the failure of Jewish leaders during World War II, he rationalizes and rejects the responsibility for the silence by mentioning the "shortsightedness and fear" of Jews in general. "The majority of the Jewish people," he says, "and its leaders, were not willing to recognize or properly interpret the symptoms."

These and similar remarks about the saddest chapter in 2,000 years of Jewish history take up only a few pages of his autobiography, with the obviously hypocritical introduction: "The chapter I am about to begin fills me with deep sadness and despondency . . . It deals with the total failure of what might be called the leadership of the Jewish people." He then says that after a long debate with himself, he came to the conclusion that the bitter and painful facts must be set forth. Of course, Goldmann does not mention the hearings in Washington, called by the United States Congress as a result of lobbying by the Irgun delegation. He was there; so was Stephen Wise. But not a word of it in their autobiographies! Why should anyone remember what really happened during that period? After all, "history" has been written by Goldmann and others who continued to control the purse of the organized Jewish people. So why bring to public attention those who during the war created such a tremendous stir and agitated for the rescue of Jews?

Goldmann speaks about the necessity of fighting the Nazis by "political means," but at least he admits, in contrast to Wise, ". . . we must stand as a generation not only condemned to witness the destruction of one-third of our number, but guilty of having accepted it without any resistance worthy of the name."

One would think that under such circumstances Goldmann would have resigned from his position. Can one imagine a prime minister or foreign minister of a country that lost one-third of its population because he failed to resist the enemy continuing in power? Yet this is precisely what happened to the organized Jewish community.

With characteristic dexterity Goldmann minimized the Joel Brand mission, which caused one of the most sensational trials in Israeli history, and in which Goldmann's close friend, Moshe Shertok (Sharett), longtime foreign minister of Israel, was never cleared of the accusation that Brand was turned over to the British by the Zionist establishment. This happened although, as Goldmann admits, there was a faint hope that Brand's mission, approved by Eichmann, could have saved more than one hundred thousand Hungarian Jews, or even more.

A master polemicist, Goldmann cleverly and admirably disposes with the Six Million in three pages. But be becomes loquacious again when it comes to describing the "Zionist" activities in America during World War II. He speaks in glowing terms of the socalled Biltmore Hotel Conference (an international Zionist meeting that took place at the Hotel Biltmore in New York, hence the name) in May 1942. One should never lose sight of the fact that this conference took place exactly four months after the Wannsee Conference when the German government instructed Eichmann and his henchmen to execute its plan for the Final Solution. Chaim Weizmann, David Ben Gurion and all the American Zionist luminaries attended the Biltmore Conference while Jews all over Europe were being shipped to extermination camps daily.

What did these Jewish leaders discuss at the meeting? According to Goldmann, they adopted, as we know it, the Biltmore Program, demanding a Jewish State in Palestine *after the war.* Goldmann then mentions that after the conference the Zionists began urging non-Zionists to support their demand. He goes on to mourn the failure of his friends, Weizmann and Wise, to obtain such support — as though this were the problem facing the Six Million condemned to death!

In the passage dealing with this era, Goldmann, ever a politician, does not fail to compliment the leaders of all the Jewish groups with which he had to deal. Speaking of a certain leader, he writes: "(He) combined a superb tactical instinct with a fighting spirit and because of that a year later we had the American Jewish Conference."

Then, with pride, Goldmann speaks of his appearance at the American Jewish Conference, where again the problem of establishing a Jewish state after the war was discussed while the House in Europe was on fire. The American Jewish Conference, he says, was "extremely successful." He also praises himself for having helped invite two leading Soviet Jews to America, poet Itzik Feffer and actor Shlomo Mikhoels. This, of course, was a great propaganda coup for Stalin during the purges. (Only Goldmann could have fabricated such a lie, that he had any contact with Stalin; that Goldmann, not the Russian dictator, dispatched Mikhoels and Feffer to America.)

But despite his *mea culpa,* Goldmann is not too bashful to tell the story of how he and others worked to persuade the Jewish public to endorse the demand for a Jewish state. Naturally, diplomat as he was, he continued "to negotiate with the State Department" — all this while the Holocaust consumed his fellow Jews.

While Goldmann, whom many considered cynical even then, at least dares hint that Jewish leaders are guilty, his senior colleague and friend, Stephen Wise in his autobiography depicts himself as one who actually sacrificed himself for the Jewish people. He also speaks unabashedly of Roosevelt's great friendship for the Jews. (One should add here the postscript that Stephen Wise was not only "the leader of American Jewry," but also a politician connected with the Democratic Party machine. He was close to Roosevelt because he always mobilized Jewish support for the president before elections.)

As in the case of all the influential Zionist leaders, Wise speaks mostly of his efforts on behalf of establishing a Jewish state in Palestine. One must remember that most of the books by Zionist leaders were written after the establishment of the Jewish state. All these leaders, without exception, tried to take credit "for their part" in establishing Israel.

When I read those books at the time, they reminded me of certain American Jewish philanthropists, or those who pose as philanthropists, who used to run to Israel to have their pictures taken with Ben Gurion so that people back home would know the extent of their great contribution to the establishment of Israel.

But coming back to the years when one had to fight to save European Jews, it makes one sad to see how, even in retrospect, such popular leaders as Stephen Wise failed to deal with the paramount issue during World War II. It was not only a Jewish issue; it was a human problem, and guilt for the death of the Six Million should never be erased from the annals of civilized humanity. Yet it was the duty of the Jewish leaders to actively press for rescue and to make it impossible for officialdom to ignore the tragedy.

Despite his claim to grandeur as a leader, Wise at least acknowledges the greatness of Justice Louis Dembitz Brandeis under whom he was active in the Zionist movement during its years of glory. But perhaps Wise praised Brandeis because when Weizmann eliminated the learned jurist from the leadership of the Zionist movement during the short period until the rift healed, Wise went down with him. At least Wise acknowledges that Brandeis was "the greatest Jew since Herzl."

It is interesting to observe, however, that most of his contemporaries did not understand what was great about Brandeis. Men like Wise, Goldmann and Weizmann fought for legalistic proclamations and resolutions when not a minute should have been lost in evacuating Jews from the danger zone. Brandeis saw it. He foresaw the volcano exploding; so did Jabotinsky and the Irgun "boys" who were inspired by his teachings and perfected them, while the influential Zionist leaders continued to talk and play politics. This is their guilt. It is not the guilt of the Jewish people, as Goldmann would have us believe.

It is interesting to peruse Wise's strange autobiography and see how he dealt with the issues during the crucial years. He says that if the president had agreed with him when he called to his attention issues that demanded immediate action, the situation could have been different. For example, in January 1937, when Polish Jews were already threatened and Jabotinsky was calling on them to evacuate, Wise urged Roosevelt, upon receiving information from Poland, to ask the Polish government to protest antisemitism and accord the Jews human rights.

Polish Jews were certainly interested in leaving Poland. But it never occured to Wise to ask the president to allow 100,000 or 200,000 Polish Jews (beyond the immigration quota) to enter the United States. The president agreed to make a statement, and informed Wise by letter that in his inauguration speech he had criticized Poland's foreign minister, Colonel Beck, who had stated that of the three and one-half million Jews in Poland, three million must emigrate.

It was clear to all acquainted with the situation that emigration was the only solution, although Beck's motives were not dictated by friendship toward the Jews. Today we know that Roosevelt's statement was meaningless. If he had announced that America would accept a number of Polish Jews, some would have been saved. And if Wise and Weizmann had supported the socalled illegal emigration to Palestine, others would have been saved; the antisemitic Polish and Rumanian governments would have helped in this "illegal" operation for obvious reasons.

Wise admits that "wherever I went I spoke of him (Roosevelt) with boundless enthusiasm." And Roosevelt knew it. Yet this unusual link with the White House was not used to help save masses of European Jews. Still, Wise dared say that except for Brandeis and Frankfurter, the Jews who had been seeing the president about the German situation were timorous. Wise says that he once considered going to Berlin himself, but was told by American diplomats that this would have created an international incident. So he did not go. But he travelled all over Europe speaking out against the Germans, agitating for the boycott of German goods and so on. At the same time, Wise says, he never failed to keep the president informed of the facts concerning "Zionism and Palestine." He says that on May 22, 1939, he thanked the president for averting a disaster which threatened the Jewish National Home because of the British immigration policy.

It is difficult to understand for what Wise thanked Roosevelt. Did he thank him for the sinking of the Struma, a boat loaded with Jewish refugees, by British ships in the Mediterranean, or for similar obstructions? Yet in his naiveté, or relying upon the short memory of the reader, or perhaps to convince the younger generation in Israel that he really did do something to help establish a Jewish state, Wise says, "The tragic plight of the Jews in Palestine caused me to seek help from the president when such help seemed the last possible hope of the beleagured Jewish people. Time and again Franklin Roosevelt responded."

It seems to me that Roosevelt, who absolutely ignored the plight of the European Jews, must have known he was making Wise happy whenever he sent him a letter for his files.

IX
American Jewish Conference

Today, when reading the records of the American Jewish Conference, the most important meeting in the history of American Jewry (the only one in which *all* Jewish organizations participated), one cannot help but ask questions: Who were those people? What determined the stance of the American Jewish establishment during World War II? Were these men and women really as bad as they appear in retrospect? Or were they cynical? Were they stupid? Were some of them war criminals in a certain sense? Should there be a Jewish War Crimes Tribunal, and should the survivors of these organizations be asked to appear before such a court?

I know all this is fantasy. Jewish leaders and professional Jews are more immune to criticism than dictators. From the records of the meetings of the American Jewish Conference, one must repeatedly come back to this query: What kind of people run what we call in the community "Jewish life?"

When the American Jewish Conference took place I was impressed by the opening meeting. I remember having written a comment, published on the front page of the daily newspaper for which I worked, in which I compared this meeting to the period in Polish-Jewish history of the "Committee of the Four Lands," the most glorious chapter in European history when Polish Jews had real autonomy and were able to act on behalf of threatened Jews elsewhere.

*　　　*　　　*

I am a Jew, so I must love rhetoric. On the evening of August 29, 1943, the beautifully lit Waldorf Astoria Hotel impressed me tremendously. What I wrote was not poetry, but it rendered my feelings exactly. I was certain then that American Jews would act while there was still time to save millions of their brethren in Europe. That was in the evening. When I rose the following morning and returned to the Conference, I looked at my own story on the front page of the paper and thought: This is the morning after; I can see more clearly now. The "leaders" are again arguing among themselves, and I am guilty of misleading those who read this newspaper. They will believe that something is being done here to rescue those in the concentration camps. (At that time we did not yet speak of extermination camps.)

Looking back on that conference, it seems to me that what was happening in Europe was as remote to us then — delegates and reporters alike — as the Uganda tragedy must have been to someone basking in the sun of the Nevada desert.

This is how the American Jewish Year Book for 1943 (an official publication of the prestigious American Jewish Committee) recorded, in part, what it called "the reaction to overseas events" by American Jews "in the past year."

The report (the American Jewish Yearbook, Vol. 46, Philadelphia, 1944.) takes up eleven pages of the 600-page book. A member of the research staff of the American Jewish Committee, Martha Jelenko wrote: "As the position of the Nazis became increasingly precarious due to sharp reverses on all battlefronts, their hope for victory waned. However, their campaign of terror and destruction continued unabated. Consequently, efforts of Jews and non-Jews in the United States were bent upon finding methods and means for the rescue of Europe's destitute Jews, and to formulate a practical program for post-war peace.

"Through vigorous and repeated protests, Jews and liberal groups generally attempted to awaken the conscience of the world. These expressions of indignation and sympathy were then followed by concrete proposals, ranging from feeding these unfortunates to facilitating their admission to the United States and other havens of refuge. As a result, a great number of suggestions were offered and discussed by government officials, political parties, labor groups, non-Jewish and Jewish organizations, and echoed by the press of the country."

Note the careful, almost indifferent tone in which the destruction of European Jewry is discussed in the official book of the American Jewish Committee. It sounds like a summary of a United Nations' debate about the starving in Africa. The author writes of a campaign of "terror and destruction." Yet the style is that of a lawyer's report or an accountant's balance sheet.

The author then relates what happened in that fateful year of 1943. First of all, she speaks of the American Jewish Conference and correctly summarizes the socalled *Six-Point Rescue Program for Immediate Action:*

"One of the first proposals was made at the final session of the American Jewish Conference, held in New York City from August 29 to September 2, 1943. Its six-point rescue program for immediate action was to be as follows: The democracies were to issue warnings that crimes perpetrated against the Jews would be punished after the war; to this end, the Allied Commission on War Crimes was to be convoked; those fortunate enough to reach Palestine were to be guaranteed the right of permanent sojourn; neutral nations bordering Axis countries were to receive financial aid and guarantees of the ultimate disposition of refugees to prevent prohibition of further entry; the United Nations were to create a special intergovernmental agency to work with Jewish organizations in sending arms and supplies for self-defense to Jews in Axis-occupied countries."

The reader must concentrate upon a few points in order to understand the psychology of the men and women responsible for these resolutions. It must also be stressed that this conference took place about six weeks after the Irgun-sponsored Emergency Conference to Save the Jewish People of Europe was held at the Commodore Hotel.

At the American Jewish Conference the phraseology of the resolutions was actually motivated by the establishment leaders' fear that unless they counteracted the impression left by the Irgun Emergency Conference, they would be lost and their names would disappear from the Jewish Hall of Fame.

It is instructive to analyze the way the author describes the two conferences.

She does not record the two events in chronological order. In an obvious attempt to erase the impression that the Emergency Committee formed by Bergson (Hillel Kook) and Merlin was first in tackling this problem vigorously and coming up with logical demands, she begins by reporting the American Jewish Conference meeting and says that "one of the first proposals in the direction of rescue was made at the final session of the American Jewish Conference." This is absolutely false. *Then* she mentions the conference called by the Irgun delegation.

It is interesting that the editor of the American Jewish Committee allowed this report to appear. The author places the Emergency Conference *after* the American Jewish Conference and unabashedly states, "Subsequently the Emergency Conference to Save the Jewish people was called in New York." From her report one is led to believe that the Irgun conference took place and Irgun activities were undertaken *after* the American Jewish Conference. In fact the Irgun Conference took place many weeks *before* and the Irgun activities took place many months *before* the American Jewish Conference. Also in her impartiality the author says that this meeting was called by a "group" of (Zionist) Revisionist leaders who had gained the support of many well-known non-Jews, moved by the *apparently* humanitarian considerations of the conference.

Thus the reader of this supposedly objective Jewish Year Book must swallow some very interesting phrases describing the organizers of the Emergency Conference. The author writes that the conference was called by a group of "Zionist Revisionist leaders." This is absolutely untrue; the Revisionists were a part of the Zionist Establishment. She continues by saying that the non-Jewish supporters of this movement were moved by "apparently" humanitarian considerations — a specious attempt to cast doubt on the Irgun delegation's motives. The true humanitarians, we are led to believe, were the organizers of the American Jewish Conference. It took these gentlemen from January 6 to August 29 to organize a meeting at the Waldorf Astoria.

The official record of the American Jewish Conference tells us that the initiative in calling a preliminary meeting in Pittsburgh, which took place on January 23 and 24, 1943, was taken by Henry Monsky, then president of B'nai B'rith. To further understand the cynicism of some of the organizers of this conference and their unwillingness to intervene with all the clout of American Jewry on behalf of those trapped by Hitler, one must carefully analyze Monsky's words in his invitation to those he asked to participate in the Pittsburgh Conference:

"American Jewry, which will be required in large measure to assume the responsibility of representing the interests of our people at the Victory Peace Conference, must be ready to voice the judgement of American Jews along with that of the other Jewish communities of the free countries with respect to the postwar status of Jews and the upbuilding of a Jewish Palestine . . . The purpose of the conference is to bring together the representatives of major national Jewish membership organizations, in order that they may consider what steps should be taken to bring about some agreements on the part of the American Jewish community."

According to the same official report, the thirty-four organizations at the American Jewish Conference were asked to reach an agreement in presenting Jewish demands at a future peace table. What demands? Were the European Jews supposed to negotiate *after* the cessation of hostilities — after their extermination? None but the Irgun delegation named the real problem: survival. In return for speaking out they were savagely attacked by the establishment bureaucracy. Pages in the conference records are taken up by speeches by leaders of the various organizations — all concerned with how they could get together *after the war* to present the Jewish demands. As Monsky said, "We have a vital stake in the peace that is to come." He did not hesitate to compare the situation of European Jewry *after the Second World War* to that *after the First World War,* when the Jewish communities remained intact. He asked us to remember that we had to fight for the right of the Jewish people to rebuild their homeland in Palestine. But what if there were no people left? How could the homeland be rebuilt? Apparently this problem never occurred to Monsky and his like-minded friends.

Significantly, at this preliminary Pittsburgh meeting a Jewish representative who was close to the Irgun delegation, Alex Wilf, blasted the demand for unity for its own sake. He reminded the delegates that they had gathered for one purpose: to save the Jews of Europe. The time was short, Wilf stated, and there was no need for a further conference. He asked that the delegates agree then and there to a concerted rescue effort. However, no such decision was taken by the American Jewish leaders — not even at this late hour.

Because Wilf was involved with the Irgun delegation, he was called to order by a New York judge who stressed the opinion of the Jewish leaders that before action could be *planned* it was necessary to record the opinion of the Jewish majority (which is, obviously, the establishment). Then he came to the point which must have at that time perturbed the Jewish leaders; that in Washington he had often been asked the question, "who speaks for the Jews in America?"

From the initial preparations for this conference, it is obvious that its real purpose was to eliminate the impression in Washington that anyone urging action to save the European Jews could not be taken seriously unless he were backed by the "majority of the Jews" . . . in America.

The Jewish leaders tried to thwart the undertakings of the Irgun delegation, but did not themselves take any real initiative. While the demanding issue was to save European Jewry, the establishment leaders bickered, in the words of Judge Morris Rothenberg, over "who shall be recognized" as the spokesman for American Jewry.

At that time more than three million Jews who were eventually liquidated were still alive. Surely those Jews were confident, if they had any hope whatsoever, that American Jews were doing everything in their power to rescue them; that Jewish leaders were travelling to the Axis countries, exposing themselves to physical danger in order to stop the mass annihilation of people. (I recently discussed this conference with a survivor of the Kielce Ghetto who now lives in Canada. I asked him how many Jews were still alive in Kielce in 1943. That was already after the *Aussiedlung.* Close to 1,000 Jews were left of the more than 2,600 who had been there previously. But those Jews who were in a slave labor camp were sure that parachutists from America would somehow appear to guide them to safety.)

At the Pittsburgh meeting, Judge Rothenberg reminisced about the American Jewish activities *in 1918,* when the American Jewish Congress demonstrated its effectiveness at the Versailles Peace Conference. He spoke movingly of the popular Jewish leader, Louis Marshall who, although a non-Zionist, joined the Zionists in supporting the Balfour Declaration. Judge Rothenberg mentioned the statement in *The New York Times* signed by some ninety rabbis who opposed Zionism. This seemed to affect the Zionist leaders more profoundly than the ominous news from Europe.

It is almost amusing to read the speeches of the leaders who stressed unity as the most important issue: a unity that would block dissident action on behalf of European Jewry. One leader even went as far as to quote Josephus, the Roman historian, who wrote that Jewish unity could have prevented the destruction of the Holy Temple in Jerusalem.

I was not there, but I am sure many must have applauded this clever remark.

*   *   *

Meanwhile the Nazi machinery continued to kill Jews by the thousands every day. The same Jewish leader who had spoken of Josephus said that the conference must work out a "plan for the rehabilitation and reconstruction of Jews in Europe *after the war.*"

Yet the *pièce de resistance* was, as always, a witty address by the most impressive speaker of them all, Dr. Nahum Goldmann. Goldmann said, "We are living in a time of unparalleled suffering, but we are also living in a time of unparalleled opportunities for the Jewish people in the future." The opportunities for solving the Jewish problem, he said, would be greater after the war, because through our tragedy "the world has learned to understand what the Jew's problem means . . . There is a feeling among the peoples of the world, and certainly among the leading statesmen of the great democratic countries — the President of this country, the Prime Minister of Great Britain — that something fundamental, radical, must be done in order to find the solution of the Jewish problem."

Whether or not our people could avail themselves of this opportunity "to lay the foundation for a radically changed Jewish future, depends primarily on the attitude of American Jewry," which he regarded as "the greatest political factor in Jewish life of today." He therefore regarded the conference as an auspicious beginning towards achieving that end.

Goldmann did not dwell on any formula or program of action that a future assembly might work out with regard to the problems of European Jewry and Palestine. He only indicated what, in his opinion, should be the spirit of such a program of action. American Jewry should advance its role of leadership in

Jewish life — a role unparalleled in the history of American Jews — "with the desire to find radical solutions for the Jewish problem." He agreed with Pittsburgh Reform leader Rabbi Freehof that this was not the time for "ideological discussions" on "the definition of the Jews in the world . . . This is the moment of all moments in Jewish history . . . when we must come forward not with palliative solutions, but with an attempt to obtain a solution of the Jewish problem which will give us what every other people will have to have in the world of tomorrow — security of life and existence and equality of position as a people among the peoples."

(The Jews in Auschwitz and Maidanek apparently did not know what wonderful opportunities were awaiting them after cremation.)

And so the leaders spoke of unity and preparing "World Jewry" for the peace talks; they spoke of a radical or less radical solution to the Jewish problem. Naturally most of the Zionist speakers discussed the problem of Palestine as a Jewish homeland and how to pressure the British into declaring it open for immigration.

One rabbi, a Zionist leader, became so excited that he blessed the assembled, telling them, "Already something has been achieved." He also stressed the strange view that Christian friends would cooperate if they knew that there was a single body representing all Jews in America.

The meeting concluded with the adoption of many resolutions, hence effectively obscuring the main problem of saving the European Jews. In relation to them, the meeting merely affirmed that it would "do everything humanly possible to alleviate their sufferings and to restore their rights." (sic!)(!?)

What physician would treat a patient facing death by offering an aspirin for his headache? Yet this was precisely the conference's role. The most important thing to emerge from the deliberations were resolutions; they were adopted "unanimously."

Was it a demonstration of cynicism when the conference concluded by sending a "message of hope to European Jewry?" The resolution included "an expression of solidarity." It terminated with "our prayer that victory may soon rest upon the banners of those who believed in a fight for justice and brotherhood among men, and that millions of our brethren may be rescued out of the Valley of the Shadow of Death."

This meeting, called in the hope of creating a greater degree of Jewish unity, could not adjourn without adding the voice of its delegates representing thirty-four national Jewish organizations to those crying aloud in horror and protest against the massacres of Jews by Nazi Germany. "The tragedy of our people does not stand alone. (sic) It is but one instance, even if the darkest and most extreme, of the persecution and slaughter of peoples in the Orient and in the Occident. To the last man and woman Jews are united in grief for the guiltless dead, in prayer for those still in mortal peril, and in petition to the United Nations to exert every effort to save those who can yet be saved. We have been enheartened by the expressions of sympathy and of a determination to help that have come from the leaders of the democratic peoples. It is our hope that the revulsion of the whole civilized world may yet serve to deter the tyrant, his allies and followers; that their own peoples may be impelled by justice and by the retribution that may be visited upon them to revolt and to put an end to this reign of terror; that the United Nations will aid refugees to escape and to find harbor; and that, wherever and whenever it can be done, they shall send food to starving Jewish and non-Jewish communities."

The messages that the conference received from the two men who were then the most renowned Jewish leaders, Dr. Chaim Weizmann and Dr. Stephen Wise, are especially significant. Dr. Weizmann, then president of the World Zionist Organization and the Jewish Agency for Palestine, had wired Monsky that he had a previous engagement and could not attend the meeting. Nevertheless he urged the representatives of the thirty-four Jewish organizations in America that *after the war* the Jews should present a common platform just as they had in 1918.

Here is the text of Weizmann's letter, quoted by the *American Jewish Conference Proceedings Book:*

"I consider it a matter of highest importance that the organized democratic forces in American Jewish life should, at this time, take counsel with each other on questions affecting the future of Jewish Palestine and the position of European and other Jewries in the post-war world. American and world Jewry, I am sure, will be deeply indebted to you and I am hopeful that as a result of this important step the great Jewish community in your country will, in cooperation with their brethren in other free countries, find a common platform just as in 1918, for the presentation of our case before the civilized nations of the world."

Dr. Wise's message had the same dramatic tone as his speeches. The delegates must have been moved when these words were read: "Our deeply wronged and cruelly smitten brothers throughout Europe can be restored in part only if the concerted action of American Jewry now becomes a prelude to united planning and action of world Jewry towards self-help and self-rehabilitation . . . With unmistakable clarity the Conference must declare that the United Nations should affirm the rightfulness of the Jewish will to establish the Jewish Commonwealth of Palestine . . . I do not doubt that this Conference will be equal to its historic task, and in time, as was done in 1918, bring about the unity of American Jews for the highest ends of our faith and people."

The president of Hadassah followed the same line: "The time has come for heart-searching discussions and thoughtful exploration of plans for American Jewry's participation in the post-war reconstruction of Jewish life." She then praised B'nai B'rith for its understanding of "common responsibility."

The conclusion was exactly like a dinner meeting of a fundraising group. The chairman did not forget to thank Monsky and B'nai B'rith for organizing the successful conference. Rabbi Freehof called Monsky "a magnificent, farseeing statesman." Of course compliments were exchanged and everybody lived happily ever after — except those in Maidanek and Auschwitz.

(Naturally the man who was in the Kielce Ghetto never received this message of hope. Instead he saw the members of his family liquidated one after the other).

The fear of being branded "adventurers" led to the postponement of action which would last as long as the leaders discussed the post-war world. Instead of immediate action, instead of embarrassing the American government for its non-action, the Jewish leadership explained to its constituency that there was nothing to be done until the end of the war. Never in the history of American Jewry were there so many meetings on the ideological differences between the various groups and organizations. The conference that was finally supposed to establish a kind of unity that could never exist in a free society caused more friction and more debates than any other initiative in the annals of the North American Jewish community. The essential debate was between the non-Zionist American Jewish Committee and the Zionist establishment which was pressured by certain leaders in Palestine to demonstrate American Jewry's interest in a Jewish State. One businessman defined the interest of American Jewry in the following manner:

"Speaking as a practical businessman, since the Jewish people have invested large sums of money in Palestine and expect to invest there even larger amounts in the future and take masses of Jews into the country, they should have a right to determine the legislation of Palestine. That is essentially the meaning, from a practical point of view, of a Jewish Commonwealth in Palestine."

How could the Jews in Europe even visualize that *this* would be the concern of American Jews at a moment when time was running out and the Nazi death machine was working day and night?

Although the conference established "unity," Judge Joseph Proskauer, the president of the non-Zionist American Jewish Committee, dissented from voting on the Palestine statement. Proskauer did not say that he considered it futile to adopt resolutions on the future of Palestine, but he was concerned that Jewish preoccupation with problems other than the war effort might jeopardize the victory at the United Nations.

Proskauer said, "At this time it is our duty to concentrate on victory at the United Nations. We are convinced that it is inadvisable to bring to the foreground of public attention at this time political matters that may divide the peoples of the United Nations and create added difficulties.

"And it is for that reason that we endeavoured, without success, in the Palestine Committee, to secure the passage of a resolution deferring action on this matter until some subsequent session of this Conference to be called by the Praesidium. We yield to no one in our devotion to the cause of Judaism and to the protection of the rights of Jews throughout the world. We have demonstrated a deep and abiding concern for the welfare of Palestine and its full and proper development. We have asked for the abrogation at once of the White Paper, and have requested that the gates of Palestine be immediately opened for the freest entry of the victims of Nazi tyranny. But because of the war considerations and the impossibility of foreseeing the quickly changing world scene, we deemed it wise to ask for the continuance of an international trusteeship to safeguard the Jewish settlement in Palestine and the fundamental rights of its inhabitants to prepare the country to become within a reasonable period of years a self-governing Commonwealth under a constitution and a bill of rights that would protect the basic rights of all."

He even promised the Jews a Bill of Rights. For the American Jews or the survivors?

*   *   *

Similarly, each of the thirty-four organizations delivered a statement and, of course, repeated meaningless messages of hope to the Jews of Europe. Yet ten months elapsed from the time of the Pittsburgh Conference to the Waldorf Astoria American Jewish Conference. During this time those to whom the messages of hope were addressed had probably been diminished by a million souls. Even so, the leaders of the conference dared remind the European Jews of Europe not to forget that *for God* the glory of Israel never fails. Pages and pages of resolutions were read and every important delegate had a chance to mount the podium and read one of the resolutions which gave him some standing in the community. Included were thanks to the Waldorf Astoria Hotel for the arrangements and the service:

"Be it resolved that the American Jewish Conference expresses its appreciation to the Hotel Waldorf Astoria for its hospitality and cooperation."

As a conference to end all Jewish conferences, the most important "political" resolution was the greeting sent to Dr. Chaim Weizmann in London. It affirmed support for this elegant and diplomatic representative of the Jews, and voiced opposition to the extremists and adventurers who would force open the doors of Palestine. No doubt the British government was pleased to have the support of the conference.

The message to Weizmann read: "In response to your message, the American Jewish Conference greets you in the consciousness that the decisions taken by this body reflect the responsibility which the tragic events of our time have placed upon American Jewry. The Conference expresses its resolve to marshal all the strength of American Jewry, and of all right-thinking men, to press before the tribunal of the Allied Nations the justice and necessity of the cause whose champion you have been for more than a generation. The American Jewish Conference pledges to you as President of the Jewish Agency for Palestine its support of the great tasks before you for the redemption of our people and the healing of its suffering members everywhere."

The conference had raised many hopes. But the average American Jew could not be criticized for failing to understand that such exercises in futile oratory were a luxury that "World Jewry" could not afford. He was too busy to be concerned about discussions at a meeting of this kind. Just as he knew Roosevelt could be trusted with running the United States and with winning the war in general, his leaders with a tremendous budget at their disposal could be trusted with winning the Jewish war against death. He did not know then and he does not know now what happened during those crucial years.

The Conference was an indirect result of the activities of the Irgun delegation in America. But instead of taking up the challenge and doing the Irgun's job, the establishment bureaucracy stifled all opposition. Many American politicians were afraid to go near the Irgun delegation offices, knowing full well that those Jews who had influence would fight them if they were to support their "competitors."

Earlier a list with the names of some leading Americans was published. This list contained names of the original sponsors of the Irgun Emergency Committee. They had asked to have their names removed under the immense pressure to which these well-meaning non-Jews were exposed. However, a number of prominent legislators such as Senators Gillette, Johnson, Thomas, Morse and Congressmen Somers and Rogers remained loyal to the "dissenters" and supported the struggle. The Zionist Emergency Council and all the American Jewish organizations maintained special departments whose task was not the rescue of Jews, but the liquidation of their "competitors," the Irgun delegation. Yet when the Emergency Conference to Save the Jewish People of Europe met in New York in July 1943, the popularity of the Irgun movement was so great that Roosevelt was on the point of acting to save the Jews. The Emergency Committee did not talk about postwar problems, did not discuss the political future of Palestine; it placed on the agenda one problem, and only one: that it was the duty of the Allies to protect the Jewish people of Europe and free them because they were prisoners of war. In a message to the Emergency Conference the American president finally said that his government expressed interest "in the terrible condition of the European Jews and of our repeated endeavors to save those who could be saved." These "endeavors," Roosevelt continued, "will not cease until the Nazi power is crushed." Likewise, Secretary of State Cordell Hull, in a message to the Irgun-sponsored conference of Jews and non-Jews, added that the governments of Great Britain and the United States had agreed on practical measures for rescue which were being put into effect.

When there was a chance for the American Jewish organizations to pressure the government into action, the establishment reacted hysterically to the sudden "popularity" of the dissenters, and the community's entire energy was mobilized in an attempt to annihilate the Irgun delegation.

(Approximately a year later I attended the International Labor Conference in Philadelphia, and it was not until this time that a resolution was finally passed to recognize the Jews in Nazi-held territories as prisoners of war. Even then the discrepancy remained between the publicly stated resolution and the imperative need for immediate action. I had a most interesting conversation at that conference with the late Jan Masaryk, the martyred Czechoslovakian foreign minister. I discussed our problems with him, and he understood my misgivings. However, when Masaryk and I ended our conversation, a Jewish official approached the famous statesman and, as I later learned, "warned" him about me because I did not speak for the Jews of America; I was a dangerous man somehow connected with rabblerousers.)

The uphill fight continued. The American Jewish Conference was soon over and forgotten, but the Irgun delegation continued its activities. How they managed to continue against this constant harassment, how all of us who supported them could have taken the abuse, I can only ascribe to our youth. Only those who are young and defiant can cope with such organized suppression of the truth.

*   *   *

Perhaps those who still do not understand what happened within the American Jewish community during that period can find a similarity in a remarkable novel. In *The Forty Days of Musa Dagh,* Franz Werfel writes about the last stand of the Armenian people in Syria during World War I, in the first modern-day perpetration of genocide — by the Turks. (Musa Dagh, the mountain of Moses, was then under Turkish administration.)

The remnant of the Armenian people could not unite even to save their own lives. They were involved in petty feuds, and not even the threat of death could eliminate the failings to which man is heir. There are moments in the history of a people where naive idealism is more vital to survival than intelligent conformity. This the American Jews lacked during the years of destiny.

*   *   *

M.J. Nurenberger.

M.J.N. with Otto Frank, father of Anne Frank, at the entrance of the Anne Frank house in Amsterdam, Holland (1961) (*Credit KLM*).

Demonstration at New York City Hall, 1943 organized by Polish Jews. The meeting
on the steps of City Hall was chaired by M.J. Nurenberger in the presence of Mayor
La Guardia, Polish senator and Mizrachi leader, Rabbi Rubenstein. In the picture,
among others, novelist Sholom Asch; Yiddish writer S.L. Shneiderman; Young Israel
leader Harry Jacobs; famous cartoonist Arthur Szyk; Polish Minister Sylvain Strakacz;
Yiddish writer Chaim Shoshkes; Cantor Moishe Oysher. (Strakacz was the Polish
diplomat who received the first cable about the extermination of Polish Jews.)

Swiss ex-president Dr. Musy who negotiated with Himmler on behalf of the Orthodox Rescue Committee.

Chief Rabbi Eliezer Silver of Cincinnati who was president of the Union of Orthodox Rabbis and head of the Vaad Hatzalah. Rabbi Silver was also chairman of the National Jewish Council of the Emergency Commmittee to Save the Jewish People of Europe and cooperated throughout the war years with the Irgun delegation, supporting all its activities.

M.J. Nurenberger with Harry Golden at Eichmann Trial.

The Greek Orthodox Archbishop Athenagoras (who later became head of the Greek Orthodox Church) was active in the Irgun Committee in New York, while in exile. With the Archbishop, Dr. Alexander Hadani (right), Rabbi P.D. Bookstater (left).

M.J. Nurenberger interviewing Albert Einstein.

M.J.N. in Vienna at the tombstone of Dr. Herzl (*Credit Signal Corps Photo, U.S. Army.*) 1945

The author with the leaders of the remnants of the Czech Jewish Community in the famous Maharal Synagogue in Prague, 1945.

Samuel Merlin. For many years, the closest collaborator of Vladimir (Zeev) Jabotinsky. Merlin came to the United States in 1940 on a mission for the French government in order to strengthen the boycott against Hitler's Germany. Merlin had been the chief executive of the Zionist Revisionist World Organization, prior to his mission to North America. In New York, he was the representative of the Irgun Tzvai Leumi in Palestine. He and Hillel Kook were the founders of all Irgun organizations established in America during World War II, including the Emergency Committee to Save the Jewish People in Europe. He and Hillel Kook also established the Hebrew Committee of National Liberation which opened, in defiance of the British, the first Hebrew embassy in Washington D.C. For the first time in history, the blue-white flag flew over embassy row in the American capital. Kook was chairman, and Merlin was Secretary-General of the Hebrew Committee.

Jacob Rosenheim. World President of Agudat Israel

Senator Guy M. Gillette; Oscar Chapman, Secretary of the Interior of the U.S.; Peter H. Bergson (Hillel Kook) and Senator Warren Magnusen; (from right to left)(*IMA*).

Weissmandl   (*LANDAU*)

Irving M. Bunim. Young Israel leader.

Ben Hecht salutes Paul Muni.   Senator Gillette and Ben Hecht.

Wartime supporters of the Irgun activities — from left to right: Harry Hershfield, Paul Muni, N.Y. Mayor William O'Dwyer, Ben Hecht and Louis Nizer.   (*IMA*)

Senator Guy Gillette. Introduced the Rescue Resolution in the U.S. Senate concerning the creation of a special governmental agency to save the Jews of Europe. (Nov. 9, 1943) (*IMA*)

Arthur Szyk's cartoon which was reproduced on the top of the Petition of the Irgun Delegation proclaiming the rebirth of a Hebrew nation, 1942.

Hillel Kook (Peter H. Bergson). Chairman of the World War II Irgun Delegation in America.

Members of the Hebrew Committee of National Liberation. Missing in this picture is: Eri Jabotinsky, who, at the taking of this picture was in the British jail in Acre.

Peter Bergson

Aryeh Ben-Eliezer

Alexander Hadani

Reuben Hecht

Samuel Merlin

Capt. Jeremiah Helpern

Yitzhaq Ben-Ami

Theodore Bennahum

David Wdovinsky

Aaron Kope

Pierre Delougaz

Albert Stara

Eri Jabotinsky

Famous Supporters of the Rabbinical Vaad Hatzalah meet in Montreux, Switzerland, 1946. In picture: Mizrachi leaders Rabbi Zeev Gold and Moshe Shapira. Between them, the late Chief Rabbi of the Holy Land, Isaac Halevy Herzog. (*LANDAU*)

Hatzalah leaders meet after the war in Paris (1945). From right to left, historian Dr. Isaac Lewin; Mr. and Mrs. Sternbuch; Dr. Lewel; and Paris Rabbi Rubinstein.

First post-war meeting of the Vaad Hatzalah in Montreux discusses situation of survivors. From right to left: Rosh Yeshiva Eliezer Botschko, Rabbi Pinchas S. Wohlgelernter of Detroit; Recha Sternbuch; Herman Landau. Standing, Isaac Sternbuch. (*LANDAU*)

Dr. Julius Kuhl. A leader in the Vaad Hatzalah rescue work.

The presentation of A Flag Is Born, which was a part of the campaign of the Hebrew Committee of National Liberation. Hundreds of thousands saw this dramatic demonstration for Jewish survival. The script was written by Ben Hecht. Its narrator was Quenton Reynolds. The stars were Paul Muni and Marlon Brando. This is the photo of the première at Madison Square Garden in New York sponsored by Mayor William O'Dwyer.   (*IMA*)

The last photo of Rabbi Benjamin W. Hendles who was the most active member of the Jewish National Council of the Emergency Committee to Save the Jewish People of Europe.

The Historic March of the Rabbis in 1943. Organized by the Emergency Committee to Save the Jewish People of Europe, in cooperation with the Union of Orthodox Rabbis and the Organization of the Hassidic Rebbes. On the steps of Capitol Hill, Vice-President Henry Wallace holds the petition signed by 500,000 Americans, asking for emergency steps to save European Jews. Behind Mr. Wallace are: Senator Edwin C. Johnson of Colorado, then national chairman of the Irgun's Committee for a Jewish Army; House Speaker Sam Rayburn.

To the right of Vice-President Wallace is Rabbi Eliezer Silver of Cincinnati, then president of the Union of Orthodox Rabbis and chairman of the Emergency Committee's National Jewish Council. Rabbi Silver read the petition in Hebrew. Partially hidden is then oldest Jewish spiritual leader of America, Rabbi Dov Ber Levinthal of Philadelphia. To the right of the vice-president is Rabbi Reuven Levovitz, then Honorary Secretary of the American Rabbinate.

The leaders of the march were received by vice-president Wallace because FDR, following the advice of the then Jewish leaders, refused to see this "horde".

The saintly Rabbi Aaron Kotler, also one of the "horde" whom F.D.R. refused to see upon the advice of his Jewish friends.

Two of the "horde" whom Roosevelt's Jewish advisors persuaded him not to receive: From left to right: the saintly Mir Rosh Yeshiva, Rabbi Abraham Kalmanowitz, and Bronx Rabbi Predmesky.

New York Rabbis and religious leaders in last appeal to Mayor O'Dwyer, City Hall, 1944. On the Mayor's left Congressman Herbert Tenzer, Rabbi Pinchas M. Teitz of Elizabeth New Jersey. Others in photo, extreme left: M.J. Nurenberger; third from left, Young Israel leader, Irving M. Bunim.

ACTION—NOT PITY
CAN SAVE MILLIONS NOW!

EXTINCTION OR HOPE FOR THE REMNANTS OF EUROPEAN JEWRY?—IT IS FOR US TO GIVE THE ANSWER

Daily, hourly, the greatest crime of all time is being committed: a defenseless and innocent people is being slaughtered in a wholesale massacre of millions. What is more tragic—they are dying for no reason or purpose.

* * *

The Jewish people in Europe is not just another victim in the array of other peoples that fell prey to Hitler's aggression. The Jews have been singled out not to be conquered, but to be exterminated. To them Hitler has promised . . . and is bringing . . . DEATH.

* * *

It is a satanic program beyond the grasp of the decent human mind. Yet, it is being carried out. Already 2,000,000 of the Jews in German-occupied Europe have been murdered. The evidence is in the files of our own State Department.

Germans Exterminating Entire Jewish Population of Occupied Europe

FACTS CONFOUND VISIONS OF HELL

WASHINGTON, Nov. 27.—News from Occupied Europe, confirmed by confidential reports to our own State Department, tells the story of the calculated extermination of every Jew in the hands of the Nazis in a campaign to make Europe Judenrein in the next year. Already two million Jews have fallen victim to the German butchers. Reports reveal:

That in Poland, the Nazis have established the price of 10 Reichsmarks (formerly $25) for each Jewish corpse and are reclaiming the bodies to be "processed into such war-vital commodities as soap, fats and fertilizer." They are even exporting the dead for the value of the corpses. While various methods are being used in this campaign, the Nazi doctors have found one of the simplest and cheapest methods is to inject air bubbles into the veins of the victims. One Nazi physician can handle more than one hundred Jews in an hour by this method.

That human slaughter houses have been organized in the Nazis. In them, men, women and children are run to death by technical means. It appears that the first of such human slaughter houses was organized at Kovno, capital of Lithuania, where Poles, many of them of Jewish faith, were killed. Another one is functioning at Belsec, where in a large building electrocutions and total gas chambers are used, some in about 10 miles from Lwow in Poland. The method used is the failure cry. The victims are ordered to strip naked "to have a bath." They are then led to a bathtub with a metal floor. The floor is lowered and an electric current is turned on. They die in agony. When the current is turned off the bodies are loaded on cars and cremated in mass graves. In addition to using spades, electrocutions and lethal gas, Jews are packed into locked freight cars 50 or 60 in a car, and long trains of these cars are driven into the country and left on sidings where the people in them are left to die! At least a million Polish Jews have been killed in Poland in these inhuman slaughter houses.

The Germans dared to undertake this process of annihilation because they knew that the Jews are defenseless; that the Jews are forgotten and deserted even by the democratic powers.

The Germans believe that the United Nations, indoctrinated by twenty years of anti-Jewish propaganda, are to a great extent apathetic and indifferent to the sufferings of the Jews. They believe that for crimes committed against the Jews, no retaliation on behalf of the Government or armed forces of the United Nations will be carried out. They know that there is no instrument of power and force on this earth with which the Jews can fight back, to avenge their dead and save the remaining millions.

Of what avail are the statements of sympathy and pity and promises of punishment after the war? Since the perpetrators of these slaughters are to be punished for the murders they have already committed, then they can lose no more by further murder.

Such mere statements of sympathy and pity are to the Germans proof that their judgment of Democracy's attitude toward the Jews is justified, and in their criminal minds they understand them as "carte blanche" to go on with the slaughter.

What can be done?

What is necessary is to impress the Germans that the Governments of the United Nations have decided to change their present policy of passive sympathy and pity to one of stern and immediate action; that they consider the cessation of atrocities against the Jews are an immediate aim of their military and political operations. Under this premise vigorous United Nations' intervention to save European Jewry would become a matter of course. Exactly as it would be if it were American

or British civilians who were being killed in a systematic campaign by the Nazis, the whole of the forces of these great democracies would be utilized to find an immediate and effective solution.

The inauguration of such a new policy on behalf of the United Nations would logically result in enabling all those Jews who have managed to escape the European-German hell, to fight back. The first dictate, therefore, would be the immediate approval of the demand for a Jewish Army of the Stateless and Palestinian Jews—an army 200,000 strong.

Suicide squads of the Jewish Army would engage in desperate commando raids deep into the heart of Germany. Jewish pilots would bomb German cities in reprisal.

A Jewish Army would imply a call to arms of all Stateless Jews living in North Africa and those that may participate in the imminent invasion of the European continent.

A Jewish Army would immediately give a decisive moral relief to the agonized Jews of Europe. Their psychology of despair and helplessness would be transformed into one of hope for revenge and survival. A Jewish Army will give a meaning to their sufferings—to their death.

They will then realize that they cease being helpless victims and become partners in the global struggle for a better world, in which their survivors will live in freedom and equality as all other human beings.

The Jews of Palestine and the Stateless Jews want to fight . . . AS JEWS. They want to prove to Hitler, and to the world, that the Jews can be more than "the persecuted people" . . . that Jews can die in other ways than through murder. They want the right to fight for the world's freedom, under their own banner.

To die, if needs be, but to die fighting.

Of course, these are not all the practical proposals which the human mind is capable of conceiving. It is unfair to ask for a single solution to such a disastrous problem. What we must realize is that it is our duty not to resign ourselves to the idea that our brains are powerless to find any solution; not to resign ourselves to the idea that the forces of Democracy are too weak to enforce such a solution.

Remember when a few thousand British soldiers were put in chains by the Germans? How swift the retaliation? ...And how practical ...

The Germans chained no more British soldiers.

Remember when a tiny town in Czechoslovakia was horribly "punished"? How swift the hurricane of world-indignation that answered ...

There have been no more Lidices.

Remember when small and encircled Sweden opposed vigorously

and stubbornly the expulsion of Norwegian Jews. The Germans abandoned their plan.

The Jews of Norway are still there.

The American sense of justice and decency and American ingenuity must also find ways to overpower the diabolical plan to exterminate the Jewish people. It must find a way now, before millions more perish.

It is, therefore, our primordial demand that an inter-governmental commission of military experts be appointed with the task of elaborating ways and means to stop the wholesale slaughter of the Jews in Europe. This must be done now—before the greatest homicidal maniac extends his policy of extermination to other peoples; before he dares to introduce poison gas and bacteriological warfare.

Remember that for years the Germans rehearsed on the Jews what they later practiced on other peoples.

Therefore we have decided to launch an all-out campaign to save European Jewry. We will spare no efforts and have no rest until the American public will be fully informed of the facts and aroused to its responsibilities.

We believe in the overwhelming power of public opinion, as the greatest, if not the only, power in democracy. Governments in democratic countries like the United States and Great Britain can act only when they feel sure that they are backed by a powerful movement of public opinion. We plead with everyone to help and to co-operate in this sacred campaign we have launched. Join in this fight—write to your Congressmen, contribute to our work, so that this message may be carried to every city and hamlet in the United States as is being done in Great Britain. You are part of the collective conscience of America: this conscience has never been found wanting.

We shall no longer waste with pity alone, and with passive sympathy, the systematized extermination of the innocent Jewish people by the barbarous Nazis.

[list of names]

And 2,401 other distinguished American leaders from all walks of life.

80 AMERICAN CITIZENS are wanted as soldiers in the Jewish Army. They fight in the Armed forces of the United States, where millions of men of all creeds have joined the struggle.

I want to support your campaign to save European Jewry by action—not pity, and to help publicize your appeal through the press, the radio and public meetings throughout the country. I am glad to enclose my check in the amount of

$

Name

Address

PLEASE MAKE YOUR CHECK PAYABLE TO THE COMMITTEE FOR A JEWISH ARMY OF STATELESS AND PALESTINIAN JEWS, 535 FIFTH AVE., N.Y.C.

Committee for a Jewish Army
NATIONAL HEADQUARTERS · NEW YORK, 535 Fifth Ave. · MUrray Hill 2-7237

Photostat of the famous Proclamation of the Committee for a Jewish Army, one of the front organizations of the Irgun, illustrated by Arthur Szyk, it appeared as an advertisement in the New York Times on Monday, February 8, 1943.

Rabbi Baruch Robbins (Rabinowitz).
Presently in Israel. During World War
II was one of the most active leaders
in the Emergency Committee To Save
the Jewish People of Europe. Robbins
supplied the author with some pertinent
facts about the Irgun activities in
Washington D.C., in which he was
involved.

Wolf Pappenheim, Agudat Israel leader in Vienna, who helped the Irgun Delegation
(in 1938) to organize illegal Aliyah.

The author with Dr. Nahman Steinberg who had been Lenin's first Minister of Justice. Steinberg was probably the only observant Jew who served in Lenin's first coalition government. The photo was taken in London in 1938.

Yosef Klarman, Herut leader, who represented the Irgun in Istanbul during World War II.

The Hebrew Embassy in Washington. For the first time the Hebrew flag was flying on Embassy Row.

Billy Rose   (*The Answer*)

Hillel Kook addressing a mass meeting in New York.

Arthur Szyk's cartoon from *The Answer* Magazine.

Members of the Irgun delegation flanked by American statesmen at a session of the Resolution Committee of the Emergency Conference to Save the Jewish People of Europe. (from right to left) Dr. Alex Hadani, Aryeh Ben Eliezer, Congressman Will Rogers Jr, Eri Jabotinsky, Senator William Langer and Prof. Max Lerner.

RESCUE OF THE JEWISH AND OTHER PEOPLES IN NAZI-OCCUPIED TERRITORY

HEARINGS $\left(3186\right)$

BEFORE THE

COMMITTEE ON FOREIGN AFFAIRS
HOUSE OF REPRESENTATIVES

SEVENTY-EIGHTH CONGRESS

FIRST SESSION

ON

H. Res. 350 and H. Res. 352

RESOLUTIONS PROVIDING FOR THE ESTABLISHMENT
BY THE EXECUTIVE OF A COMMISSION TO
EFFECTUATE THE RESCUE OF THE
JEWISH PEOPLE OF EUROPE

———

NOVEMBER 26, 1943

———

Printed for the use of the Committee on Foreign Affairs

UNITED STATES
GOVERNMENT PRINTING OFFICE
92577   WASHINGTON : 1943

CHAIRMAN
DR. STEPHEN S. WISE

SEP 29 9 42 AM '44

RECEIVED

September 26, 1944.

The President
The White House
Washington, D. C.

Dear Mr. President:

Six months have passed since we were privileged
to meet with you to discuss the future of Palestine
and the settlement there of hundreds of thousands of
homeless Jewish refugees. At that time you authorized
us to say on your behalf that "when future decisions
are reached, full justice will be done to those who
seek a Jewish National Home."

In the meantime events have moved fast and today
the liberating forces of the United Nations have already freed considerable areas of Europe from Nazi
domination. The problem of what is to be done with
the surviving Jews in these and in other areas about
to be freed is a matter of immediate moment. The
intergovernmental bodies concerned are formulating
plans and are taking measures designed apparently to
return the refugees to their places of origin or of
first refuge. But many of the refugees desire above
all to rebuild their shattered lives in Palestine.
This opportunity is being denied them and action is
being taken which later will be irreparable.

The problem is becoming more acute with every
day that passes and it would appear to be of immediate
urgency that steps be taken to deal with a situation
that is causing widespread disquiet. As heads of the
combined Zionist organizations in this country it is
our earnest request that you accord us the earliest
opportunity of meeting with you in order to submit to
you our views on this and on related matters.

Yours faithfully,

Abba Hillel Silver

Abba Hillel Silver

Stephen S. Wise

Stephen S. Wise
Co-Chairmen

X3186

x Gen
x PPF 4520

September, 1944 — a few months left to rescue the remanants of European Jewry. The
Irgun Delegation urges F.D.R. to evacuate European Jews on Lend-Lease boats, retur-
ning from Europe. The Official Zionist leaders, Abba Hillel Silver and Stephen S.
Wise, are pre-occupied with the future of Palestine. (*F.D.R. Archives, Hyde Park, N.Y.*)

BALLAD OF THE DOOMED JEWS OF EUROPE

FOUR MILLION JEWS waiting for death.

Oh hang and burn but—quiet, Jews!

Don't be bothersome; save your breath—

The world is busy with other news.

Four million murders are quite a smear

Even our State Department views

The slaughter with much disfavor here

But then—it's busy with other news.

You'll hang like a forest of broken trees

You'll burn in a thousand Nazi stews,

And tell your God to forgive us please

For we were busy with other news.

Tell Him we hadn't quite the time

To stop the killing of all the Jews;

Tell Him we looked askance at the crime—

But we were busy with other news.

Oh World be patient—it will take

Some time before the murder crews

Are done. By Christmas you can make

Your Peace on Earth without the Jews.

by BEN HECHT

Vertrauliches Protokoll der Besprechung mit alt Bundesrat Dr.Musy im Hotel
Continental,am 1.5.1945. in Anwesenheit von
Dr.Musy, Dr.Weingort,Herrn Donnebaum, Dr.Hecht, in Lausanne:

Herrn Musy gab eine historische Uebersicht über seine Verhandlungen.
Zunächst hatte ihm Himmler zugesagt, alle Juden aus Deutschland herauszu=
lassen, wenn die Amerikaner sich bereit erklären, sie aufzunehmen und wenn
eine wohlwollende Presse im Auslande, besonders Amerika, über dies Entgegen=
kommen berichte.
Ursprünglich verhandelte Musy wegen Kompensationen: Trektoren, Werkzeugma=
schinen, etc, doch waren diese Verhandlungen und die Durchführung der event.
Resultate sehr schwierig. Auf die Frage Musys, ob stattdessen den Deutschen
Devisenzahlungen genehm wären, erhielt er die Antwort,dass kein Interesse
an Devisenzahlungen bestünden; Deutschland bedürfe dieser nicht. Musy infor=
mierte sich hier bei Verhandlungen,ob Paris für die Kompensation von Trakto=
ren und Werkzeugmaschinen geneigt sei und sprach auch über Arzneimittel.In
Basel verhandelte er mit dem Generaldirektor der CIBA,die bereit war, bis zu
Sfr. 10 Millionen Geg=nwert Cibazol zur Verfügung zu stellen,da die deutschen
verwandten Fabriken kaum den Bedarf decken konnten.
Erneut in Berlin, verhandelte Musy mit Himmler,der behauptete, "nicht so böse
zu sein,wie man sagt", worauf Musy wörtlich geantwortet habe: "Sie haben es
verdammt nötig,nicht so schlecht zu sein,wie man sagt". Himmler habe dann eine
Deckung von 5 Millionen Sfr.zur Enhaltung der Verpflichtungen verlangt, wobei
von einer kleinen Gesellschaft inBerlin, für die diese 5 Millionen in der
Schweiz zu deponieren wären,gesprochen wurde. Die 5 Millionen seien ja gekom=
men, doch "können Sie nun darüber verfügen", da die Gegenseite ihre Zusagen
nicht einhielt. Musy habe auf eine grosse Geste gedrängt, und es war abgemacht,
ebenfalls als Geste,die ganze Sache dann dem Internationalen Rotkreuz zu
übergeben (d.h.die Durchführung der Menschenausreise aus Deutschland). Darauf
kam der erste Zug aus Theresienstadt, dem wöchentliche Züge laut Zusage folgen
sollten.
Wahrscheinlich habe man jemand aus Hitlers Umgebung errangiert,dass im Atlan=
ticsender als Gegenleistung für die von Musy erreichte Befreiung der Juden
von einem Alibi für die dabei mithelfenden Nazis gesprochen wurde.Auf jeden
Fall wurde dies Hitler hinterbracht, worauf dieser wütend wurde. (Die Ameri=
kaner hätten ja auch,laut Musy, dies Entgegenkommen wohlwollend abgewogen).
    Erneut in Berlin, erfuhr Musy von Schellenberg, dass Httlers Wut gegen Musy
sehr gross sei,da Musy Hitlers Kampf gegen die Juden gebrochen habe und Hitler
ein Todfeind und wütender Hasser der Juden ist. Musy wollte Hitler sprechen.
Man sagte ihm: "Wenn Hitler es wagen würde, würde er Sie erschiessen lassen",
auch Schellenberg fühlte sich direkt in bedrohter Lage,wenn er weiter für die
Juden einträte. Musy meint heute,man hätte Becher heranziehen müssen, doch
wollte dies Schellenberger - als Becher vergeblich um eine Besprechung mit
Musy nachgesucht hatte - nicht,da Becher dem Schellenberger unterstellt sei
und diesem Bericht geben müsse. Man sagte Musy,die Aktion könne weitergehen,
wenn die USA-Zeitungen gut schreiben würden, Musy fand die Berichte der USA-
Zeitungen genügend freundlich,die Deutschen nicht.
Nachdem man im Moment nicht alle Juden befreien konnte, wurde abgemacht,dass
eingereichte Listen akzeptiert würden, die Schellenberg und Goering erhielten.
Benoit war nachts lange mit diesen zusammen,und Goering versprach bei den
Musys feierlichst,diese Leute zu befreien. Madame Bolomey habe Musy erklärt,

Confidential Minutes of a secret meeting in which Swiss ex-President, Dr. Musy,
reports to Dr. Weingort, Mr. Donnenbaum and Dr. Hecht on his negotiations with

er solle unbedingt einige Franzosen mitbringen, damit ihm in Paris keine
schlechte Presse für die Aktion mehr entstünde. So habe er den Neffen des
Nuntius,einen Neffen von Frau Bolomey (Leutnant,Kriegsgefangener), eine Frau
für die sich von Steiger einsetzte, befreit,doch sei ihm feierlich die Befrei=
ung der ganzen Liste zugesagt worden.
Nun erfuhr Musy,dass Hitler selbst befohlen hatte, alle Lager zu räumen und
die Insassen zu Fuss nach dem Süden ins Reduit zu schicken. Schellenberg und
Goering erklärten ihm,dieser Befehl müsse ausgeführt werden. Von Buchenwalde
nach dem Reduit z.B. müssten die Juden 300 Km mit ihren Sachen zu Fuss gehen,
und Musy sah selbst über 1000 Elende auf den Landstrassen sich hinschleppen
und protestierte energisch. Schellenberg sagte Himmler,Musy finde dies skan=
dalös. Nach Schätzung Schellenbergs würden von 18.000 Juden aus einem Lager
8000 unterwegs sterben. 15 Lager sollten so zu Fuss auf den Landstrassen ge=
trieben werden. Schellenberg ging zu Himmler,der sich hinter Hitler verschanz=
te. Vorher hatte Himmler Musy erklärt, er könne alle Juden ohne Hitlers
Zustimmung befreien. Jedoch war Hitlers Macht wie Berg und Tal auf=und abstei=
gend,und manchmal merkte Musy,dass Himmler,dann wieder dass Hitler die Macht
hatte. Hitler sei imstande gewesen,seine besten Freunde erschiessen zu lassen,
wenn sie sich seinen Befehlen widersetzten. Nunmehr wurde verlangt, dass,wenn
man Musys Wunsch nachkomme und die Leute nicht mehr auf den Landstrassen nach
dem Reduit deportiere sondern in den Lagern belasse, die SS an Ort und Stelle
bleiben und die Ordnung aufrecht erhalten könne und dass die SS wie Soldaten
behandelt würden und nicht von den alliierten Truppen erschossen würden. Musy
erklärte,dass alle in Uniformen sein müssten,nicht schiessen und die Waffen
abgeben müssten. Himmler forderte,dass dann die SS als Soldaten behandelt
würden und nicht erschossen würden. Musy erklärte,dass sie,wenn sie sich Ver=
brechen schuldig machten, verantwortlich seien, jedoch nicht sofort erschos=
sen werden dürfen,wenn die Truppen kommen,sondern als Soldaten einem Kriegs=
gericht unterstehen. (Dies wurde auch eingehalten,sogar Kramer, der SS-Leiter
von Bergen Belsen wurde nicht direkt erschossen,sondern als Kriegsgefangener
verhaftet).
Musy führte aus,dass nach dem Kriege Rache und Empörung der Welt gegen Deutsch=
land eingestellt sei und es nötig sei,alle Gefangenen, Politische,Kriegsgefan=
gene,Zivildeportierte,Juden, freizulassen,direkt in ihre Heimatländer, wofür
einige Korridore bestimmt würden durch die Frontlinien, an denen einige Tage
dazu das Feuer beidseitig eingestellt werde. Himmler war hierzu voll bereit,da
man nun an die Auswege des Friedens denken müsse. Hitler war strikte dagegen.
Benoit fuhr, während Musy bei McClelland war,zum Rendezvous nach Weimar zu
Goering,am 9.April, trotz der Warnung des Bezirkshauptmanns von Konstanz,wobei
Benoit die angebotene bewaffnete Begleitung ablehnte. 2 Funktelegramme nach
Berlin wegen des verschollenen Benoit waren erfolglos. Musy glaubt,dass er nach
Theresienstadt fuhr,um im Camion unsere Leute nach Liste abzuholen,die man dort
hin verbracht hatte. In St.Margarethen gab schliesslich Heckener(?)Frau Stern=
buch ein Visum nach Deutschland,doch wäre es grundfalsch gewesen,wenn sie als
Frau gefahren wäre. Da das Benzin nicht reichte,fuhr Musy nach München,wo er,
wie schon in Konstanz, jemanden traf,der Benoit in Berlin im Hauptquartier der
SS bei Goering und Schellenberg gesehen hatte. In München war Musy auf der
Sicherheitspolizei,Geheimpolizei der SS,beim Chef derselben,doch waren Himmler
und Goering wie Schellenberg nicht in München (Himmler einige Stunden vorher
abgereist).Auf der Rückreise gab es Halte und Komplikationen im Durcheinander
Deutschlands. Musy ist bereit,wieder zu fahren,Leute zu bringen und für weite=
ren Schutz zu sorgen.(Unzusammenhängend damit erzählte Musy,dass Schellenberg
ihm sagte,die Deutschen wollteneinen Film über das gute Lager Landsberg machen.
Benoit und Musy wollten die Lager Dachau,Bergen Belsen,Buchenwalde besuchen,was
ihnen untersagt wurde).
Vertraulich erzählte Musy noch,dass Hitler und Goebbels - entgegen den bisheri=
gen Zeitungsmeldungen,die unrichtig seien - letzten Mittwoch, 25.4.,abends
gestorben seien.Danach erst habe Himmler sein Angebot machen können.Freitag
14 Uhr sei er von München über Prag nach Berlin geflogen).

Himmler. Musy reports that Himmler was ready to allow all Jews to leave on the condition that the United States be willing to receive them. (*Dr. Julius Kuhl Archive*)

X
Roosevelt and Frankfurter

I know that some may question my contention that during World War II the Jews closest to F.D.R. failed to act on behalf of the Jews of Europe.

I would suggest that those who consider this an indefensible allegation read *Roosevelt and Frankfurter* (by Max Freedman) where the letters of the famous United States Supreme Court Justice, known as a "Zionist" to Franklin D. Roosevelt, are reproduced. Some of his letters deal with Jewish and Zionist problems as well as the question of antisemitism; some deal with the Holocaust.

Those familiar with recent American history know that Felix Frankfurter considered himself a very loyal Jew. When I met his sister, Marion, in Jerusalem some years after the War of Independence, she told me how much Frankfurter had believed in and hoped for the establishment of a Jewish sovereign state in Palestine. The entire Frankfurter family was dedicated to Jewish survival. I quote Frankfurter's letters to Roosevelt, from which his absolute lack of understanding of the emergency in Europe becomes clear. The Justice was the typical "prominent," influential American Jew of that era, who did exactly what eminent Zionist leaders asked of him. How could Frankfurter have understood that it was not Weizmann, the respected world leader of Zionism, but a group of rabblerousers who were fighting for Jewish survival in Europe? These letters demonstrate that during the Holocaust years Frankfurter asked the American president to consider only those issues thought *relevant* by the Zionist leaders.

Frankfurter was not an expert on Jewish affairs, and he believed that Weizmann and Wise gave expert advice on how to deal with the problems of Jewry. Justice Frankfurter was no less active in Zionist affairs than Justice Brandeis. Yet while Brandeis was a political thinker in the Zionist sense of the word, a theoretician of the Jewish problem, Frankfurter was more of a follower of the establishment, albeit a well-meaning one. As a young man he had attended the Paris Peace Conference as a representative of the World Zionist Organization and of Dr. Chaim Weizmann. He also successfully negotiated an agreement with Lawrence of Arabia who had acted as spokesman for King Faisal.

As one of his biographers observed, Frankfurter very much resented the accusation by some Jews that he displayed timidity in the struggle against Nazism. His biographer, Max Freedman, is right in observing that Frankfurter was Roosevelt's "faithful and vigilant ally" in that struggle. His failure to grasp that European Jewry might perish in the war against Hitler was the fault of the American Jewish establishment. Also, no matter what might be said about Roosevelt's callousness in dealing with the Jewish problem, he did not act without pressure from his friends in the organized Jewish community. Certainly

Frankfurter was no less or more a "Zionist" than the other conventional Zionist leaders. Yet in the contest with Nazi Germany he was more realistic than most Zionists because he was able to present the case against the Nazis not as a Jewish case, not as a threat to Jewry alone, but as a danger to freedom itself. Freedman is right, then, when he observes that "on this larger issue ultimately on the fact of freedom itself" Frankfurter must have felt personally involved in presenting his case to a deeply concerned Roosevelt. There is no doubt that he influenced Roosevelt towards action against Hitler.

There is no question in my mind that if Frankfurter had comprehended that the European Jews would not survive to see the establishment of their own commonwealth, he would have been active in the Irgun movement. Yet fate willed it that the best among the Americans were influenced by the machinery of the professional Jews who cannot be absolved from responsibility for their "neutrality" towards the European Jew from 1939 to 1945.

As I said, Frankfurter considered himself a deeply committed Jew. In 1934 he wrote to Roosevelt: "My wife and I are making a flying visit to Palestine . . . if perchance a near-eastern war breaks out while I am there . . . please remember that I am a Major in the Reserve Corps . . . you can reach me care of the King David Hotel, Jerusalem."

Certainly these are not the words of a timid Jew.

Brandeis was more militant: a political Zionist who recognized Jabotinsky as an heir of Herzl. Unfortunately, during World War II he was old and disillusioned. He did not have Frankfurter's political influence, although he towered over him in the legal profession.

*   *   *

It should be remembered: A Jew in that era, who had reached such eminence, saw the future of Jews linked to the progress of democracy in the United States. Frankfurter viewed himself as the Jew who had proved beyond any doubt that belonging to a minority did not prevent anyone from reaching the top. Thus, when such Jews, without fear of endangering their position, took an outspoken stand towards their coreligionists — on Zionism, for example — they did so only because they believed it to be the solution to the Jewish problem. They, like the Jewish leaders, forgot that the wartime struggle was not for a postwar political solution to the Jewish problem, but for the bodily rescue of men, women and children. The paradox here is that politically Herzlian Zionists during World War II became pragmatic Jews refusing to discuss postwar aims, while the "practical" Weizmann Zionists spoke of politics only — in the future tense.

Following Hitler's rise to power, Frankfurter began to think of rescuing prominent individuals, although such action was a far cry from action to rescue the masses.

Frankfurter helped save Albert Einstein, and aided in getting Sigmund Freud to England. He also helped find positions in America for famous writers and scholars trapped by Hitler. While his biographer maintains that Frankfurter "helped not only the famous . . . but also the obscure and frightened," there are very few facts to corroborate this.

As an American Frankfurter understood American problems, but knew very little of the situation of European Jewry. In fact, some maintain that he had warned Roosevelt about Japanese treachery long before Pearl Harbor. Frankfurter was respected in the White House because of his influence in appointing members of the cabinet; the president very often listened to his advice. Roosevelt always remembered that Frankfurter, together with a few other liberal Jews (the most famous being his ghostwriter, Judge Samuel Rosenman, and Herbert Bayard Swope), had worked incessantly for his election. These men believed, and rightly so, that Roosevelt would change America.

*   *   *

At the very beginning of Hitler's rule in Germany, Frankfurter did not hesitate to speak out against antisemitism. In one of his letters to the president, in the fall of 1933, Frankfurter wrote: "The significance of Hitlerism far transcends ferocious antisemitism and fanatical racism . . . The attack against the Jew is merely an index to the gospel of force (now in Germany)."

However, it is remarkable how little he understood the threat of Hitlerism to the Jews. Perhaps he did not really believe that the Jews in Germany, in Europe, would be exterminated. In the same letter Frankfurter tells Roosevelt that Berlin's attitude towards the disarmament conference could be largely explained by domestic circumstances. Later he admitted that he had made the same incorrect evaluation of Hitlerism as "a number of distinguished German exiles," but grants that "the forces of violence and showmanship of the Hitler regime will be intensified." And yet Frankfurter had the incredible naiveté to suggest that because the German people "live in darkness," the president should broadcast in German, presumably to lift the darkness from the German nation.

*   *   *

One of the men who recognized the danger to Jews in Germany was James G. MacDonald, who later became the first American ambassador to Israel. MacDonald, who had been appointed the League of Nations High Commissioner for German Refugees, was the only man who ever spoke to Hitler about Jews. This was in 1933. Frankfurter must have been impressed by MacDonald's first report, for he asked the president to read it carefully. Did Roosevelt read it? No one knows to this day.

(I would like to mention two encounters I had with James MacDonald, the first when he was a member of the mission appointed by U.S. President Truman to the European D.P. camps; and later when he was the first American ambassador to Israel.

(When I spoke to him in 1946, at the Bristol Hotel in Vienna, about his encounter with Hitler, he confirmed his impressions of 1933. He told me that Hitler had frankly stated that he would make no compromise on the Jewish question.

MacDonald reported this to Roosevelt. Yet it seems that MacDonald was the only one who believed Hitler; the Jewish leaders did not.

(I learned how profoundly MacDonald was involved with the destiny of the Jewish people when I visited him at his home in Ramat Gan during his tenure as ambassador.

(It was a Friday night I will never forget. MacDonald, who remembered me from the time I had covered his mission to the camps, jested lightly and said, "I have to apologize because I have no kosher food; I cater mostly to Jews." Then he invited me to follow him to the roof of his house from which, on that clear night, clear as only Israeli nights are, he pointed to Jordan and said, "All this will one day be Israel; only the blind cannot see it.")

Yet MacDonald was the lonely Prophet of Doom. Everybody else, including Frankfurter, returned to business as usual, trying to influence the president to do something for "important refugees," not for the masses trapped by Hitler.

Those who understood, and they were a small minority, realized from the start that the Commission created by the League of Nations to help the German refugees (of which MacDonald was High Commissioner) would fail because no country was ready to admit Jews. MacDonald was helpless; he tried but failed. In fact, in a letter to Justice Frankfurter in 1933, MacDonald warned "that the German government is contemplating the issuance in the near future of decrees establishing formally a second-class citizenship for German Jews." In his letter, MacDonald also said: "Such action once taken would not only further humiliate and degrade hundreds of thousands of men and women; it would make much more difficult any softening in the German government's attitude later. Such retrogression to the inhumane and unchristian practices of an earlier age should, I think, be forestalled if there is any conceivable way of doing so.

"Moreover, I, in my official capacity as High Commissioner for German Refugees, have a special interest that this definitive action be averted. Under present circumstances the refugee problem is too large to be handled satisfactorily, but if conditions for the Jews become worse in Germany, there is a grave danger that something like an exodus — panic in character and proportions — may be precipitated. This would create a situation in the bordering countries beyond the possibility of ordered control. You will at once sense the tragedy of such a situation.

"In addition to all this, one can be quite sure that such an exodus would embitter further the relations between the Reich and many of its neighbors. It would tend to jeopardize every effort now being made to settle the more acute political questions such as disarmament — in which our own government is so much interested.

"Have you any possible suggestions as to what might be done to help avert such a blow? I should be most grateful for any help you may be able to give me."

*   *   *

During his activities on behalf of Zionism, Frankfurter introduced Roosevelt to another Jewish judge from New York, Julian W. Mack, a leading Zionist. Frankfurter was well acquainted with Roosevelt's personal secretary and intimate friend, Miss M.A. LeHand, and from her he must have learned how much Roosevelt shared his love of good food and the best wines. He also knew, probably from LeHand, that Roosevelt detested his wife's "unexciting food." Mack was an expert in French wines. Franklin D. Roosevelt was very grateful for having met Judge Mack, to whom he wrote:

"Felix Frankfurter has been spending some time with me and I was much interested to learn that aside from being one of our best jurists, you are also a connoisseur of wines. I am hoping that as soon as things quiet down you will come to Washington to see me. I have some 'wine tester' stories that I think will amuse you."

Like Justice Louis Brandeis, Judge Julian W. Mack was at one time president of the Zionist Organization of America. Indeed, Brandeis brought many American Jewish intellectuals into the Zionist movement. He influenced this San Francisco-born jurist to join the Zionist movement, where he stood somewhere between Frankfurter and Brandeis.

But these personal relationships were not used to tackle the Jewish problem. Only once did Frankfurter ask for the president's help, in assisting the Rumanian Jews in 1936. However, when Roosevelt requested the Justice to define American freedom "without attacking by name either Nazi Germany or Fascist Italy," he complied.

Frankfurter was also concerned with the danger to Austria, a center of anti-Jewish conspiracy. Yet the fact that there was no time to be lost escaped him. Frankfurter loved, it seems, Roosevelt's famous saying that "this generation of Americans has a rendezvous with destiny," but the Justice never realized that our generation of Jews also had a rendezvous with destiny.

By 1938, the precariousness of European Jewry, especially those under Hitler, was self-evident. Yet then, at the very beginning of Frankfurter's rendezvous with Jewish destiny, he failed in the most important task: to evacuate those endangered by Hitler. Frankfurter's biographer says that while Frankfurter "knew that Roosevelt had been outraged by the Nazi persecutions," this eminent Jewish friend of the president "also respected the political caution imposed on the president by a divided Congress and a troubled country . . . The suffering of the refugees in the spring of 1938 complicated Roosevelt's position. For most of the refugees were Jewish and this was a desperate period when antisemitism was showing an alarming increase." So the biographer interprets Frankfurter's opinion that, "Roosevelt, despite all his goodwill, could bring only a small portion of the refugees into this country . . . a great mass of the refugees would have to remain in Europe."

It seems to me that during those fateful years, when Jewish destiny in Europe was on the scales, Jewish leaders throughout the Free World pressed for the admission of Jews into any country other than their own, in order "not to undermine" their own position. For example, it was very easy for American Jews to propagandize against Britain for keeping the doors of Palestine closed. But there were no wild demonstrations against Roosevelt when he ordered the ship St. Louis, loaded with German refugees, back to Europe. Despite the cruelty of this action, there is no record of Justice Frankfurter's protesting to Roosevelt or to Roosevelt's beloved assistant, Missy. Instead, Frankfurter subconsciously (I do not believe it was intentional) began his "postwar" Zionist political agitation. I must underscore this: There was no malevolence in this attitude, only a certain stupidity, considering that Jewish lives were at stake.

In 1938, according to Frankfurter's biographer, the eminent Justice of the Supreme Court, "proud of his Zionist faith," began to speak out concerning his "dismay at the English attitude towards Palestine." In Frankfurter's judgement, England had "violated and betrayed her obligations as a mandatory power. No one could match Frankfurter's constant influence on the highest echelon of the Roosevelt administration in pleading the case of Zionism or in helping the refugees."

Roosevelt never embraced the cause of Zionism; in fact, he openly stated that he understood the King of Saudi Arabia much better than he did Stephen Wise. Roosevelt did not help the refugees. And, if Britain was guilty of "betraying her obligations" vis-à-vis Palestine, Roosevelt was guilty of betraying the faith of millions throughout the world who believed that he would show compassion towards those threatened by Hitler. This betrayal constituted Roosevelt's Munich — a Munich not dictated by a naive belief in the possibility of peace in our time. His lack of action, his abandonment of the millions in Europe, was caused by the political fear that he might lose the votes of some antisemites.

Frankfurter's attitude, I believe, stemmed from a belief in the perennial generalities concerning liberalism and freedom. *Philosophy* of freedom never freed men; *action* did.

So again the machinery of the Zionist movement proclaimed Palestine as the only haven for the Jews. Had the gates of Palestine been open at that time, Jews would have been saved. But while the United States maintained a closed-door stance, Britain could not have been expected to change its policy. If Roosevelt had opened the gates of America to some refugees and challenged the antisemites and bigots, Chamberlain would have had no choice but to alter his policy on Palestine.

At the end of November 1938, Frankfurter again writes about Britain's bad faith concerning Palestine. But not a word about *American* indifference to the Jewish fate in Europe. Still, Frankfurter continued to press the president on the "new wave of persecution in Germany." It was Dr. Weizmann and Ben Gurion who had asked him to transmit their opinions to the president and insist that Roosevelt press Britain to change its Palestine policy.

*   *   *

We are now in the middle of the war. The Jews are trapped. No one speaks anymore about releasing the hostages. In the meantime, Russia is attacked and persecution turns into extermination. But what does Frankfurter say? He compliments Roosevelt that he, "in lonely statesmanship," saw that Hitler's "treatment of the Jews" was more than a prelude to the first stage of his war against civilization. In January 1942, Frankfurter praises Roosevelt "for the wonderful goal" incorporated in the Declaration of the United Nations. Should those in Auschwitz not have been consoled by the Declaration of the United Nations?

Thus in June 1942 Frankfurter urges Roosevelt, upon pressure from Ben Gurion and Weizmann, to consider the Zionist demands for Palestine. Naturally, Roosevelt reported to Frankfurter that he found "discouraging opposition" to the Zionist cause in the Washington establishment. All Frankfurter achieved was the authorization to inform Weizmann and Ben Gurion about this situation in Washington.

In 1942, then, Frankfurter is busy with postwar problems. Palestine and the punishment of Nazi criminals occupy his mind, but not a word is said about saving the Jews in Europe. He is also informed by the White House that the president refuses to see Ben Gurion because Roosevelt would not make any statement about Palestine in the middle of the war. In October 1942, Roosevelt thanks his dear friend Felix for the book *Brandeis on Zionism*. Whether Roosevelt read it or not we do not know, but it gave him cause to crack a joke about his friend Henry Morgenthau, Jr., then Secretary of the Treasury, who, according to Roosevelt, "became the next leader of Zionism." Roosevelt tells Frankfurter that when Morgenthau returns from his vacation in Miami "Eleanor and I will telegraph him congratulations."

This was all Frankfurter got on behalf of the Jews in Europe from his friend, Franklin D. Roosevelt. And Frankfurter "achieved" more than any other American Jewish leader.

Roosevelt was obviously annoyed with the American Zionist leaders. When he cracked the joke about Morgenthau, the next Zionist "leader," it was, I believe, the result of the socalled successful Zionist lobbying in Washington. Roosevelt was involved in the greatest war recorded in human history. He was the leader of the Free World confronted by Hitler and his powerful armies. He had to win the war against Nazism. Therefore, any problem which did not affect the conduct of the battle against the Hitlerites did not attract his earnest consideration. Thus, while the official Zionist machine continued to bombard the White House with demands that the American policy regarding the *future* of Palestine be defined, the president of the United States apparently looked upon all this as baby talk. Especially during moments when the Allies were in a precarious situation, when an effort had to be made to save strategic positions, how could Roosevelt have seriously entertained the postwar demands of the Zionist leaders, including Weizmann and Ben Gurion?

In a secret communication to the Secretary of State in July 1942, Roosevelt, clearly annoyed by Zionist political pressure, said: "The more I think of it, the more I feel that we should say nothing about the Near East or Palestine or the

Arabs at this time. If we pat either group on the back, we automatically stir up trouble at a critical moment."

The error committed by the Jewish establishment at that time becomes even more glaring when one studies some of the inter-office memoranda circulated among the State Department officials. Time and again American leaders responsible for our diplomacy told Zionist visitors that "the United States now was interested only in the minute-by-minute issues directly connected with the war." They were simply embarrassed and often hurt by the lack of understanding on the part of Zionist propagandists when it came to problems related to the conduct of the war. After all, there was only one issue, one challenge: to win the war against Hitler.

Above all, the Jewish establishment failed to demonstrate that the rescue of the Jews in Europe, the legal classification of the Jews trapped by Hitler as prisoners of war, Allied hostages, should have been part and parcel of the war effort. Six million Jews in Europe had the same right to be included in a proclamation for liberating populations enslaved by Hitler as had the Poles, Czechs and others. The Zionist task should have been to prove, to impress upon the Allied governments, that rhetoric concerning refugees or religious and racial minorities was dangerous to the Jews locked within Hitler's Europe. It was dangerous because there was a declaration of war against the Jews, irrespective of their official national allegiance. If the Zionist leaders had followed the classical Zionist teachings, they would have pointed out to Roosevelt and others that the Jews of Europe — although they were not concentrated in one territory, in one country, and although they formed no majority of the population in any land — were a nation for all practical purposes. Instead, the leaders lobbied to permit the settlement of Jews in Palestine *after* the war. In fact, Roosevelt was so disgusted with this pressure that he sent a memorandum to the Department of State ordering a cessation of the discussion on the Palestine problem.

It was dishonest on the part of Jewish leaders in America to demand, purportedly on behalf of European Jewry, a redefinition of the political status of Palestine. The Jews of Europe had one hope: that the United States and her Allies would proclaim *urbi et orbi* that the Jews locked within Hitler's Fortress were prisoners of war, that the Red Cross had a duty to report to the Allied governments on their fate and that the extermination camps would be bombarded.

These demands were made by the Irgun delegation in public advertisements in American newspapers. But each time such demands were stated, the Jewish establishment not only refused to support them, but denounced the Irgun delegation as irresponsible adventurers. This was the essential, the actual crime committed by those who purported to speak on behalf of the Jews trapped by Hitler. Of course it was easy to formulate postwar demands. And it became very easy for Roosevelt to refuse to consider the Irgun demands, for he could always dispense with them by stating that they came from unauthorized Jewish sources. However, when it came to taking action with regard to Zionist demands for political solutions regarding Palestine, the president was honest in saying it was too early to discuss postwar considerations.

Thus the Jews of Europe lost their war for survival because those who claimed to speak for them did not even mention their plight.

XI
Final Solution: The Confirmation

The Emergency Conference to Save the Jewish People of Europe, called upon the initiative of the Irgun delegation in America (at that time still operating as the Committee for a Jewish Army), was a direct result of the Bermuda fiasco. At that time the Irgun delegation published a very interesting, factual brochure, *From Evian to Bermuda,* which struck the balance of five years of frustration among those who hoped for intergovernmental action to save the hostages from Hitler.

Documents now declassified prove beyond any doubt that State Department bureaucrats, especially Breckenridge Long, who continually acted against the interests of the Jews in Europe, used the British-American Conference on Refugees in Bermuda as yet another device to make people believe something was being done to counteract Hitler's war against the Jews. (Dept. of State memo; Feb. 23, 1940). As in Evian five years earlier, the show was directed by the British Foreign Office and the State Department. Reaching any decision of consequence was impossible; the president of the United States was to be informed that the American government had done something to save "those unfortunates."

The chairman of the American delegation to Bermuda, Professor Harold W. Dodds of Princeton University, was chosen by Breckenridge Long, the intransigent opponent of any large-scale activity on behalf of attempts to rescue European Jewry. The lone Jewish member of the delegation, Congressman Sol Bloom, had become what Samuel Merlin of the Emergency Committee called the "shabbos goy" of the State Department. The Irgun delegation made Bloom very angry by calling him the "shabbos goy," but even today, after so many years, it seems to be the *mot juste* to describe Bloom's role.

It is my view that Breckenridge Long and his immediate superior, Secretary of State Cordell Hull, made sure the members of the American delegation in Bermuda remembered that nothing should be done to "interfere with the war effort." In State Department parlance, "interfering with the war effort" was a euphemism which signified opposition to the rescue of the Jews. And, when adapted to the situation, it explained why nothing, absolutely nothing, could be done.

One should remember that the Bermuda Conference and the subsequent nonsectarian Emergency Conference called by the Irgun delegation took place approximately half a year after the Department of State and the leaders of American Jewry were informed of the Final Solution. They all knew that the war of extermination against Jews continued unabated, that Auschwitz and the other extermination camps were working to full capacity, that there was no let-up in the Nazis' determination to destroy the Jews. Dr. Stephen S. Wise, who was at that time the recognized spokesman for American Jewry, had also heard the ominous news months before. (This was before Gerhard Riegner of the World Jewish Congress in Geneva sent the information to New York. It is now public knowledge that the State Department withheld these messages from Wise for many months.)

The Committee for an Army of Stateless and Palestinian Jews and the American League for a Free Palestine became more active. They continuously "embarrassed" the American government by sponsoring fullpage advertisements in *The New York Times* in which the macabre facts were publicized. Wise became so angry on account of these advertisements, on account of all this "irresponsibility" on the part of socalled unauthorized Jewish groups, that he attacked the Emergency Committee. Of course, each attack by Wise and his friends against the Irgun delegation strengthened the position of Secretary Hull and Breckenridge Long, who could well afford to continue being tolerant towards Germany's war of extermination against the Jews.

Despite ongoing harassment by the Jewish establishment, the Irgun delegation mobilized public opinion and kept on demanding that action replace mere sympathetic murmurs. Although the establishment of the War Refugee Board was the result of the propaganda campaign conducted by the Irgun delegation, one should not forget that it actually took two years — and probably three or four million corpses — before this American government agency to rescue the Jews became operational. It was too little and too late — all because of sabotage by the Jewish establishment, which feared competition and was intent upon maintaining its position as the mouthpiece of American Jewry no matter what the cost.

At the time, Rabbi Benjamin W. Hendles, executive head of Agudat Israel, became very active in support of the Irgun delegation and fought relentlessly for the recognition of the Jews' extraordinary situation. His connection with the Emergency Committee stemmed from his deep disappointment, beginning in 1941, with the Jewish leadership.

At the beginning of the war, Agudat Israel, through its connections in Switzerland and Hungary, found a way of sending food packages to Jews in Poland. Agudat Israel, Hendles explained, believed that the Polish Jews had the same right to receive food packages as the Yugoslavs or Allied war prisoners in whose interests the blockade regulations had been waived by the Allies. Hendles thought that by sending food parcels to Nazi-occupied Europe, a situation might be created where Jews, the recipients of these packages, would become prisoners of war, *de facto* if not *de jure*. Such systematic supplying of food packages would have had to involve the International Red Cross which, as we know today, played a very questionable role with regard to European Jewry. (It never reported what was happening at Auschwitz and Maidanek.) In fact, the systematic shipment of packages would have convinced Nazi officials (who eventually saw that no one was interested in the fate of the Jews of Europe), that they could not completely disregard the Allies' concern for the survival of the Jews.

Just as the blockade regulations were waived on behalf of the Greeks and

Yugoslavs, Hendles saw no reason why they should not have been waived in the interests of the starving Jews in Poland. Agudat Israel became especially active when official reports from Poland informed the American Jewish communities that during the first year of German occupation in Poland, more than half a million Jews had died of hunger.

The activities of Agudat Israel brought Orthodox Jewry, then a loosely-organized community without much influence in the United States, into open conflict with the World Jewish Congress and the American Jewish Congress. I wonder how many remember those dark days of the feud among Jews, when the Boycott Council of the World Jewish Congress in New York picketed the offices of the Agudat Israel in front of the Broadway Central Hotel because "Agudat Israel helped the Nazis by sending food to the Jews in Poland." The chairman of the Boycott Committee of the World Jewish Congress had the temerity to write in a Jewish newspaper, *Der Tog:*

"Even if it should mean that we will pay the price with lives in Poland or elsewhere, Jews cannot feed the Nazis."

The boycott committee of the World Jewish Congress also published statements in many newspapers stating that the British War Cabinet had asked them to see to it that no such packages slipped through to Poland. Yet the same newspapers carried an appeal to send packages to Yugoslavia. At the same time the boycott committee of the World Jewish Congress and American Jewish Congress were fighting Agudat Israel, the British government was allowing the shipment of food to prisoners of war and the civilian populations of Yugoslavia and Greece.

The Union of Orthodox Rabbis of America and Canada blasted the demagoguery of the World Jewish Congress Boycott Committee. If one remembers the atmosphere of 1941, this small community of Orthodox Jews fighting the Boycott Committee were called "agents of Nazis." It is important to stress this point because we are dealing here with a psychological attitude which hastened the doom of European Jewry: that nothing must be done to "interfere with the war effort."

The starving Jews should be allowed to die; no concessions should be made. It is my considered opinion that this was the attitude of Cordell Hull, Breckenridge Long, and most American Jewish leaders who spoke of the postwar aims of the Jewish people while conveniently neglecting to demand the rescue of those threatened by Hitler.

As one analyzes the situation more than forty years later, it becomes evident that had the Nazis known the Jews in Europe were a commodity, worth something to the Allies, many of these criminals would have had second thoughts when it came to collaborating fully in the socalled Final Solution. But how could the Nazis have known this, when the European Jews were seemingly worthless to their overseas brethren?

So Hendles, who had waged his private war with the Jewish establishment, became involved with the Irgun delegation as soon as Ben Hecht, Peter Bergson

(Hillel Kook) and Samuel Merlin initiated the campaign for immediate, concrete action.

When it became clear that the Bermuda Conference had ended with no decision taken to rescue Jews, the Irgun delegation succeeded in mobilizing many Americans — Jews and non-Jews — on behalf of the millions of Jewish hostages in Europe. Despite the campaign of the Zionist establishment to discredit "dissident" activities, the Emergency Conference that took place in July, 1943 attracted some of the most prominent Americans. Still, while the Irgun delegation was busy with the task of moving America to help save the Jews in Europe, the Zionist establishment engaged in propoganda "to prevail upon our government to help in eliminating the British White Paper on Palestine." They wanted to see resolutions being taken on Palestine and its future, and constantly attacked the Irgun delegation. The Emergency Committee that sprung from the Emergency Conference warned American Jews against these tactics, but was relatively helpless as the Zionist organizations had at their disposal tremendous subsidies from the United Jewish Appeal.

Nevertheless the Emergency Conference attracted such men as former President Herbert Hoover, who addressed the meeting. Hoover dared to state that food relief to starving women and children in the occupied countries would help the Jews. He mentioned that the Greek people were being helped; yet the State Department officially proclaimed that this in no way benefitted the Germans.

Many other prominent Americans were involved in the campaign to save the Jews. So tremendous was its impact that the Conference received messages from the President and Secretary of State Hull. The next day, however, the Zionist establishment began harassing all non-Jews who had endorsed the resolution of the newly-formed Emergency Committee. Some of the participants reacted with "a plague on both your houses," and many became so disgusted with the internecine Jewish war that they abandoned the rescue effort.

Had there been no influential Jewish opposition against the Emergency Committee at that time, a special government agency would have been formed immediately — against the wishes of the State Department. Roosevelt was finally convinced that something should be done, but the State Department found allies in those Jewish politicians who opposed the Irgun delegation. One of the stalling maneuvers was the House Committee on Foreign Affairs hearing, organized by Congressman Bloom with a design to diminish the impression made by the Emergency Conference. The hearings effectively postponed action for another year.

XII
1943: Lost Opportunities

Nineteen forty-three was the year of lost opportunities with regard to saving Jews from the Nazis.

In Europe there were still four million, doomed by the Nazi war machine to die as "enemies of the Reich". In every corner of Nazi-occupied Europe, a special department of the German government, directed from Berlin by Adolph Eichmann, was working full-time to round up Jews for the slaughterhouses. Special agents of the Gestapo were employed to ferret out Jews from hiding places. The plan for the Final Solution was being put into practice with proverbial German efficiency. In countries where antisemitism was traditional — tolerated, if not encouraged, by the Catholic Church (Lithuania, Poland and Slovakia, for example) — local bigots were actively helping the Germans to detect Jews who had no Jewish features. Even in countries where democracy and tolerance had been traditional, such as Holland, Belgium, and France, daily *razzias* were a common occurrence. Men who "looked Jewish" to German agents were picked up in the streets and often taken to headquarters to make sure they did not belong to the "circumcised race."

Those who lived through those years of unparalleled German tyranny remember the *law* according to which a Jew had to die; it was illegal for a Jew to survive. According to Nazi law, all Jews living today are "illegal survivors" of the Holocaust.

This was the picture in Hitler's Europe in that fatal year of 1943, when the campaign to exterminate the people of Abraham, Isaac and Jacob was in full gear.

Yet even on the continent there were loopholes through which most of the Jews could have been rescued. Success in evacuating the doomed depended upon two factors: first, an understanding throughout the Free World, especially in North America, of the urgency; and second, the determination of Jews in the Free World that the rescue of their brethren become an international issue.

Very few understand that from 1933 onwards, Nazi policy regarding the Jews was not a Jewish issue, just as the German attack against Poland in 1939 was not a Polish issue. There was a war against the Jew, but those who made a living out of "solving" Jewish problems never grasped the essence of the question. The Irgun, the underground Jewish armed forces in Palestine, a relatively small organization, had already forseen the need for a Jewish revolution — a revolt against both obsolete Jewish "political" groups and the traditional gentile concept of the Jew as the eternal scapegoat. Yet in 1943, the Jewish psyche was not ready for revolution.

*   *   *

The fact that a few thousand were saved was entirely due to the efforts of a small number of activists in Switzerland, led by Belgian-born Recha Sternbuch of Zurich, who represented American Orthodox Jews. For three years, from 1941 to 1944, the "Joint" in America refused to support this "illegal" activity. But if the Orthodox Vaad Hatzalah (Rescue Committee) was hampered by a lack of funds, the "official" Jewish Agency Vaad Hatzalah in Jerusalem was paralyzed by lack of authority and a sense of defeatism. Although it had no connection with the Vaad Hatzalah of the Orthodox rabbinate in America, this Rescue Committee was established following a campaign of Agudat Israel and Zionist-Revisionist opposition in Palestine.

Only towards the end of November 1942, did the British censor and certain officials of the Jewish Agency finally permit the Palestinian press to release the news concerning the extermination of Jews in Europe, at which time Agudat Israel immediately demanded the creation of an Emergency Committee. Under pressure of public opinion, the Jewish Agency at last gave in, and the Revisionists and Agudat Israel were finally invited to sit in on the Palestinian Rescue Committee, formed not according to the competence of its members, but following a "party key" used at Zionist Congresses. (To this very day, funds from the United Isreal Appeal are distributed by the Jewish Agency according to this "key".)

The World Zionist Organization (Jewish Agency) and the National Jewish Council of Palestinian Jews were allotted eight of the twelve seats. Four representatives, two of each group, were from Agudat Israel and the Zionist Revisionists. However, the secretariat in charge was pure establishment.

Thus, at its very birth, the committee was plagued by party politics. The leaders of the establishment in Palestine knew what was going on in Hitler's Europe, but the members of the Committee — and even their representatives sent to Istanbul to "organize rescue" — began fighting each other, defending their own parties and political interests. From the point of view of mass rescue, the Committee was stillborn. The Jewish Agency's Vaad Hatzalah was never given the authority to act, and even under the most perilous conditions "recommendations" had to be approved by the Jewish Agency. A historian of the Palestine Rescue Committee of the Jewish Agency says that suggestions for a solidarity strike in Palestine or a public march in Jerusalem were rejected by Jewish Agency politicians on the grounds that they would imperil the "good relations" between the Palestinian Jews and the British administration.

Each time a resolution was passed by the Agency's "Rescue Committee," its chairman, Jewish Agency executive member Yitzhak Greenbaum, always referred it to the "Agency" for clearance. The Jewish Agency made sure that all secretaries employed by the Jewish Agency were responsible to no other organization. Funds had to be turned over to the Jewish Agency. Indeed, it took this "Rescue Committee" a full year to establish its office in Istanbul — a full year, from November 1942 to November 1943! According to the arithmetic of the Holocaust, it took two million Jewish corpses before the delegates met in Istanbul.

The entire operation was under political control. For example, each Zionist political party had to have a representative in the delegation dispatched to the Turkish capital. The members of this first delegation were H. Barlas, representative of the Jewish Agency Immigration Department; J. Goldwin, representative of the Palestine office (a Jewish Agency branch that distributed immigration certificates received from the British); V. Pomerantz, a representative of Mapai (Labor Party); M. Bader, representative of the extreme left Mapam Zionist party belonging to the establishment. To these were added two representatives of groups outside the Jewish Agency: Jacob Griffel of Agudat Israel and Joseph Klarman, representing the Zionist Revisionists (today known as Herut).

The records of the meetings of this group divulge the internal feuds between the parties. Each committee that was appointed had to be under the supervision of the "Labour Zionists." No instructions of this "Rescue Committee" were to be carried out if they were found to be in opposition to the policies of the representatives of the leftist groups.

This Rescue Committee, under the leadership of Yitzhak Greenbaum, apparently refused to engage in any political moves on behalf of Jews before consulting the British. All action, of course, should have been taken entirely without British knowledge. In America the State Department tragically echoed the British policy that the "problem" of European Jewry must be postponed until after the war.

According to the study published by Aryeh Morgenstern, who wrote a doctoral thesis on the rescue policy of the Jewish establishment in Palestine (1943-1945), the representatives of the leftist parties among the Palestine rescue delegation in Istanbul opposed every move towards independent, secret deals aimed at saving lives. Consequently the representatives of Agudat Israel and the Opposition Zionist Revisionists appeal for support from Istanbul to the Irgun "Emergency Committee" in New York. Subsequently Ben Hecht shocked many people when his advertisement appeared in the *New York Times*. Then he was accused of being "irresponsible," but time has proved him right. Jews were for sale in Eastern Europe, and one could buy a Jew for seventy dollars. If, at the very least, the official American Jewish establishment had refrained from publicly opposing the unorthodox, though imperative campaign of the Irgun delegation, the State Department could not have gotten away with prolonged inaction. A War Refugee Board would have been created at the beginning of 1943, and temporary camps would have been set up to receive Jewish refugees in the neutral countries of Europe, North Africa and, perhaps, even in parts of Latin America. Indeed, it was rumored that Canada was once ready to permit the immigration of a number of European Jews.

Yet while the European tragedy grew more and more hopeless, the leadership of the Jewish establishment in Palestine did not even comprehend the challenge. The most cynical statement was made by the same Yitzhak Greenbaum who, before escaping to Palestine, was the undisputed leader of the Polish Zionists. On August 26, 1942, when the Zionist leaders in Palestine already knew the full horror of the Final Solution, Greenbaum told Rabbi Isaac Meyer Levin, a leader of the Agudat Israel, at a meeting of the Jewish Agency Rescue Committee, "I do not believe that we can save Polish Jewry or even help them." Greenbaum said he saw no reason to continue the public campaigns on behalf of Polish Jews. He even stated that people should not continue to support the negotiations being carried out by Rabbi Michael Dov Weissmandl in Slovakia. Later Greenbaum also stated that he did not approve of Joel Brand's rescue mission.

In another official record (secret reports of the Jewish Agency's Palestinian Rescue Committee dated March 23, 1943) Greenbaum indirectly confirms Weissmandl's later accusations that the World Zionist leaders and professional Jews refused to engage in any serious negotiations of the type which had previously led to the rescue of a number of Jews. Today we also understand from Greenbaum's statement (he was later to become minister of the interior in the first government of Israel) why the Zionist leaders in America, acting under orders from Palestinian Zionist leaders, did not engage in any earnest rescue work, but rather in the futile discussion of Zionist postwar policies that should have been left until the Allied victory. We can also understand why Joel Brand was turned over to the British.

This attitude stemmed from a delusion that prevailed among Jews prior to the establishment of the State of Israel that non-Jewish powers would liberate the Jewish people. The belief that liberty is given and not taken constituted the essential difference between those who clung to the nineteenth-century version of Jewish politics and the men and women of the Hebrew underground in Palestine who launched the Jewish revolution of our time. This explains how, in 1947, prior to the establishment of the Jewish state, a man like Moshe Shertok (later Foreign Minister Sharett) could have voted against the declaration of Jewish independence from Britain only because U.S. Secretary of State George Marshall advised him of the American opposition to such a measure.

So the tragedy continued. At numerous meetings, Yitzhak Greenbaum reiterated his theory, later to become the official policy of the Zionist establishment in Palestine, that "the rescue will come only following the military victory of the Allied powers." As historian Aryeh Morgenstern points out in his study, this viewpoint was also espoused by the chairman of the World Jewish Congress, Dr. Nahum Goldmann, who lived in the United States. Goldmann, who, according to his autobiography, was afraid to remain even in Switzerland, stated: " . . . We cannot expect the majority of the Jews in Europe to survive except in the Soviet Union and England."

A profoundly religious Zionist leader in Palestine, Moshe Shapiro, said in a moment of truth, "What we are doing is just something to lighten our conscience."

Greenbaum was even more explicit. He said there were two areas of Jewish combat, two tasks, two challenges: Palestine and the rescue of the diaspora. "We cannot postpone the first because of the second. Zionism must be above any other consideration." As Morgenstern points out, the Rescue Committee of the Palestinian establishment, operating from Istanbul, simply carried out the instructions of the Jewish Agency and was active only in bringing individual Jews to Palestine.

Morgenstern writes, "It must be said with full responsibility that the leadership of the Rescue Committee of Palestinian Jewry did not believe in rescue, just as plain as that. It is difficult to assume even for one moment that such views about the prospects of rescue did not influence the rescue activities themselves."

The lack of belief in investing funds in rescue, in a preference given to the requirements of the Jews of Palestine, naturally weakened the rescue effort.

Morgenstern continues: "It is significant that Griffel and Klarman (the opposition to the Jewish Agency) were never admitted to the inner councils of that Committee. They didn't even become members of the Action Committee."

Reports reached Palestine — and this was confirmed by Chaim Barlas himself — that everything in Istanbul was conducted according to party considerations. This was especially the case in the matter of sending funds to underground groups in Europe. The emissaries of the leftist parties made sure that funds went to their own people. Only after the American Joint Distribution Committee protested to the Jewish Agency was Rabbi Isaac Meyer Levin of the Agudat Israel included in the finance committee.

How tragic that these circumstances prevented the kind of action that should have been taken — while there were still so many opportunities to save lives! It came to the point where Klarman contacted the Irgun delegation in New York, while Griffel contacted the Orthodox Vaad Hatzalah. Such connections gave these men the opportunity to act without red tape. However, since it was "illegal" to live as a Jew in Europe, all activities to free the European Jews were likewise regarded as "illegal." Yet the Jewish Agency, due to political considerations, was never ready for "illegal" activities, and any messages from occupied Europe, suggestions for rescue missions, were never made public. Indeed all information was censored before it reached the Jewish Agency Rescue Committee. This is why, Morgenstern says, Joel Brand's mission was sabotaged; apparently it had been kept secret by Moshe Sharett.

Yitzhak Greenbaum himself, who was supposed to be the chief savior of European Jewry, enunciated his policy as early as August 1942. He sabotaged the initiatives of Rabbi Weissmandl and Gizi Fleischmann in Bratislava, and opposed Joel Brand as well. Greenbaum, a leader of the Jewish Agency, adopted the same tone as Cordell Hull, the American Secretary of State, who declared that the rescue of European Jewry would only come about "after the military victory of the Allies."

The identical opinion was voiced by Dr. Nahum Goldmann of the World Jewish Congress. In a cold and frightful manner he said:

"I think we have to take into consideration the extermination of the majority of European Jews, except those who are in the USSR and England."

Nahum Goldmann admitted, years after the war, that he "made a mistake" during World War II — just a tiny error. Morgenstern believes that some members of the committee actually used it for one purpose: to quiet their consciences.

Greenbaum openly told the Rescue Committee that "Zionism must take precedence over anything else; Zionism means building Palestine, and no money from the United Palestine Appeal should go towards the Diaspora."

In a confidential memo, the members of the Palestine Rescue Committee were advised as follows: Seven million Jews could perish in Europe. These Jews could not be saved. Even if the big powers had wanted to save masses of Jews, they were not in a position to do so. Only a few tens of thousands of Jews would be saved. A plan to save the Jews of Slovakia would not succeed. It was impossible to evacuate Jews from Bulgaria and Hungary.

At the crux of this approach was Greenbaum's declaration: "The Bermuda Conference has proved that there is no will and no possibility to save Jews and that all these rescue activities are only philanthropic efforts and have no political or social significance."

"This calamity," the Zionist leader concludes, "will prove the Zionist point of view that only Palestine can save Jews and that only a number of them will be saved. However, the Rescue Committee must continue to operate in order to prove to the world and to the Jewish people all over that the Jewish Agency is the only one that acts on behalf of saving Jewish lives."

It is doubtful whether Machiavelli could have written more cynical prose.

However, the Jewish Agency memorandum also contains notes of "optimism." It is an optimism that makes one cry in despair. We are told that the Holocaust will raise the prestige of Zionism as the only solution to the world Jewish problem. Palestine will be recognized as the only country to which Jews can turn in order to save themselves. However, even if there were a possibility, the Jewish Agency was not ready to rescue all those who could be saved. First and foremost, Morgenstern writes, was a truly incredible stance: "An effort must be made to save those from whom the rebuilding of Palestine and the rebirth of the people could profit."

The "practical" suggestion, therefore, was to try to save children: the pioneering youth, spiritually prepared for Zionist work. Again, "selective immigration" for utopia. And then there was the moral duty to save active Zionists, "because they would understand and forgive Palestinian Jewry."

The political insinuations could not have been clearer. The political parties in control wanted to save their own people in order to consolidate the establishment. The memo states candidly that one must first save "the good element," and give up the effort to rescue the "destructive element" . . . which obviously means political opponents.

No wonder Sally Mayer, the representative of the American Jewish Joint Distribution Committee (part of the United Jewish Appeal) in Switzerland, refused to allocate funds to save lives, if Greenbaum declared that Zionism meant building Palestine, not spending money to save the diaspora. The Irgun delegation in America, and this cannot be stressed too often, believed in rescuing the people for whom the state was being built. The official Zionist establishment recognized only postwar aims.

*   *   *

This, in brief, was the atmosphere in Palestine. But how did it affect the battle in the United States?

On April 25, 1943, the Irgun delegation in America called an emergency meeting at the offices of the Committee for a Jewish Army in New York. The following Irgun emissaries participated: Peter H. Bergson (Hillel Kook), Samuel A. Merlin, Yitzhak Ben Ami, Arieh Ben Eliezer and Eri Jabotinsky. From the American Friends of the Irgun, the following took part: Dr. Maurice Williams, Alex Wilf, Michael Potter and Frances Gunther, wife of the author.

Samuel Merlin, the theoretician of the group, prepared a statement and resolutions demanding that the Committee immediately abandon, for the duration, Palestinian politics and concentrate all its efforts on saving the Jews in Nazi-held Europe. He called for the creation of a non-sectarian committee for this purpose.

However, before the problem of European Jews could be set before the public, the meeting had to clear up several problems resulting from their harassment by the Jewish establishment — as usual. As more and more declassified government documents continue to indicate, the Irgun delegates were accused of misappropriating money, and were troubled by the attentions of the Internal Revenue Department. In fact, at the meeting Bergson asked that the firm of Lovejoy & Niden, Accountants, and the law firm of Potter & Potter be thanked for their help in preparing a memorandum for the Internal Revenue Service .

Also at this meeting, copies of several interesting letters were read. These letters had been sent to prominent Americans from Jewish leaders *warning Jews* against supporting the Irgun delegation. Yet the Irgunists were determined to act, and they did. They decided to organize a national conference for the rescue of European Jews. (This meeting took place after the successful Washington production by the Irgun delegation of Ben Hecht's play, *We Will Never Die,* in which Paul Muni and Edward G. Robinson appeared. A number of foreign ambassadors and five or six members of the United States Supreme Court attended a performance.)

Bergson (Kook) informed the gathering that unless the gentile friends of the Jews were told they had to act, they would remain under the impression that influential Jews were already tackling the problem. Non-Jews could hardly have been expected to believe that Jewish "statesmen" were not involved in rescuing their brethren.

This meeting took place at the same time as the Bermuda Conference, and Bergson warned his friends of the danger of Congressman Sol Bloom's participation there.

Congressman Andrew Sommers disagreed with Bergson; he believed that Bloom "would surely fight to save the Jews." But Sommers was a gentile and did not understand Jewish politics. Bergson insisted that the Committee go directly to non-Jewish friends, that otherwise the cause was lost. "We should not stop nagging them!" he stated. "We have to do it, for we are the only ones representing the interests of European Jews."

Eri Jabotinsky disagreed with Bergson's analysis that Jews could prevent non-Jewish Americans from acting. After all, the Jews, Jabotinsky argues, had been opposed to his father's Jewish Legion established by the British during World War I.

Merlin, in his analysis of the situation, declared: " . . . the stateless Jews, the European Jews, are a nation; no one defends them or represents them!"

Ben Eliezer (who later became vice-president of Israel's parliament) cautioned the Committee against negotiating with Jewish organizations. "They would only look upon us," he stated, "as competitors."

During 1943 the Zionist organization and the American Jewish Conference continually undermined the position of the Irgun representatives. For example, every time a prominent American lent his name to the Committee, he would receive a letter from Stephen S. Wise urging him to resign.

Dr. Wise, in a memorandum to Harold Ickes, Roosevelt's Secretary of the Interior, had this to say: "I was sorry to note, as were others among your friends, that you had accepted the chairmanship of the Washington Division of the Committee to Rescue European Jews. I am enclosing a copy of a statement about to be issued by the American Jewish Conference which virtually includes all organized, responsible and representative Jewish groups and organizations in America.

"I do not like to speak ill to you, not of us, concerning a group of Jews, but I am under the inexorable necessity of saying to you that the time will come and come soon when you will find it necessary to withdraw from this irresponsible group which exists and obtains funds through being permitted to use the names of non-Jews like yourself.

"I wish I could have seen you before you gave your consent. I know your aim is to save Jews, but why tie up with an organization which talks about saving Jews, gets a great deal of money for saving them, but, in my judgement, has not done a thing which may result in the saving of a single Jew."

This campaign on the part of the Jewish establishment was so intense that the issue was taken up in the Senate of the United States.

After the Committee for the Jewish Army and the Emergency Committee published advertisements in which exerpts from the statements of friendly senators were quoted, these legislators were bombarded with letters from Jewish organizations to the effect that they were being used for fundraising and personal enrichment. Some were practically forced to make statements from the Senate floor in order to defend themselves against influential Jews.

The campaign against the Emergency Committee in the Senate was led by Senator Lucas of Illinois. However, some senators understood that there were other motives behind this smear campaign than the supposed defense of their integrity. So Senator William Langer declared that while he did not see the advertisements of the committee prior to publication, he could not help but stress the fact that the Bermuda Conference reports had been kept secret. "On the other hand," Langer said, "we are urgently reminded of the fact that two million Jews in Europe have been killed off already and that another five million Jews are awaiting the same fate unless they are saved immediately. Every day, every hour, every minute that passes, thousands of them are being exterminated."

In discussing the Bermuda Conference, Langer declared its scope to be so narrowly circumscribed that the objective could not be adequately dealt with during its sessions. The fact that the issue of rescue presented by the Irgun committee, as distinct from the general "refugee problem" raised by the State Department, was not to be dealt with, was clearly stated in a Department of State memorandum. Even the excerpts of the reports of the Bermuda Conference which the Senator from Illinois read from the floor of the Senate failed to mention the word "Jew."

Langer, influenced by his friends in the Irgun delegation, declared, "Should we not wish to take on ourselves the moral responsibility of being passive bystanders to the continued slaughter of the surviving five million Jews, we can and should see to it that all who can still escape their tormentors have some way open to them."

In speaking about Palestine, Langer refused to engage in polemics with Britain, an ally of the United States, about the White Paper. He was pragmatic and mentioned Palestine as a natural home for the escapees because of its nearness to the European continent, but he also recalled that there was a lack of ships to take these people there.

Again attacking Senator Lucas, Langer said that Lucas himself had admitted that (in Bermuda) "he was not given the power to make any committment or decision." Langer concluded by urging Lucas to consider the demand of the Irgun delegation that a special American agency of military and diplomatic experts be created to save the remaining millions of Jewish people in Europe.

Langer informed the Senate that the Irgun's Committee for a Jewish Army was ready to undertake the task. There were volunteers, he said, potential suicide commandos, eager to attack the extermination camps and pilot retaliatory bombing missions.

However, the Senate debate on the Bermuda Conference terminated with a "victory" for the State Department and the Jewish establishment. Lucas won the battle against those who demanded immediate Allied intervention on behalf of Hitler's Jewish hostages. He and other spokesmen for the Administration succeeded in postponing a decision to establish an American or United Nations' agency to rescue the Jews in Europe.

Lucas also triumphed by maligning Peter H. Bergson (Hillel Kook) from the Senate floor (Senate Debates 1943-44). Lucas said he had ample "information" from leading Jews about the personality of Bergson, the terrible man who was responsible for the newspaper advertisements attacking the Bermuda Conference. Lucas said, "The advertisements were written by a man who is not even a citizen of this country . . . he, and four or five other Palestinians, are in this country at the present time preparing full-page advertisements, among which was the one we discussed on the floor of the Senate. It seems to me to be rather unusual to find citizens of another country coming here and doing what was done in this particular instance. I did not know this when I made my speech or I would have made reference to it then . . . I may have more to say about Bergson before this matter is finished." Lucas, who was a member of the American delegation at the Bermuda Conference, continued by threatening Bergson and others who were in the United States on a visitor's visa that the time had come "for a showdown."

When one reads the statements published by the official American Zionist Emergency Council, by the American Jewish Zionist Emergency Council and, later, by the American Jewish Conference, it becomes clear from where Lucas and the others received their "information." For example, in one of the American Jewish Conference press releases, the Emergency Committee was attacked because it "assumed" the right to speak for American Jewry "without a mandate." It never did.

The Zionist statement mentioned the names of other committees and insinuated that "their leadership included members of a small political party, the Irgun, which was in conflict with constituted Jewish leadership." It also "informed" Americans that this group, in Palestine, opposed the "official Zionist policy of disciplined restraint" against Arab rioters. In other words, the American Jewish Conference denounced the Irgun for what it was: a fighting underground movement.

The statement then expressed the regret of its authors that so many men of goodwill were supporting this Committee. And, in perhaps the most biased remark of all, the statement denounced the Ben Hecht advertisement in which it was implied that 70,000 Romanian Jews could be saved at a cost of seventy dollars each.

Today we know that this was true. Nevertheless, the Jewish establishment won a battle against the Irgun. For a short period it succeeded in discrediting the Emergency Committee, thus postponing action on behalf of the European Jews. No wonder Weissmandl felt such bitterness towards the American Jewish leaders, for thousands of copies of their statement were distributed to people throughout the United States to warn them against the Emergency Committee — instead of supporting its effort to establish a powerful agency to save the Jews of Europe.

XIII
On a Train to Washington

November 1943. Along with several leaders of the Emergency Committee to Save the Jewish People of Europe, I was on the congressional train from New York to Washington, D.C. The hearings called by Sol Bloom, New York Congressman and Chariman of the Foreign Affairs Committee of the House, were to begin November 19. And, as honorary secretary of the National Jewish Council of the Emergency Committee, a small group of friends of the Irgun delegation, I thought the few hours on the train might give me deeper insight into what could well become the most important event in the battle to save European Jewry.

The National Jewish Council was the little-publicized Jewish arm of the Emergency Committee, a nonsectarian organization. Among the small group active on this Committee was Isaac Zaar, a journalist with whom I worked on the same newspaper. In his youth Zaar had been one of the leaders of the Labor Zionist movement in America, and during World War I he had worked with Ben Gurion to promote Labor Zionism on this continent. Zaar was also the founder and first editor of *Yiddisher Kemfer,* the Labor Zionist weekly. During World War II he was active in all the organizations established by the Irgun delegation and worked full-time to promote the Hebrew Liberation Movement. He was deeply disappointed with the leadership of the Labor Zionists, and reportedly told Ben Gurion so during one of the latter's visits to America.

Another outstanding member of this committee was Rabbi Benjamin W. Hendles, the only survivor of the official leadership of the prewar Jewish Community Council in Warsaw (kehillah). In Warsaw he had been a leader of Agudat Israel, the Orthodox religious movement which had achieved great influence in prewar Poland. Both Zaar and Hendles were idealists of the old school, dedicated to the task of Jewish rescue. They saw in the activities of the Irgun delegation the only way to arouse public opinion in favor of the Jews embattled in the Fortress Europe.

The most outstanding member of this National Jewish Council was its honorary chairman, Rabbi Eliezer Silver of Cincinnati. A true patriarch, a personal friend of the late Senator Taft and the recognized leader of the Orthodox Rabbinate in America, Silver was a human dynamo. During World War II he was busy day and night, working for the rescue organizations, and was active whenever there was hope of saving even a single individual.

Rabbi Silver was one of the few Jewish leaders in America who realized from the beginning that the Jews in Hitler's Europe must be rescued, that their situation was hopeless while they remained under German rule. Perhaps some day Rabbi Silver's story will be written, and it will become public knowledge how many individuals Silver personally saved from Europe and Japanese-occupied Shanghai, where many refugees were stranded during World War II. In order to help the needy, Rabbi Silver gave not only his time, but his personal income as well. Along with other members of the Emergency Committee, Silver was en route to Washington to demand the creation of a governmental agency that would deal exclusively with the problem of Jewish rescue from Europe. In fact, Silver had personally delivered a message of support for the demands of the Emergency Committee to Congressman Sol Bloom before the opening of the congressional hearings, and was instrumental in obtaining a statement of support from the Chief Rabbi of Palestine, Dr. Isaac Herzog.

Following the successful conference of the Emergency Committee to Save the Jewish People of Europe and the tremendous publicity it received from the American press and other media, the State Department could no longer ignore the movement. Thousands upon thousands of Americans began asking embarrassing questions. Was it true that millions were doomed? Was it also true that the United States would not lift a finger to save them?

(After the Emergency Conference in New York at the Commodore Hotel in July 1943, the Committee for a Jewish Army, which had launched the movement to rescue European Jewry, adopted the title of Emergency Committee. Many criticized the fact that the Committee for a Jewish Army had changed its name. Like others who were interested only in saving lives, I supported the change. The Committee understood very well that imparting any political connotation to the rescue work would make it difficult, perhaps impossible, to obtain universal support. It was also taken into consideration that many people, Rabbi Silver among them, were not Zionists, and that they supported the Emergency Committee only because of its militant position on behalf of the millions of Jewish hostages in Hitler's hands. They and other prominent Americans, non-Jews, were interested in saving Jewish lives, not in discussing the future of Jews after the Allied victory.)

At the time of this trip to Washington, the American public was ready for a revolutionary step in the struggle to rescue Europe's Jews. For a long time before the Congressional Hearing, full-page advertisements were placed in *The New York Times* and other newspapers, first by the Committee for a Jewish Army, then by the Emergency Committee.

These appeals to the conscience of America and to the President of the United States made a tremendous impression upon the public. In fact, despite the ongoing campaign of vilification against the Irgun delegation by the establishment, and despite pressure from the Committee's opponents, men such as Herbert Hoover, a former American president, participated in the Commodore Hotel Conference. Like many others, Hoover understood that this was a humanitarian, not a political, movement.

Taking into account the unabated hostility of the State Department towards any further practical moves to save Jewish lives (the State Department even hid documents confirming the slaughter from the American public), the Emergency Committee decided that two of its members, both congressmen, should introduce a resolution in the House urging the American government to act. Simultaneously, two prominent senators connected with the Committee proposed a similar resolution in the Senate.

Unfortunately, Assistant Secretary of State Breckenridge Long was in charge of the "Jewish problem" at the Department. Long was a typical conservative who happened to be a protége of the Roosevelt Administration and a personal friend of the president. A very wealthy man, Long frequently contributed to Roosevelt's campaign funds. I maintain, after studying Long's then-secret memoranda concerning the Jewish problem in Europe (memoranda now declassified at the F.D.R. Library in Hyde Park, New York, and the Department of State in Washington) that the exercise of this man's power had consequences for the Jews of Europe almost as tragic as the Nazi occupation of the Continent.

Long lied before the hearing. He obstructed every effort to help Jews and made certain that no extra visas were issued to people who could be saved. Even the very conservative and extremely cautious *American Jewish Year Book* (Vol. 40), a publication of the American Jewish Committee, said regarding Long's testimony, " . . . In November 1943, former Assistant Secretary of State Breckenridge Long had created a sensation by giving, to a congressional committee, erroneous figures of the number of refugees admitted to the United States during the decade 1933-1943. His statement that 'we have taken into this country since the beginning of the Hitler regime and the persecution of the Jews until today approximately 580,000 refugees, gave the erroneous impression that the total immigration from 1933-1943 was refugee immigration and that it was all occasioned by anti-Jewish persecution."

Because of this intentionally misleading statement by Breckenridge Long (the *American Jewish Year Book* termed it the "confusion created by Mr. Long's incorrect data"), the House Foreign Affairs Committee hesitated to approve resolutions introduced by Representatives Will Rogers, Jr. and Joseph C. Baldwin, providing for the establishment by the Executive of a commission to effectuate the rescue of the Jewish people of Europe. Toward the end of the war Secretary Henry Morgenthau, Jr., accused Long of antisemitism.

Certainly Long was obsessed by a xenophobia characteristic of a particular WASP group in prewar American society to whom everything "foreign" was obnoxious and to be kept in quarantine. Whenever he spoke of Hitler's war against the Jews, he assumed the paternalistic tone of one moved by the tragedy of "those poor Jews." However, he always remembered to stress that nothing could be done for them except winning the war.

In the decisive year of 1943, Long found allies who, by their very positions and interests, should have opposed him: leading members of the American Jewish establishment. Afraid that Americans would support the Irgun delegation and the Emergency Committee, the professional leaders of the establishment were convinced that the Irgun men represented a threat to their "rightful" leadership in the community.

*   *   *

The Commodore Hotel Conference was a direct answer and challenge to the State Department and Foreign Office after the misleading information concerning the alleged achievements of the Bermuda Conference was made public.

The Bermuda Conference, held in the spring of 1943, did not make any practical attempt to relieve the plight of the European Jews. It was just as sterile and meaningless as the first international conference on refugees held in 1938 in Evian, France. No decision was made to move Jews from Hitler-occupied territories. Long falsely testified at the Senate hearings that the Bermuda Conference had given the intergovernmental committee on refugees in London the power to act "within and without Germany and the occupied territories." He then concluded that there was no need for a new executive committee to deal with the problem of saving Jews from Nazi Europe. Later on, when Jewish organizations discovered that Long had made such unfounded statements before the Foreign Affairs Committee, many of them protested. Yet because of his influence he managed to slow the process of establishing government machinery for the purpose of rescue. The Jewish Establishment, fearful of its position because of the tremendous publicity given the Emergency Committee due to its nonsectarian character, called an American Jewish Conference in the fall of 1943. The conference, however, essentially discussed the post war aims of the Jewish people, stressing the need for a political solution to the Palestine question instead of dealing with the crisis facing European Jews.

This helped the State Department bureaucrats sabotage any concrete plan to relieve the European situation as far as Jews were concerned. The Emergency Committee, however, did not rest; it relentlessly pursued its task despite the smear campaign directed against its leaders. Eventually Senator Guy Gilette introduced a similar resolution, that an executive committee deal with the problem of saving the Jews.

On the train trip to Washington, we felt that obstacles were being put in the way of achieving a concrete plan to counter-attack Hitler's genocidal campaign against the Jews. Since I was the only one in the group who personally knew Sol Bloom, I told my friends what kind of man he was. He loved to do a favor unobstrusively, but did not understand the challenge of the hour.

While the Emergency Committee strove endlessly to persuade America and its president to take concrete action to save European Jews, Nahum Goldmann sent a memo to the State Department proving that the Jewish establishment had been fighting the "Bergson group" since its activities began. A few weeks before the hearings started, Goldmann wrote the following letter to Mr. Wallace Murray of the Department of State:

"In the course of the conversation which I had the pleasure of having with you last week, you expressed the wish to see the statement in which all Zionist organizations in this country repudiate the Committee for a Jewish Army."

In the same letter, Dr. Goldmann stressed that this statement against the Committee for a Jewish Army was issued as early as February 27, 1942 — one month after the German government held the infamous Wannsee Conference. The sins of the Committee for a Jewish Army must have been very grave indeed for all Zionist groups in America to issue a statement denouncing them. One only wonders what would have happened to the Jewish people in Europe if the Jewish Agency and similar organizations had supported the demands of the Irgun delegation instead of continually fighting their efforts on behalf of European Jewry — or if these organizations had never even existed at the time!

When Bergson (Hillel Kook) appeared before the Foreign Affairs Committee, he did not know, as we know now, that the Department of State took all the insinuations against Bergson and his friends very seriously indeed. None other than Cordell Hull, the Secretary of State, wrote to Attorney General Francis Biddle on August 6, 1943, asking him to check on Bergson. Also, the Acting Secretary of State, Mr. Stettinius, wrote to the American Consul General in Jerusalem requesting confidential information on Bergson, Samuel Merlin, Arieh Ben Eliezer, Eri Jabotinsky, Ben Ami and Hadani — all the members of the Irgun delegation in the United States.

These investigations were a direct result of the campaign of vilification against the Irgun emissaries. In a special memorandum from the State Department stamped "strictly confidential" and addressed to the Justice Department, the following observations were made: The Department of Justice has been carrying out an investigation of Bergson and his friends; Bergson was invited to visit the Department of Justice to discuss his position; the Department regretted the fact that it was very difficult for them to act in this case because "prominent American citizens, particularly certain members of Congress, act as a front for Bergson's different organizations."

It was also impossible to prove any financial misconduct against the Irgun delegation despite all the allegations of its opponents. The Department believed that Bergson, Merlin, Eri Jabotinsky and others were members of the Irgun Zvai Leumi, "an illegal military organization in Palestine." This, however, could not be established officially.

The Department also sought intelligence from the British authorities in Palestine, suggesting that "certain persons" be contacted in order to provide further information regarding Bergson and his associates.

I remember saying to Merlin on the train, "I wonder how you are able to function and do what you are doing." Whenever I visited the offices of the Committee, I found Merlin in conference with investigators from the Treasury Department checking the books. They did not find anything, but they must have been responsible for the depression that I often saw in the faces of those involved in the rescue work. I asked, "How can you survive?"

I remember Merlin's answer: "What else can we do when we know what is happening in Europe?"

By then Stephen Wise, Nahum Goldmann and other leaders of the American Jewish community had all the facts about the systematic slaughter of European

Jewry. Yet they were still busy with Jewish politics.

At that time it was already known that certain neutral European powers were ready to admit Jewish refugees from Hitler-occupied countries, providing the United States would guarantee the temporary nature of these admissions. Here was a definite possibility of rescuing hundreds of thousands. Many Germans and Nazi officials realized that the war was lost, and some of them were seeking contact with Jews in order to establish an alibi for the day of reckoning. Some Germans in high positions were willing to, and in fact did, negotiate for the release of the Jews, but the State Department's indifference to the fate of European Jewry suggests that Washington indirectly consented to the Final Solution.

On the eve of the Wannsee Conference, the viewpoint of those Nazis who had always demanded the extermination of the Jewish people was seen as justified in the eyes of the Nazi leaders and, in January 1942 in a Berlin suburb, the decision was made to exterminate the Jews.

When the Bermuda Conference took place, *The New York Times* warned that this meeting should not settle on a palliative to relieve the conscience of the "reluctant rescuers." But Breckenridge Long and Cordell Hull saw to it that this conference ended without any decisive results.

XIV
The Bloom Hearings

November 19, 1943 is a date very significant in connection with the efforts to rescue the Jews of Europe. At that time there were still millions alive.

On November 19, 1943, Sol Bloom, chairman of the powerful Foreign Relations Committee of the House of Representatives in Washington, opened the hearings on a resolution demanding that the American government establish an agency to deal exclusively with saving the remnant of European Jewry from the slaughterhouse. The hearings were a clever State Department tactic to postpone action on behalf of Jews — to delay it until the end of the war.

The resolution, introduced jointly in the House by Congressmen Will Rogers, Jr. and Joseph Baldwin, co-chairmen of the Irgun's Emergency Committee, provoked a fanatically heated battle within the American Jewish community. I covered the hearings in the Capitol Building and remember both the atmosphere and the activities surrounding this initiative.

As with all great ideas, the House resolution, and a similar one introduced in the Senate by Senator Guy Gillette of Iowa, was a very simple proposition. It demanded that the United States government finally recognize the urgency of the issue: that European Jewry had been singled out for total elimination by the Hitler regime. Since the Jews were declared enemies of the Reich, the resolution proposed that the Allies consider them *de facto* prisoners of war. If American Jewry had been leaderless at that time, if it had not been endowed with the paraphernalia of several Jewish organizations supposedly engaged in defending the rights and the lives of Jews the world over, such resolutions might have passed without opposition a year earlier. But the congressional resolutions were sponsored by the Emergency Committee to Save the Jewish People of Europe. And this Committee, it should not be forgotten, was established by the Irgun delegation. Thus the professional Jewish establishment of the War Refugee Board was delayed for more than a year.

One should remember that ever since late summer in 1942, all American Jewish leaders, as well as the leaders of the Jewish community in Palestine, had known the terrible truth about the Nazi extermination program. They knew that every day, while they were debating Zionism and non-Zionism, thousands and tens of thousands of Jews were being condemned to the furnaces of Auschwitz and Maidanek. Yet Zionist business, Jewish community dinners and testimonials for important philanthropists continued as usual. No neurosis engulfed the Jewish community. All Jewish offices continued to function as in yesteryear. But in Europe the German machine functioned with unabated efficiency.

The belated hearings in the House were concocted by the influential chairman of the Foreign Affairs Committee, Congressman Sol Bloom of New York. Bloom was a confidant of President Roosevelt. He was also what one calls "a very good Jew" — an important point because of the position Bloom took on the rescue issue. To have to criticize Bloom *post mortem* is especially painful, for in certain respects Bloom was a personal friend. Because of his intervention in 1940, I did not have to wait more than four weeks for my immigration visa when I decided not to return to Europe and settle in the United States. Bloom also intervened later on my parents' behalf. All he asked was that my father (a Torah scribe) write a special prayer for him on parchment. My father was happy to comply, and Bloom always carried the prayer as a good luck charm.

Yet the truth demands that I fully describe the role of Congressman Bloom in the most important chapter of contemporary Jewish history. His was a negative role and, no matter how profoundly I feel for the man — and he was a good man — I must say that he was one of the two American Jews who held the key to the salvation of European Jewry. But, because of political motives, Bloom failed. The other influential American Jew who had access to the White House was, of course, Stephen S. Wise.

Perhaps it was Sol Bloom who, during World War II, typified the fears and the subconscious terror of the average American Jew: Let us keep Nazism and all its problems in Europe overseas; otherwise the horror might engulf us here.

Sol Bloom considered himself an Orthodox Jew; he belonged to an Orthodox Jewish congregation. In April 1943, when he was sent as Roosevelt's emissary to the Refugee Conference in Bermuda, he went there not as a Jew demanding that the British and the other Allies join the United States in an effort to rescue his brethren, but as an American diplomat. The very appointment of Sol Bloom to this conference was a misfortune. Not only the Irgun delegation but even the old, established American Jewish organizations resented the fact that Bloom was the "representative of the United States Jews" in Bermuda.

Yet Bloom never really understood his responsibility in Bermuda. In his defense I must say that he was a little man catapulted into a position which could have been decisive as far as the European Jews were concerned. But he remained the little man who liked to help people, do favors for constituents and obtain visas for would-be immigrants. He even intervened to secure the release of the hassidic Gerer Rebbe from Warsaw. But Bloom could not visualize the full extent of the slaughter overseas. His limited vision of history did not allow him to perceive the macabre picture of the millions locked in Hitler's Fortress Europe.

In a sense he was a State Department boy as far as the Jewish issue was concerned. And so, while the State Department continued to frustrate any earnest effort to rescue masses of European Jews, its bureaucrats found in Bloom a Satan's gift — the ideal instrument to thwart a declaration that the rescue of European Jewry was an important aim of the Allied Powers.

Bloom was a truly pathetic figure. I can still see him presiding over committee meetings. He was a small man, always impeccably dressed. Elegant and well-mannered, Bloom was a true gentleman. His trademark was the perennial cigar in his right hand.

Bloom sincerely believed that his position as chairman of the powerful Foreign Affairs Committee should be appreciated by the Jewish people as recognition of their standing in American society. To Bloom, and he believed this sincerely, the proud Roosevelt Jew in Bermuda was an achievement *per se* from the perspective of American Jewish interests.

He did not understand irony. He was Sol Bloom, the little New York politician who, because of certain maneuvers within the Democratic Party, rose to prominence during the Roosevelt years.

Had the chairman of the Foreign Relations Committee been a non-Jew, the demand for action to rescue the Jews of Europe probably would have been expedited, not thwarted. But Bloom was not thinking of the Jews in Europe; his concern was how the entire problem would effect him and the American Jewish community. He considered it "dangerous" for American Jews to become identified with European Jews, people condemned to die by a "civilized" government.

Whether it was *The New York Times* or Congressman Bloom or prominent members of the Jewish community, during the years of struggle for the lives of the Six Milllion, there was widespread, subconscious fear that to even discuss the plight of European Jewry might jeopardize American Jews. It is not an accident of history that from 1933 to 1945, no important Jewish organization ever demanded that the United States open its doors to the Jews threatened by Hitler. It may sound cynical, but the continuing demand of some American Jewish leaders that Britain admit Jewish refugees into Palestine was, to a certain degree, a safety valve which they exploited in order to avoid the clamor for an American immigration policy. Here, too, was another subconscious rationalization: Throwing the responsibility for action on the shoulders of others saved the consciences of those who should have acted.

After a year of lobbying by the Irgun delegation in America for the creation of a government agency to save European Jews, Bloom finally found a "diplomatic" solution which pleased the State Department: namely, to call hearings on the issue. An American reporter, Arthur Hale, at the time the most popular radio broadcaster, described his impression of the congressional hearings:

" . . . The divergencies among Jewish organizations and groups over what, if anything, should be done to rescue the Jews still alive in Europe, has now developed into an open split. Evidence of this is apparent in the sudden maneuver by Congressman Sol Bloom who, as chairman of the House Foreign Affairs Committee, has called a public hearing to start Friday on the resolution recently introduced in both houses of Congress, which would urge President Roosevelt to create a joint commission to deal with the European Jewish refugee problem. The proponents of the resolution had counted upon a reasonable lapse of time to permit an adequate organization of their witnesses and experts who would be called upon to testify in the open hearings. Representative Sol Bloom, however, forced the issue by scheduling the hearing before the House Foreign Affairs Committee to commence November 19. Congressman Will Rogers is still engaged in urgent matters in California and must abandon these matters and jump aboard a plane to get back to Washington in time to lead the forces that are seeking to bring prompt and favourable action before it is too late to save the Jews, marked for slaughter, remaining in Europe.

"Large Jewish groups are said to be identified with the attitude of Congressman Bloom in opposing any action by the United States government to help rescue their compatriots. However, thus far, no spokesman for this group has ventured to explain openly how the policy of rescue is opposed and it is probable that the Congressional hearing now about to begin will uncover the real reason for such opposition." (*Answer* Magazine)

From the onset it was clear that these hearings concerning the establishment of a *Special Agency* to Save the Jewish People of Europe were meant to prolong the debate on the situation in order to take the pressure off the State Department. In a confidential memo to his staff prior to the Emergency Conference called by the Committee for a Jewish Army (which had taken place a few months before the hearings), Secretary of State Cordell Hull asked that publicity be given to the unfortunate Bermuda Conference — the inter-governmental conference — which concluded with no decision of importance. As Hull says in his memo, it was important to publicize this conference so that the people of the United States would believe the Allied governments were actually doing something to save the Jews of Europe. Also, on other occasions, the State Department asked that Congressman Bloom himself be given some publicity so that those in the Jewish community who questioned his role would be appeased.

In its incessant war against the Irgun "troublemakers," the State Department enjoyed the ongoing support of the Zionist leaders. For example, at the height of popularity of the Jewish Army Committee, the representative of the Jewish Agency informed the Department that the Jews were against these people. In fact, Nahum Goldmann, in a confidential memo to the Department of State, informed the United States government "that all Zionist organizations are opposed to the Committee for a Jewish Army," and all Irgun activities.

Thus the American government, and especially the State Department bureaucrats, found allies among the Jewish establishment in their opposition to taking any concrete steps on behalf of European Jewry. It was very convenient for the American establishment to rely upon the Jewish establishment when deciding to postpone action "until the end of the war."

Here is the basic conflict. The Irgun delegation pressed for the immediate rescue of the Jews in Europe, because otherwise those to be rescued would not live to see the victory over Germany. The State Department, echoing the interests of the British who were afraid that a mass exodus from Europe through neutral countries would force London to admit some Jews to Palestine, maneuvered for delay. Jewish organizations with vested interests, equally fearful that a successful conclusion of the Irgun delegation's efforts would diminish their prestige within the Jewish community, fought the Emergency Committee instead of fighting those within the State Department or the Foreign Office who would sabotage the rescue effort.

This is how a spokesman for the Jewish establishment, Boris Smolar, editor of the subsidized Jewish Telegraphic Agency, dealt with the problem: "The American Jewish Conference," he wrote, "may soon issue a statement which will come as quite a blow to the groups which have branched out from the Committee for a Jewish Army.

"Jewish leaders are especially incensed at the Emergency Committee to Save the Jews of Europe because of the fact that this Committee was responsible for the introduction of a resolution in the Senate and in the House which urges the creation of a special commission to plan the rescue of Jews in Nazi Europe — excellent as this resolution may seem, important American Jewish leaders consider it harmful . . . In fact we understand that Senator Gillette, who introduced this resolution in the Senate, was asked by well-known Jewish leaders to abstain from doing so . . . so was Representative Will Rogers, Jr., before he introduced the resolution in the House . . . Both preferred, however, to act on the advice of the Emergency Committee and against the will of the American Jewish Congress, the American Jewish Conference and others."

Thus we see the beginning of the drama with its tragic connotations — and consequences. On one side a group of dedicated young Irgun emissaries made an effort to move heaven and earth to have the United States government give priority to the rescue of European Jewry. On the other hand, the Jewish establishment, afraid of losing its influence upon the community, instead of supporting these resolutions mobilized all its power *not* to save the Jews in Europe, but to save the prestige of its own leaders. This effort was financed from public funds collected among Jews to help the refugees.

I followed the hearings very closely. However, at that time I did not fully understand the situation. For example, the chairman constantly tried to hint to the members of his committee that Peter H. Bergson (Hillel Kook), head of the Emergency Committee, was *not so kosher*. Indeed, during the entire period of this decisive battle for Jewish survival on the continent, all "decent" Jewish leaders were spreading rumors about Bergson and his boys collecting money under false pretenses, misappropriating funds for personal expenses and so on. Thus it was no accident when, at the beginning of the hearing, Chairman Bloom asked Bergson what his salary was and how much he was drawing for expenses. Shocked silence pervaded the room as Bergson "admitted" how much he was drawing: less than fifty dollars a week!

This kind of questioning should not be ascribed to malice on Bloom's part. He was put up to it by the professionals in the Jewish organizations who saw in the Irgun's American operations a danger to their very existence; he was told that they were con men. Jewish professionals used to salaries larger than those paid to members of the United States Congress would not have survived if the Irgun policy had become their financial policy. Of course, the shock among the opponents of the Committee was greater because Bergson's statements were made in the presence of members of Congress who were affiliated with the Emergency Committee and knew that Bergson was telling the truth.

Thus the hearings proceeded, and Bloom and the State Department made every possible effort to prolong their duration. They called upon all the Jewish leaders to testify. When Stephen Wise appeared, it became clear that the Jewish establishment was out to kill the initiative contained in the resolution. While every congressman was approached behind the scenes by Jewish organizations to oppose the resolution, Wise devised a very diplomatic solution. He knew that he could not publicly oppose a resolution establishing a government agency to save the European Jews, but could kill it by lending it a political character. So Wise declared that he spoke on behalf of the American Jewish Conference, "the most widely democratic representation of Jewish organizations," and that he approved of the resolution on one condition: that it be modified "to include the opening of the gates of Palestine for these Jews."

When a member of the committee called Wise's attention to the fact that such a change might destroy the resolution by giving it a political anti-British tenor, the Jewish leader declared, "If we thought the addition of such an amendment would jeopardize it and might bring about its failure, we should certainly reconsider our recommendation."

Those who lived in America during the war years remember that it was the Emergency Committee, through the initiative of the Irgun delegation in general, that placed the Jewish question on the agenda of American politics. Until the arrival of the Irgun delegation, American Zionist leaders operated in a ghetto. It never occurred to them that to achieve tangible results, they would have to create an atmosphere in which all Americans would be traumatized into awareness of the situation, that only then would they be able to understand the responsibilities of the Free World towards a people doomed to die. The New Deal, so to speak, of the Irgun delegation, mobilizing non-Jewish personalities on behalf of Jews, constituted a radical innovation. Today it is a matter of record that until the Irgun committee became active in America, the most ominous news about the persecution and even murder of Jews was either ignored by the press or buried near the obituary columns. The less said about it, the better. Hence the Irgun delegation not only shook the American public from its lethargy, but stirred the Jewish leadership to action as well. The official Jewish leadership, however, instead of fighting the Nazis, instead of changing its apparatus and altering its activities, mobilized its power and financial resources to combat the threat against its image posed by the Irgun. There was a war against the entire Jewish people — an openly declared war. Meanwhile, the Jewish leadership was busy playing the futile game of Who's Who in American Jewry. Today they know that the members of the Irgun delegation never had any ambition to become Jewish leaders. In fact, most of them were the only "Zionist leaders"; they left America and settled in Israel after it became a state. Hillel Kook (Bergson) and most of the others became extremely successful businessmen there. Yet the American Jewish professionals thought that these boys were after their jobs in the various Jewish organizations.

The House Committee's hearing, with the help of the Jewish establishment, fulfilled the State Department's purpose precisely and proved itself an instrument to further postpone action while millions perished. Yet despite all this maneuvering, the hearings brought to public attention for the first time what was really going on in Europe. Many prominent Americans, members of both Houses of Congress, impressed with the idealism of the Irgun emissaries, joined them. Men such as Senators Taft, Thomas and many others, despite denunciation by the Jewish establishment, supported the "dissidents." At this point the position of the Jewish establishment became so shaky that Wise went to see Roosevelt to explain who represented the Jews.

The story of the Irgun delegation's operation in America during World War II parallels that of the Irgun and the Stern group within the general context of the Jewish revolution in Palestine. There the Irgun sparked the revolt which led directly to the reestablishment of a sovereign Jewish state. However, in Palestine, as in America, politics prevented the Irgun from completing its mission.

The same fear that guided the opponents of the Irgun delegation to America during World War II, the fear that unorthodox activities would tarnish the image of Jews as nice people, was to a certain degree the undoing of certain establishment Zionists in Palestine. Yet there the situation had to change when the opponents of the Irgun were forced to accept the Irgun way of doing things in order to survive.

During World War II American Jewish leaders echoed the feelings of the Jewish masses in that they were guided by fear, although it was subconscious. Among my contacts within the American Jewish community, I noted the majority was somehow afraid to speak of the events in Auschwitz and Maidanek. This fear can now be articulated brutally but openly: Save the Jews in Europe, if possible, but please don't tell the *goyim* what is really going on there; otherwise they may do the same thing to us here in America!

If it were not so, why did the non-Zionist Jews refrain from demanding a change in American immigration policy that would have opened the doors of the United States to Europe's Jews? The Zionists could be absolved from absolute guilt because they were following policy established by the World Zionist Movement, which concentrated on changing British policy through protest meetings and protest resolutions. This could be understood, though not forgiven. But where were the Jews who opposed Zionism, who were against settlement in Palestine, who were against unnerving the British? Why did they not speak up on behalf of Jewish immigration into the United States?

Jewish politics, as strong today as ever, has been dictated by the fear of the *goy*. What will the *goy* say if I fight in order to live? Will I still be a *nice Jew* who will receive a greeting from the president on the Jewish New Year, stressing the historic contribution of the Jew to Judeo-Christian civilization? Will the politicians still continue to put on yarmulkas at political meetings in order to impress the Jews that they recognize the socalled Hebrew contribution to their civilized society?

In reality, however, the way the Irgun spoke to the non-Jewish world, both in the United States and Palestine, is the only language that the non-Jews, especially our true friends, understood. They know that liberty has never been given; it can only be taken. They also know that oppression has never been lifted by political means in any society in recorded history, except through violent opposition. In this connection, it is worthwhile to note the opinion of Winston Churchill.

The writer Ben Hecht, who probably did more than anyone else in Zionist history to publicize the Jewish struggle in Palestine and the battle for the rescue of European Jews, thus described Churchill's reaction to the Irgun:

" . . . During one of his visits to New York in the late 40's, Sir Winston Churchill spoke to Billy Rose in the home of Bernard Baruch. He said he had heard that Mr. Rose had been involved in some fashion in the Palestinian fracas. Billy Rose, who had worked with me in the Irgun propagandist committees captained by Peter Bergson and Samuel Merlin, stuck to his guns, but a bit modestly, before England's greatest man.

"'Yes,' said Billy Rose, 'I became involved by my friend Ben Hecht in that Irgun business, without quite knowing what was going on,' which was the truth.

"Churchill answered: 'If you were interested in the establishment of an Israeli nation, you were involved with the right people. It was the Irgun that made the English quit Palestine. They did it by raising so much hell that we had to put 80,000 soldiers into Palestine to cope with the situation. The military costs were too high for our economy. And it was the Irgun that ran them up.'"

XV
The Rabbis' March:
A Washington Scandal

By the fall of 1943 it was clear to the Irgun delegation that the European situation had deteriorated. At the same time, efforts of the Emergency Committee were being fought tooth and nail by the establishment. Accordingly, at this eleventh hour, a decision was taken to hold a March of Rabbis in the streets of the capital. The purpose of the demonstration was to generate support for the establishment of a special government agency to aid the remnant of European Jewry. Organizational details were placed in the hands of the Emergency Committe's National Jewish Council, of which I was an honorary secretary.

Tremendous support for this undertaking came from the Union of Orthodox Rabbis of the United States and Canada and the Organization of Hassidic Rabbis, as it did from all traditional Jewish groups, including Young Israel. Others committed to the cause were the members of the Jewish War Veterans of the United States.

It is not widely appreciated that during World War II there was one segment within American Jewry that used every possible means to save Jews: the Orthodox Jewish groups. At that time traditional Jewry in America was very weak in the organizational sense, yet, despite its relative weakness in the field of public relations it constituted an exception to the rule when it came to supporting the Emergency Committee of the Irgun delegation. In fact, the traditional Jews maintained their emergency committee, the Vaad Hatzalah, which saved a number of Jews from Hitler's Europe through its Swiss representatives. An Israeli writer, Moshe Prager, who compiled (in Yiddish) *A History of The Orthodox Vaad Hatzalah*, displayed the usual anti-Irgun bias when he claimed that the Washington March was organized by the Union of Orthodox Rabbis with the "co-operation" of the "Emergency Committee to Save the Jewish People in Europe." It should be stressed that the Emergency Committee took the initiative; thereafter it was supported by the rabbinical organizations and other groups.

In my role as honorary secretary of the National Jewish Council, I obtained the support of prominent Jews in the traditional community. Our honorary president was Chief Rabbi Eliezer Silver of Cincinnati, Ohio, an unusual man, renowned for his piety and revered as a sage in Israel. Whenever there was a chance of saving someone from Hitler, Silver borrowed money from the bank and paid for rescue efforts himself. At the time he was the most influential Orthodox Rabbi in the United States and leader of the most numerous and important rabbinical organizations in North America. Rabbi Silver, along with Rabbi Benjamin W. Hendles, assisted with preparations for the march. Rabbi Silver gave me carte blanche to use his name, and I helped draft several resolutions which were subsequently read in Washington.

Both Kook and Merlin expected the demonstration to bring pressure to bear on Roosevelt, and a committee of rabbis was formed to seek an audience with the president. Yet until the last moment we were in the dark as to whether he would actually receive the delegation.

On October 7, 1943, the capital of the United States witnessed perhaps the most unusual spectacle in its history: Approximately five hundred Orthodox rabbis, dressed in traditional garb, descended upon Washington. This was the first rabbinical demonstration of this kind, not only in the United States, but anywhere in the world. Some of the religious leaders were true patriarchs, elderly men. They led the procession, walking the distance from Union Station to the Capitol.

In its coverage of the march, *Time* noted that upon the rabbis' arrival at Union Station the demonstration aroused universal respect: People must have realized that something unusual had happened or was about to happen, to make these sages undertake such a pilgrimage. "Clear the way for those rabbis," the station-master shouted.

The five hundred Jewish spiritual leaders, most of them bearded, many in silken cloaks with thick velvet collars, filed silently through the hurly-burly of the Washington streets. As *Time* remarked, the president had no time to receive them. The magazine then described the discrepancy between the cold-shoulder treatment the president gave to the most moving demonstration in American Jewish history and the reception accorded the rabbis' "foes."

Time reported: " . . . a few days before, the two main foes of the Jewish idea had been feted, dined, greeted and generally given the full red-carpet treatment. The foes, Prince Feisal, Foreign Minister of Saudia Arabia, and his younger brother, Prince Khalid. For these people FDR had ample time."

Time could not have known then that it was not only "oil imperialism" that had dictated this policy of disdain for the revered representatives of the Jewish faith. Someone within the Jewish community, someone among its "recognized" leaders, must have made it easy for the president to publicly insult the most respected spiritual leaders of American Jewry. Probably then and there F.D.R. and his State Department advisers decided that they could do "anything against these Jews" once they satisfied the enormous appetite for honor and personal recognition of some of the leaders of the Jewish establishment.

What actually transpired was revealed by an obscure Hebrew monthly, *Bitzaron* (edited by a professor of Dr. Stephen S. Wise's Reform seminary in New York). In a leading article, the editor celebrated this public offence to the men who, by their appearance, by their style of life and by their learning and scholorship truly represented Historic Israel. While the entire American press agreed that the Rabbis' March was one of the most significant demonstrations ever seen in the capital, the satirical editorial in *Bitzaron* was reminiscent of the style used in internecine sectarian feuds. The editor, while forgetting that the purpose of the rabbinical demonstration was to urge revolutionary action to save the remnant of European Jewry, "reminded" the pious rabbis that they had "no right" to go to the president without the approval of the men close to the American government — the Jews who knew the leaders of America. He told the demonstrators in this *post factum* editorial:

"The keys to the White House — never forget it! — lie in other hands. There is only one rabbi," *Bitzaron* stated, "who has the key to this kingdom." And this rabbi, the editorial intimated, makes sure that unless *he* turns over the key, no one in the Jewish community sees the President.

Who remembers now that while someone was making it easy for F.D.R. to ignore the demands of the rabbis, tens of thousands of Jews were being slaughtered every day? Yet the rabbi who had "the key to the White House" was busy with one preoccupation only: closing the gates of Pennsylvania Avenue to those men who had travelled to Washington from, literally, the forty-eight states in the Union to demand that the American government finally act on behalf of the Jewish hostages in Hitler's gangster empire.

The "rabbi" to whom *Bitzaron* was referring was not the *only* Jew who kept the keys to the White House in his pocket. Another Jew among Roosevelt's advisers — the one closest to the president — Judge Samuel I. Rosenman, F.D.R.'s speechwriter, also had a hand in this Machiavellian undertaking. He was asked to intervene so that the president would not have to receive a rabbinical delegation. For a time, it seems, F.D.R. (perhaps because of his American upbringing or his misgivings about offending the clergy) was ready to meet with the rabbis. In fact, until their very arrival in the capital, it was understood that the president would receive them; in fact they had been promised an audience. But at the last moment Rosenman burst into the president's office and warned him against seeing "this horde."

This is how the president's assistant, William D. Hassett, described Rosenman's intervention: "Judge Rosenman . . . said the group behind this petition was not representative of the most thoughtful elements in Jewry. Judge Rosenman said he had tried — admittedly without success — to keep the horde from storming Washington . . . the leading Jews of acquaintance being opposed to this march on the Capitol."

"But the rabbis' hope of publicity out of their visit to the White House was dashed . . ."

Leading "this horde" were such "mobsters" as L.B. Levinthal, of Philadelphia, then the oldest rabbi in the United States, the father of Judge Levinthal; Israel Rosenberg, the President of the Union of Orthodox Rabbis in the United States and Canada; Eliezer Silver of Cincinnati, a close friend of Senator Taft and a renowned Talmudic scholar; Rabbi Wolf Gold, president of the Religious Zionist Mizrachi Organization; and Solomon H. Freedman, president of the group of Hasidic Rabbis, who was known as the "Byaner Rebbe."

The distinguished rabbis had been told by the Presidential Secretary, Marvin McIntyre, that the Chief Executive was unable to meet the delegation because of the pressure of other business. A spokesman for the March then told the reporters that there was considerable resentment among the rabbis who had called at the White House under the assumption that they were to see Mr. Roosevelt. Some delegates speculated that the failure of the president to receive their representatives may have been dictated by the presence in Washington of Arab cabinet ministers. They could not believe that *Jews* were intervening in order to keep them from meeting with F.D.R.

Naturally not all Zionist leaders knew that "the rabbi who had the key" to the White House, or Judge Rosenman, had made sure that this "horde" should not be received by the president, and that they should not be given any publicity. For example, Dr. Samuel Margoshes, a Zionist leader and an editor of the Yiddish daily, *Der Tog,* who covered this march, commented in his column:

" . . . The pilgrimage of Orthodox Rabbis to Washington to hand President Roosevelt and vice-president Wallace as well as the leaders of Congress a petition on behalf of the doomed Jews in Nazi-held Europe, will forever stand out in my memory as the most notable adventure it has been my privilege to witness during a fairly varied and adventuresome life. To say that it was dignified and impressive is to be guilty of an understatement. To characterize it as grand and glorious is, to my way of thinking, to come nearer the truth . . . What was even more heartening than the amount of attention showered on the pilgrimage was the attitude displayed by the populace to the procession of Orthodox rabbis, as it moved through the streets of the capital. There were absolutely no snickers, no smirks on the faces of the onlookers. There was interest, wonderment and there was respect. As the five hundred rabbis, wearing their hassidic garb of long silk and gabardines and round plush hats, moved along Pennsylvania Avenue, they certainly presented a picture which for its exotic quality was unprecedented even in such a cosmopolitan city as Washington. I seriously doubt whether most of the bystanders had ever seen anything like it before. Yet they did not gape or guffaw as almost any crowd in a central or East European land most decidedly would have. They watched in wonderment and in respect. The traffic stopped, and here and there a burgher removed his hat. I myself saw many a soldier snap to salute as the oldest Rabbis, remarkably reminiscent of the patriarchs in Doré's Bible, passed in review. There was something of the quality of a religious procession that characterized the rabbinical pilgrimage and compelled the respect of every passerby.

"The only disappointing aspect of the rabbinical pilgrimage was the failure of the rabbis to hand their petition to the President directly and to be received by him personally, just as they were received by the vice-president and the leaders of the House and the Senate. But if the five hundred rabbis, representing the foremost religious leadership of American Jewry were disappointed, they were free from blame. The fault was not theirs that they were snubbed as no other religious representatives of their rank and standing would be, if they made their pilgrimage to the White House. Somebody has failed us, and it was not the rabbis."

When this demonstration was held, there were still millions of Jews alive in Hitler's Europe. Yet every effort by the Irgun delegation to change the traditional approach to Jewish politics and to convince influential Jews and non-Jews that this was no time for politics was met by either lack of understanding or outright hostility.

I recall the depressing atmosphere at the last meeting of the National Jewish Council of the Irgun Emergency Committee before the pilgrimage, the meeting at which it was decided to go through with the March of the Rabbis despite the attempts at sabotage. Hillel Kook and Samuel Merlin explained the urgency. There was not a minute to lose, they declared. We agreed.

When we of the National Jewish Council decided to become involved in organizing the Rabbis' March, we knew that the Jewish establishment would never support it. Therefore Hillel Kook asked my friend and colleague on the Council, Samuel B. Rose, to travel to Cleveland to discuss the situation with Rabbi Abba Hillel Silver, the Zionist leader who had competed with Stephen S. Wise for first place within the establishment. (The conflict between Wise and Silver even had an echo within the White House. Of the two Silver was considered the most militant Zionist leader, but as a Republican he had no "key" to the White House.)

Sam travelled to Cleveland and was received by Dr. Silver in his study at the temple. Dr. Silver, instead of discussing the situation calmly and earnestly, said he would never accept suggestions from the Irgun delegation. "They are all charlatans," he told Sam, who will never forget the meeting. "If you are a good Revisionist, leave them."

When Sam, a born PR man, suggested that Silver head the March — not the Irgun delegation — the "militant" Zionist leader remained unmoved; he repeated that he would not even deal "with charlatans and racketeers."

Such epithets were often hurled by Zionist leaders — and not only against the "charlatans and racketeers" of the Hebrew underground in Palestine and its emissaries in America. The competition for leadership was just as intense among the "important men" during that period of Jewish history. Weizmann used Stephen Wise to dethrone Silver. Then Silver and Ben Gurion, acting together, dethroned Weizmann at the World Zionist Congress in 1946. It is doubtful whether Weizmann ever forgave them. Even Weizmann, ever the diplomat, became very offensive in describing his opponents within the Zionist movement. He was quoted by C.L. Sulzberger of *The New York Times* as having described Ben Gurion as "that damned fascist." In the same interview Weizmann did not hesitate to speak of the "racketeers of the Irgun."

This was in 1947, a year before Weizmann accepted Ben Gurion's offer to become President of Israel, a largely ceremonial post. At that time Weizmann, whom many considered the wisest of all Jewish statesmen, still believed that if the Stern group had not executed Lord Moyne, Churchill and Lord Moyne would have helped establish a Jewish State during World War II.

*   *   *

Yet, despite all the obstacles, the march took place.

For the first time, tens of thousands of Washingtonians "got to know that millions of Jews were done to death in Nazi-held Europe and that millions more are in jeopardy . . . and that the Jews of America are profoundly agitated by what is happening to their kin . . . that they are appealing to the government and the people of the United States for help in saving their brethren from eminent doom."

Although the president was "too busy" to see the rabbis, something must have happened within the White House. F.D.R. was already out at an airfield looking over some airplanes to be shipped to Yugoslavia; he had left through a back door with several White House correspondents. The rabbinical delegation and the Irgun representatives who had hoped for an audience refused to turn over the petition to F.D.R.'s secretary. They walked back to the Capitol where Vice-president Henry Wallace and several members of the Senate, including Senator Johnson, came out to welcome them. Despite all the efforts of the Jewish establishment to the contrary, the press published the most moving photographs of the demonstration.

From the experience of the Rabbis' March, Roosevelt must have learned that as long as he listened to the establishment Jews who had "the key to the White House," he could continue to fool the Jews of America by publicly telling them one thing and doing otherwise behind the scenes.

The campaign of the establishment against the demonstration prompted Hillel Kook to summon Dr. Stephen Wise to a Beth Din (rabbinical court) in order to prevent a public debate on such a sensitive issue. Wise refused to appear, and the Emergency Committee, having other problems in its campaign to pressure the government to change its policy, dropped the case.

In his autobiorgaphy, Wise, the recognized leader of American Jewry during the F.D.R. era, devotes one chapter to what he calls "Resistance to Hitlerism." Wise, who failed to clearly see the challenge and the means to fight the Nazi threat, could not have originated this title without recognizing that there was no American Jewish resistance to Hitlerism.

Hitler's ascent to power in January 1933 was accompanied by an unequivocal declaration of war against the Jewish people the world over. If the Jewish leadership of the time had been capable of understanding the challenge, we would have witnessed the creation of a wartime cabinet — an organizational instrument eschewing meaningless public statements while secretly planning and directing active resistance.

Wise's recitations in his *Resistance to Hitlerism* seem absurd when his story is analyzed more than forty years later. However, one episode he mentions is tragic in its implication. It shows how little this naive man understood in terms of the relentless Nazi war against the Jewish people. Wise admits he was informed by the American Assistant Secretary of State, Sumner Welles, that reports of the physical extermination of the Jews, the Final Solution, were confirmed by sources close to the State Department. In the chapter "Death by Bureaucracy," he relates the story. According to Wise himself, he first learned of this war of extermination in the fall of 1942. Several months later he was told by his own representatives in Switzerland that Jews were about to be deported to extermination camps where they would be liquidated through "prussic acid and (in) crematoria." (The cables were held by the State Department and delivered only a few months later).

In November 1942, Welles wired Wise to come immediately to the State Department. Upon his arrival in Washington, Welles told him the following:

"I hold in my hands documents which have come to me from our legation in Berne. I regret to tell you, Dr. Wise, that these confirm and justify your deepest fears." Wise says that Welles then presented him with original documents from Switzerland, documents that substantiated all "our dreadful apprehensions."

Welles then added that, for reasons that Wise would understand, he could not give these to the press, but suggested there was no reason why Wise should not do so, in which case the State Department would not deny the facts if queried.

Wise called a press conference, indicating the source of the documents: " . . . namely the State Department." However, he did not ask why, a few months earlier, Cordell Hull had assured him that the Rosenheim report was "war propaganda."

Thus Wise, who was so close to Roosevelt, conveniently relieved the American government of its obligation to tell the world about the extermination of the Jewish people. Wise knew, and he admits in his autobiography, that earlier in the war bureaucrats in the State Department had tried to minimize the horror and withhold information from the American people. Wise did not go to his friend Roosevelt and demand that the President of the United States publicly announce the news. He simply gave a statement to the press. Nor did Wise protest to Roosevelt against the criminal attitude of certain State Department bureaucrats.

After hearing such ominous reports, how could Wise leave Washington and return to New York to busy himself once more with Zionist politics? Should he not have stayed at the gates of the White House to picket and, if necessary, to act —as did the hero of the Book of Esther, Mordecai, when he heard the news about the conspiracy concocted by Haman? One should not forget that the biblical Haman had only an extermination *plan* whereas, while Wise was sitting in Welles' office, thousands of Jews were being killed every hour of every day. Wise's response to the slaughter of his brethren was to occupy himself with attacking the Irgun delegation, which had charged Roosevelt with personal responsibility for the lives of European Jewry. This charge was made public in full-page advertisements published in *The New York Times* and signed by Ben Hecht. The Irgun refused to relieve the American government, the Allies and the Red Cross of the responsibility for the lives of Jews who were Hitler's prisoners of war.

In the same chapter, "Death by Bureaucracy," Wise mentions the opportunity to "buy" the lives of some seventy thousand Jews in France and Romania: funds could have been deposited in the names of certain Nazi officials on the condition that their names be released only after the war. Wise spoke to the president about this, and F.D.R. agreed that these funds should be deposited in a Swiss bank. Henry Morgenthau, Jr. gave his permission but it took the State Department several months to obtain a licence. Wise says it took "five full months" after the president had approved the issue of a licence, and says that history should record this irresponsibility, this "callousness" on the part of the State Department.

Yet Wise failed to understand that he, too, was responsible for withholding this information from the American people. Why did he keep it secret until after the war? Why did he not go to Roosevelt and demand that rescue money be made available within twenty-four hours? Is this why he was given the "key to the White House?"

During this period both Stephen Wise and Nahum Goldmann (who had received the same information from the World Jewish Congress in Geneva) were busy with preparations for the Zionist "Biltmore Conference."

According to Goldmann, "I conceived the idea of convening a democratically elected Conference of all American Jews where the chances that a large majority would vote for a Jewish State were much better."

It is obvious, then, that the issue before the Jewish leaders was not how to work twenty-four hours a day to stop the slaughter in Europe, but to formulate postwar programs for the establishment of a Jewish state. As if the Jewish revolution in Palestine could not have materialized after the war without their meetings and debates!

As I look back on the days and months of our existential solitude in the struggle to rescue our brethren, I cannot help but remember the eloquent silence of *The New York Times*, the newspaper that supposedly published all the news "fit to print." Certainly *The New York Times* knew or could have obtained more information than all of us about the "progress" of this Final Solution. But the *Times*, reflecting the fears and complexes of its publishers, was "a Jewish newspaper." It printed everything of news value without censorship — everything except "Jewish news." When it came to "Jewish news," it became "a Jewish newspaper" in the tradition of the pre-war *Berliner Tageblatt*. Journalistically speaking, it suffered from a Jewish complex and followed the German-Jewish tradition of keeping quiet when Jewish issues were at stake. Throughout all the years of the struggle to rescue the hostages from Hitler, *The New York Times* had to be fought as well.

It was no accident that *The New York Times* was consistently opposed to the establishment of a Jewish state until the very end. In fact, all the movements in the American Jewish community which contributed to the Hebrew renaissance and Jewish survival did so contrary to the editorial advice of *The New York Times*. In its editors' desire to counteract the view that it was "a Jewish newspaper," *The New York Times* went out of its way to criticize any manifestation of Jewish self-affirmation.

Following in the footsteps of the legendary Adolph Ochs, George Ochs-Oakes, the famous *New York Times* editor, strongly opposed the Zionists and all the other advocates of a Jewish state in Palestine until his death in 1931. When Arthur Hayes Sulzberger became publisher, he made speeches urging Jews not to support the idea of a Jewish state in Palestine. In 1939 he was among a group of influential Jews who urged President Roosevelt not to appoint Felix Frankfurter to the Supreme Court because they believed his appointment might lead to an increase in antisemitism in America.

In 1946 *The New York Times* cancelled an advertisement submitted by the American League for a Free Palestine. Sulzberger went as far as to explain the refusal to publish this ad by declaring that the "anti-British charges could not be supported by facts . . . and (the newspaper) could not be responsible for the ill will that the advertisement . . . would stir between Britain and the United States."

Thus *The New York Times,* always sensitive to the accusation that it was considered a "Jewish newspaper," actually acted like a Jewish newspaper by editorializing on what was good or bad for the Jews, and by taking an intransigent stand on issues affecting the future of the Jewish people. Not only did *The New York Times* make sure that its policy on Zionism prevailed within the Jewish community and impressed the rest of America, but during World War II its silence on the slaughter of millions certainly reflected the fear that the Jews who ran the newspaper would lose their own influence in society if they did not keep quiet.

Nothing could be more cynical than the memoirs of C.L. Sulzberger, who during the Holocaust years, travelled the world as the chief foreign correspondent of *The New York Times.* In his memoirs, Cy Sulzberger, covering the years 1934-1954, does not mention a single word regarding the Final Solution and the extermination of the Jews in Europe. He speaks movingly of the sufferings of many peoples under Hitler, but has no word for Jews, the prime victims of the Nazis. A clever juggler of words, he must have felt, before publishing his memoirs and diaries of that period, that "as a Jew," someone might wonder whether he had never heard of what happened in Europe. So he constructed a chapter about a secret visit to the morgue of the Jewish cemetry in Vienna. This was in 1938, after the first coffins filled with the bodies of Dachau victims were shipped back to the Austrian capital.

In his best prose, Sulzberger tells the morbid story of what he saw in the cellar of the Viennese morgue. He "checked five of these bodies — all five were recorded as suicides . . . I have never known a man to kill himself by putting out his own eyes." Did C.L. Sulzberger report this to the United States? No. He says, "It was my intention to write a sensational series of articles," but suddenly he suffered "a traumatic experience from which it would take weeks to recover . . . what technical name psychologists give this condition I do not know, but I was unable to master it and finally chucked the project, writing nothing . . . this was neither courageous nor helpful to those I wished to aid by describing the Nazi brutishness, so I shed it, all of it, and rode off to Carlsbad with a Czech major, focussing my attention on the lovely grain and hop fields of Sudetenland."

Not a single word about the Final Solution. Absolutely nothing! Nowhere in his writings is there even a suggestion that during his many trips to Russia Sulzberger might have noticed the destruction being wrought upon Jewish communities by the Nazi invaders.

Naturally, this attitude was reflected in *The New York Times*. Sulzberger's relatives among the publishers lived in constant fear of losing their jobs if they spoke up, so they kept quiet.

This was yet one more front on which the Irgun delegation had to fight. Therefore its campaign to acquaint the American public with the facts through paid advertisements in the *Times* was so important during the conspiracy of silence surrounding the extermination of Jews.

XVI
The Sternbuch Saga

Now, forty years after the Holocaust, newly-available documents make it possible to establish to what degree the Swiss government (and some Swiss Jewish leaders) should be held responsible for the inhuman treatment of Jewish escapees from Hitler during World War II. The same could be said concerning the Swiss guilt for deporting back to Germany, back to hell, Jews who had succeeded in reaching Switzerland. Yet Swiss officials were conniving with Germans to keep Jews out; this is now a matter of record. While Switzerland "inherited" billions of dollars in secret accounts deposited there by Jews murdered by Germans, it made sure that the smallest number of living Jews were saved. We will never know how much heirless Jewish money is bulging in the safes of Swiss banks, but slowly the picture unfolds of a cynicism and a cruelty during World War II that very few would believe possible when looking at the pastoral picture of a land of milk-chocolate and beautiful Swiss villages.

In the late fifties, following demands by liberal Swiss circles that the government make public all facts concerning the treatment of Jewish refugees during World War II, Professor Carl Ludwig was commissioned to undertake a thorough investigation. His report, submitted to parliament, contains the most sensational revelations about the conduct of the Swiss authorities toward Jews from 1933 until 1955.

A few facts from his book *Die Fluechtlingspolitik der Schweiz seit 1933 bis zur Gegenwart* (The Refugee Policy of Switzerland from 1933 until the Present) are most pertinent when one analyzes the surface innocence of the Swiss during the darkest period in European history.

Following are some relevant points made by Dr. Ludwig:

1. When the Swiss authorities decided (as early as 1933) to keep out Jews fleeing Germany, they were under the influence of xenophobic and antisemitic campaigns against the "danger of Judaizing" Switzerland. Certainly, says Ludwig, at that time there was no such "threat" to Switzerland . . .

2. Switzerland pursued a secret policy against naturalizing Jews of Eastern European origin "because they were considered foreign elements." After Hitler's takeover of Germany, German Jews were considered undesirable elements. Later on, this policy was extended to all Jews in Western Europe trapped by the Nazis.

3. What Dr. Ludwig states about the role of the Jewish establishment in Switzerland during that period is more shocking than his accusations against his own government. He says, "It is a fact that in the circulars advising officials of these regulations, it is stated that this policy . . . was fully understood by the official representatives of Swiss Jewry." Here Dr. Ludwig adds, "This author

must confirm this fact on the basis of his own experience." According to Ludwig, the president of the Swiss Federation of Jewish Communities informed the Police Department in Basle that "Swiss Jews are definitely interested that as many refugees be admitted into Switzerland, but also that they *be shipped out of the country as soon as possible."*

At a meeting of the Swiss Parliament, M.P. Bringolf stated that Swiss Jews are of the opinion that the "undesirable immigration of Jews be halted."

4. In 1938, Dr. H. Rothmund, head of the Police Department, told the German Ambassador in Berne that "Switzerland is in need of those Jews . . . as much as is Germany." This was the period when Austrian Jews were fleeing Vienna. Then the German Ambassador in Berne wired the Foreign Office in Berlin that the then president of Switzerland, Baumann, protested to him that Jewish emigrants are assisted by German authorities to enter Switzerland illegally: "President Baumann considers this to be an unfriendly attitude towards Switzerland." (These documents were found by the Allies in the secret archives of the German Foreign Office. In fact, following this intervention, the Swiss Consulate in Vienna would accord visas only to those Austrians who could produce documents stating they were "Aryans.")

5. Concerning the attitude of the Swiss Jewish establishment, Dr. Ludwig makes the following points:

(a) The President of the Union of the Swiss Jewish Communities officially informed the authorities in the spring of 1939 that the growing immigration of refugees "has caused concern in Jewish circles" because they "cannot possibly cope with a further invasion neither financially nor technically." Says Dr. Ludwig: "Although the police regulations then already meant danger to the lives of thousands, the Jewish community leaders did not protest against this policy."

6. The leaders of the Jewish community in Switzerland even had the temerity to ask the leaders of the Jewish community in Vienna — by wire — that they discourage the illegal emigration of Jews to Switzerland!

7. An official Swiss circular directed to all diplomatic representatives abroad "explained" its anti-Jewish policy by stressing the information that the representatives of Swiss Jewry recognized "on their own initiative" the necessity to impose such regulations. The circular to the Swiss diplomatic representatives demanded that this attitude be explained in a manner that Switzerland does not "suffer morally" in France, England and America.

The same policy prevailed almost until the end of the war although, as Dr. Ludwig maintains, the Swiss authorities cannot claim they did not know what the Germans did to Jews during the last three years of the war.

*   *   *

On a recent visit to Geneva, a Swiss friend and I discussed this black chapter in the history of Switzerland. Symbolically, perhaps, our discussions (sometimes acrimonious) took place about three o'clock in the morning near the monument commemorating Jean Jacques Rousseau. Our café next door had closed, so we continued to argue at the foot of the monument, probably to the annoyance of the sleeping Geneva burghers.

When I mentioned this cruelty of the Swiss authorities, he replied, "How can you, an American Jew, accuse little Switzerland of cruelty and inhumanity towards escaping Jews, when the United States set the example of shipping the S.S. St. Louis back to Europe? Have you forgotten that all your Jewish leaders ever did was to protest — to the Cuban government! — for refusing to admit the nine hundred and thirty refugees who carried Cuban visas?

"I remember one philanthropic organization offering to deposit bonds for each passenger. Yet when an additional ransom of a few hundred thousand dollars was asked in the traditional pre-Castro, Batista-Cuban manner, your leaders refused to pay that bribe, and let the Jews be sent back to Europe! So what do you want from the Swiss? Maybe I'm wrong, but I never heard of stones being hurled at American government offices at the time for refusing even temporary admittance to these unfortunates."

Maybe my friend was right. Is it not true that the period from 1933-1945 must be recorded in history as an era of complete insensitivity to human suffering, of an era when might meant right? However, from the pile of documents and books written about the official Swiss reaction to this problem emerges a picture of complete disregard for the sufferings of Jews. Only towards the end of the war, when the Swiss realized that the Germans were finished, did they appear to be "moved" by the Jewish tragedy. Certainly President von Steiger could not have been more cynical about his role and his country's attitude during World War II when he told the Swiss parliament on November 12, 1947, "If what was going on there in the Reich had been known, the range of the possible would have been broadened."

Von Steiger conveniently forgot that he himself, as federal councillor (president), had defended Swiss cruelty towards escapees from the bordering Reich with a glib statement he often repeated in parliament during those years of trial and suffering, that one "must reconcile heart and reason; one cannot always give in to feelings of pity."

This policy of "not surrendering to the heart" cost innumerable human lives. From the records of that dark period emerges the almost unbelievably sinister figure of the chief of the Swiss Fremdenpolizei, Dr. Heinrich Rothmund. To Jews who were deported during the period of the Final Solution back to German-occupied countries, and who survived by some miracle, this policeman with a Ph.D. remains the symbol of Swiss inhumanity.

I spoke to two men who had dealings with Rothmund during World War II when they were involved with this problem in Switzerland, and who compared him to Eichmann. According to Swiss historian Alfred A. Hasler, Rothmund, as early as 1938 (following the German take-over of Austria) until the end of 1944, consistently practiced an anti-Jewish policy with regard to refugees. There are differences of opinion as to whether his cruelty, unmatched by a man in a similar position in a free country, was his own doing or whether he was only the executor of policy established by the Federal Government of Switzerland. Thus we ask concerning Rothmund: Did he enjoy persecution or was he the typical Eichmann who was doing a job?

The fact is that Switzerland was the country that pressured Nazi Germany to issue special passports to Jews who travelled abroad so that the Swiss authorities would be in a position to turn back unwanted Jews. The "J" that eventually appeared on such travel documents was a direct result of persistent, ongoing demands by Swiss officials that Germany "properly" identify a Jew's passport.

During these negotiations a Swiss official explained to his German counterpart that Germany also should "be interested in preventing an agglomeration of such emigrants in immediate proximity to the Reich."

In 1938, another Swiss official reported to the Federal Council that "the simplest solution would be to restrict the requirement for a visa to non-Aryan Germans."

This same official, a Swiss diplomat, Dr. Dinichert, admits that although such practices were "repugnant to our principles," it was also in the interest of Swiss Jews "to be protected against any further influx of foreign Jews." Dinichert continues by quoting the example of such countries as Hungary and Romania in order to have "more and more special restrictions against Jews." These words, including the using of the Nazi term "non-Aryan," come from the man who was at that time Switzerland's envoy to Berlin.

The policy continued under the new ambassador, Dr. Hans Froelicher. But Froelicher, it should be noted, went further than his predecessor. It was he, the Swiss ambassador, who suggested "a special mark in Jews' passports."

At that time the Germans encouraged the emigration of Jews. The poor Swiss, the guardians of the swollen bank accounts of so many, had to struggle with the Nazis in order to have more restrictions imposed upon Jews who might trickle into Switzerland!

In order to impress the Germans that the Swiss needed help keeping out Jews, Dr. Rothmund had no hesitation in conferring with the infamous Dr. Hans Globke, the author of the notorious 1935 Nuremberg racial laws.

At that early hour in Geneva, my friend had to listen when I quoted these and other, similar facts mentioned in the book of historian Hasler. Rothmund even said (and this today is also a matter of record) that if he had had a cheque for one hundred thousand francs for Jewish refugees, he would have "kept it in my pocket." Rothmund himself, at a later date, described the manner in which the Swiss harbored those refugees who succeeded in remaining in Switzerland legally. They were kept in camps where they had to work from daybreak to nightfall. The barracks were so constructed that they could be kept under surveillance from a watchtower day and night.

Rothmund also admitted that the inmates had been deliberately "thrown together in a planned heterogeneity." Jews, antimilitarist bible students, incorrigible criminals, "all had been jumbled together." This was Swiss "hospitality" for the Jewish escapees from Hitler-occupied countries.

*   *   *

Here arises the problem of the attitude of the official leaders of the small but influential Jewish community in Switzerland during that epoch. Rothmund later defended his own policy by stating that "Swiss Jews had understood this and also made considerable effort to explain the Swiss view . . . to foreign circles." According to Rothmund, any other Swiss policy would have "imported" antisemitism and threatened the position of the Swiss Jews.

What are the facts?

Here commences the Sternbuch saga:

Recha Sternbuch, the Belgian-born daughter of Antwerp's Orthodox Chief Rabbi Rottenberg, and her Swiss husband, Isaac Sternbuch, who lived in Montreux, Switzerland during the war years, will probably be remembered as the most dedicated, most selfless, most idealistic couple in the rescue work on behalf of Hitler's Jewish hostages. Many times Recha was arrested by the Swiss police.

At one point during the latter part of the war she was ready to travel to Berlin in order to negotiate for the release of extermination-camp inmates with archenemy Himmler himself.

I dare say: Had Recha Sternbuch obtained some support from the Jewish establishment in the United States, Palestine and Switzerland, we would not be talking about the Six Million today.

These efforts, as our report will show, induced Heinrich Himmler to enter into a secret deal with the Orthodox Vaad Hatzala: He thought that through this contract he might produce an alibi when the day of reckoning arrived. Unfortunately, the Sternbuchs and their committee members (Dr. Reuben Hecht, Dr. Julius Kuhl, the Laudau brothers) were not supported by the Swiss Jewish establishment and the international Jewish leaders. Quite the contrary: They were harassed, actually persecuted as "competitors" of the "new class" of professional Jews.

We are beholding a scene from Kafka: The Sternbuchs and their friends are on trial — by Jewish leaders — because they are involved in saving Jewish lives from Hitler. They don't know *why* they have to fight not only the enemies of the Jews, but their own "leaders" who control the purse strings.

*   *   *

Sternbuch never forgave Mayer. Sternbuch knew it was out of the question to obtain Mayer's support for any "illegal steps" to save the Jews. Recha Sternbuch remains the heroine of this era. It is difficult to believe that this elegant, handsome woman was the Joan of Arc of Jewish rescue in World War II, but she was.

In 1938 Recha was travelling in and out of Hitler's Germany smuggling Jews into Switzerland. The fact that she spoke both French and German without a trace of an accent helped. Following one of her trips she was denounced to the Swiss police by someone within the Jewish community. She was arrested and held incommunicado for a few months. The infamous Dr. Rothmund himself interrogated her in prison several times, and threatened to keep her locked up until she died unless she turned over to him the names of those who had entered Switzerland "illegally."

Rothmund did not succeed in obtaining any information from her. She told him that if she died in prison she would not be the first Jew to die for her people. She certainly would not become an informer for the police. She reminded him that she was a Swiss citizen, married to a citizen of Switzerland, and insisted on her rights. Finally she was released and resumed her activities.

A personal observation:

Toward the end of 1945 I met Recha in Prague. She said she had invited me to her friends' house because she heard that I was to accompany Justice Jackson of the Nuremberg Tribunal to Poland at the invitation of the Polish government. Until this day I don't know how she found that out. The only person who knew it was the American Ambassador to Czechoslovakia, Lawrence A. Steinhardt, who had a message from Nuremberg asking me to report to the Tribunal. Of course, I promised to travel with her to Poland in order to help save Jews. She said, "You don't know what an American uniform means there."

However, when I arrived in Nuremberg, I heard that the Polish government had cancelled the invitation to Jackson. This was the time when Polish bands were roaming the cities trying to kill the few surviving Jews who had escaped the Nazis.

The Polish attorney-general, Jerzy Sawicki, who was then in Nuremberg representing Poland (secretly a very dedicated Jew with whom I used to discuss commentaries by the rabbis on biblical themes), confided in me that the Polish government did not like the delegation that would accompany Jackson, including some who understood Polish. Maybe they were referring to me because when I visited the Polish Embassy in Prague to get my visa, an employee made an antisemitic remark, thinking I did not understand her. When I said that I would report this to the American Embassy, her face flushed and she started apologizing by saying that her best friends were Jews, etc. I took my visa and left without saying goodbye.

Nothing came of this trip. But Recha Sternbuch went to Poland and smuggled out hundreds of Jews, mostly children.

XVII
The Musy Mission to Himmler

Here begins the most exciting part of the Sternbuch saga: Himmler's Secret Deal, the socalled Musy Mission.

This secret deal with Himmler constitutes the most intriguing chapter in the history of the struggle on behalf of the Jews doomed by Hitler. It also presents the most tangible proof that it was possible to buy lives from the Nazis.

The facts were confirmed after the war by Jewish participants in this operation and, among others, by a Nazi who was directly involved in this deal.

One of the most infamous butchers of the gangster empire, S.S. General Walter Schellenberg, Himmler's assistant, relates the events in his memoirs. He speaks of the contacts with Musy and mentions the opposition from Schellenberg's own "competitor," Kaltenbrunner. Schellenberg describes the negotiations involved in the agreement, which provided for releasing twelve hundred Jews each week. He also confirms that Himmler and he had agreed that the ransom money should not be paid to the Germans, but be deposited in Switzerland with Musy acting as trustee. I found a document left by Musy himself, a typewritten report in French in which this pro-fascist former president of Switzerland (engaged in rescue activities on behalf of the Orthodox rabbis in the United States) relates the story of his negotiations.

Who was Musy?

During World War II, when he learned the true facts concerning the Final Solution, Dr. Jean-Marie Musy, a friend of the Nazis before the war, had second thoughts about their racial policy. During his rescue mission Musy personally negotiated with Himmler for the evacuation of Jews from Germany and/or for their release from the death camps. One must remember that Musy was not a minor Swiss official; he was a former president of the Swiss Confederation, one of the outstanding lawyers in his country, and had most unusual connections in the leading fascist circles. The Sternbuchs and their friends approached him *because they knew* that before the war he had been a sympathizer of the fascists and that he was a personal friend of Himmler from the days when they sat on the socalled International Anticommunist Committee.

The story begins with a Swiss Jewish couple, Mr. and Mrs. Loeb from Berne who had visited Musy and begged him to intervene with the German authorities for the release of their sister and brother-in-law from a German-controlled prison in France. As Musy recalls, they were apprehended only because they were Jews. It was with some hesitation that Musy went to occupied France to intervene with the chief of the Parisian Gestapo, a certain General Hoberg. Hoberg told him quite plainly that "a Jew once sent to a concentration camp can never come out of it."

Nevertheless, "I did not lose my courage," Musy relates. "Insisted and even said that one of the arrested was of Swiss origin." In Musy's words, this argument proved "an unexpected success." The Jewish couple was liberated from the camp and taken to Switzerland.

It seems, Musy continues, that news of this successful intervention which was "without precedent" somehow reached certain underground circles in Paris. This is how Mrs. Bolomey, the Paris contact of the Sternbuch committee in Montreux (representing the Vaad Hatzalah of the American Orthodox Rabbinate), came to see Musy and asked him to undertake a major effort on behalf of Jews in the German extermination camps. According to the surviving members of the Sternbuch committee — Reuben Hecht, Julius Kuhl, Herman Landau and others — before the war Musy had been known as a social antisemite. He did not like associating with Jews and welcomed "certain restrictions" against them, but was truly shocked when he heard the facts about the "extermination program." To this fascist sympathizer, as to other fascists in Romania and Hungary, genocide was intolerable. (Sternbuch, Hecht, Kuhl and Landau accepted Musy's statement that the entire initiative for negotiating with Jews to free hostages in Germany came from Musy himself.)

No matter how one regards Musy in retrospect, no matter what his motives were, facts prove that the last million of the doomed Jews in occupied Europe would have been saved if Jews had not bickered among themselves.

Here, according to Musy's secret report, are the facts:

In 1944 the Nazis intensified the extermination of Jews, especially after they heard that the Allies refused to bombard Auschwitz.

Musy accepted the invitation to attend a meeting in Berne with Isaac and Recha Sternbuch and others. "I was told," Musy continues, "that it was necessary to intervene in Germany for the liberation of Jews. Hundreds of thousands of them, I was told, are in concentration camps." Musy had never seen a concentration camp, and was repeatedly refused a permit to visit one. Although he was afraid of both the Germans and the Allied bombardment, he undertook this "delicate mission."

Musy reports: "I immediately wrote to Reichsfuhrer Himmler telling him that I had an important message for him."

Fifteen days later, Himler replied, saying that he was ready to receive him. Musy left immediately for Berlin, taking along his son Benoit, "who spoke perfect German and who was an excellent driver."

Upon arrival in Berlin, Musy was welcomed by General Schellenberg. Schellenberg told Musy that Himmler would receive him within the next few days and that he should prepare for a long journey to Himmler's headquarters. Finally, two days later, at 4 A.M., General Schellenberg took Musy in a military car to Breslau (now Wroclaw), in Silesia, where they boarded a train. Himmler was waiting for Musy in a compartment and they spoke throughout their journey to Vienna.

Musy describes their conversation: "We had a long discussion, very long, in which I explained to him why, from my point of view, even disregarding all humanitarian considerations, Germany had a major stake in closing all concentration camps and to profit from an exceptionally favourable opportunity to regulate the Israelite problem."

Musy prepared a memorandum for Himmler in which he stated that there were Americans ready to pay the expenses for the transportation of all liberated Jews. In the same memo Himmler was told that the United States was ready to accept all Jews who could not find places in Europe or in Palestine.

"At moments," Musy says, "the conversation with Himmler was very lively, but it was always very courteous. The attitude of Himmler was even benevolent. He listened to me attentively and made an effort to understand my viewpoint, very far from his."

This conference in the train continued for two hours, and Musy was left with the impression that his arguments had "touched" the Reichsfuhrer. At the end of the conversation, Himmler came to an agreement with Musy, who had been officially authorized to act on behalf of the American Orthodox Rabbis.

The agreement contained the following points:

1. The Germans undertook to free immediately all Jews from concentration camps in all territories under German rule. (At that time, Musy observes, there were still six-hundred-thousand Jews in the camps. It was extremely important, according to Musy, that such a step be undertaken without the authorization of Hitler.)

2. The liberation of the Jewish prisoners would begin immediately once the organization of the Orthodox rabbis in America accepted the basic points of the deal.

First, Himmler wanted trucks, tractors and cars as compensation. Yet Musy rejected these conditions outright. For obvious reasons it would be impossible to deliver such material to the Germans, the Swiss ex-president said. Instead Musy suggested that the Germans accept money in foreign exchange and some medical supplies. It took time, Musy says, to convince Himmler, but the suggestion was accepted. Musy rushed home via Berlin to report to the Sternbuchs, and also contacted a pharmaceutical firm in Basle asking for the medicine he had promised.

At a second conference with Himmler in Wildebad, in the Black Forest region, Musy confirmed that no trucks could be delivered; only some medicine and cash in foreign currency would be forthcoming. Again Himmler accepted the terms: *money for blood.*

At the Wildebad conference Musy again reminded Himmler of the political advantages of the transaction. It was imperative to stress humanitarian rather than material considerations. The Reichsfuhrer was convinced, Musy reports, that it was necessary "to profit from the opportunity, to resolve in an 'elegant manner' the Jewish problem in Germany."

Musy, in his naiveté, again assured Himmler that the American government was ready to receive these Jews in case they did not find homes in Europe, and that it would pay their travelling expenses.

Apparently, throughout all these negotiations Himmler was impressed only because Musy could produce letterheads of the Union of the Orthodox Rabbis in America which the Nazi probably regarded as a very important power. After all, he was a fanatical Hitlerite who believed in some kind of a "secret international Jewish government . . ."

Himmler's price was five million francs ($1,250,000). This was to be deposited in Switzerland in Musy's name, with Musy acting as trustee. Musy believed that such a situation was unbecoming to him, and he preferred to have the money deposited in the name of Sternbuch of the Montreux Committee, the representative of the rabbis. Sternbuch managed to raise the money and deposited it. During Musy's third trip to Berlin, he was able to show Himmler the bank records. It was understood that the money would be released to the Germans only after the end of the war. Everything seemed to point to an eventual solution and to the rescue of the Jews. But, as Musy says, no one could have expected the new and very serious difficulties that arose.

A Nazi official by the name of Franz Gehring, an emissary of Himmler's aide, Schellenberg, received the order from Himmler to release a number of Jews and dispatch them to the Swiss border where they would be turned over to Musy. The first problems occurred with concentration camp officials who were unwilling to release their victims. Nevertheless, some Jews (all the names are in the document), were taken to the border.

According to Musy, Gehring and Schellenberg continued to organize other transports of Jews for movement to the Swiss border. But there new opposition manifested itself in the person of one of the worst Nazi killers, Kaltenbrunner, Himmler's deputy. This complication arose directly because of the bickering among Jewish organizations.

It seems that part of the money deposited by Sternbuch was lent to the rabbis (after long negotiations and pressure) by the American Jewish Joint Distribution Committee. When the Joint representative in Switzerland, Sally Mayer, heard about it, he decided, according to Musy, to take over the entire operation. Maybe there were also some instructions from New York not to let the Orthodox rabbis "get away" with such a tremendous achievement. Why shouldn't the *official* Jewish community at this late hour take credit for this performance?

Musy accuses Mayer of practically sabotaging the entire enterprise. Himmler was informed by people close to Mayer that they represented a more important organization of American Jews than the Orthodox rabbis; therefore the Nazis should negotiate with them, not with the Sternbuch Committee!

Musy was summoned to Himmler, who demanded immediate information about the "importance" of the Orthodox organization. It seems that Musy succeeded in eliminating the Nazis' doubts when he again showed Schellenberg the very impressive letterhead of the Union of Orthodox Rabbis of the United States and Canada. But, says Musy, wherever there was trouble in such situations, it was created by Sally Mayer.

In Toronto I asked Herman Laudau, who had negotiated with Mayer, whether these accusations were true. Instead of giving me a direct answer, Landau said, "Once there was an opportunity to do something concrete. I had a cable from Weissmandl. It was a Friday afternoon and I phoned Mayer in St. Gallen.

"Mayer, the Swiss representative of the Joint Distribution Committee and the American United Jewish Appeal, told me, 'Let's wait until after Shabbat.' I knew then that this was a lost cause."

*   *   *

Who was Sally Mayer?

During the war years he was a Jewish community leader in Switzerland as well as the represenfative of the American Jewish Joint Distribution Committee (JDC) there. In order to understand the present criticism of the role of Sally Mayer, it must be remembered that Switzerland remained the only country bordering on Germany which was not invaded by the Nazis. It was the listening post for spies of both camps, but at the same time a centre from which rescue operations could have been directed. Sally Mayer, as the man trusted by the Joint leaders in New York, had the authority to spend money for rescue. After the war, the JDC public relations offices in New York released stories to the effect that Sally Mayer had outsmarted the Nazis by continuing to hold back the ransom money which was to have been paid to the Nazi gangsters in return for the release of Jews. Even the American representative of the War Refugee Board, Roswell D. McClelland, admitted that Mayer protracted these talks too long. According to the JDC, however, he was a hero who "refused to give money" to the Nazis.

While Mayer was still alive and the accusations against him were rampant, he never sued anyone for libel; nor did any of the leaders of the JDC.

Irving M. Bunim of New York, leader of Young Israel who was involved in all this, received a report on Sally Mayer's activities from the Orthodox Vaad Hatzalah representatives in Switzerland. When asked to help bring Jews to Switzerland from Eastern Europe, Mayer said, "Wer Braucht hier die Ostjuden?" (Who needs the Jews from Eastern Europe here?) Somehow this report appeared in a Jewish Telegraphic Agency dispatch, Bunim recalls.

Mayer, by the way, was "a friend" of Dr. Heinrich Rothmund, head of the Swiss Federal Alien Police. In this capacity Rothmund was the Swiss official responsible for an active policy of persecuting the Jews fleeing Hitler. After the war, Rothmund defended his policy by blaming the official leaders of Swiss Jewry for suggesting antirefugee regulations. Despite the diverse explanations, one must wonder: Sally Mayer was the representative of the JDC. Why did the JDC in New York have no information from him regarding the extermination of Jews in Eastern Europe, the kind of information that was transmitted to New York by the Vaad Hatzalah representatives and the World Jewish Congress agents in Geneva? What was Mayer doing in Switzerland during those years? What reports did the JDC office demand of him?

In November 1943 there was an opportunity to save some French Jewish children. At that time, under pressure of public opinion, the Swiss government issued a permit to the Jewish communities of Switzerland allowing the immigration of all the children they could bring in from France. There was one condition: that Jews should be responsible for their upkeep. This was the response of the Union of Jewish Communities in Switzerland to the government: The community is too small to accommodate all these children. The letter was signed by Dr. George Brunschvig and Sylvain S. Guggenheim, leaders of the Jewish Community in Switzerland!

Thus the official Jewish community rejected in writing an offer by the Swiss government to help save Jewish children.

Yet, during all these years, Dr. Rothmund and his Jewish friends had very determined enemies who never tired of fighting for the rescue of Jews. First there was Recha Sternbuch and her husband, Isaac. They formed the nucleus of the Vaad Hatzalah, a self-appointed local rescue committee that had no funds, no prestige within the community and very little support except in some synagogues. What they did have was the moral and physical strength to face the wrath of their fellow Jews. They knew that Switzerland was the only centre to which reports from the valley of death could be sent and from where they could be relayed to the great Jewish centers. So the Sternbuchs, together with several friends such as Dr. Reuben Hecht, Heinrich and Herman Landau, and Dr. Julius Kuhl, tried to move heaven and earth on behalf of the Jewish hostages in Hitler's Europe.

Herman Landau, who lives in Toronto, and Julius Kuhl, who recently passed away in Miami, were themselves foreigners in Switzerland: the Landaus were refugees; Kuhl, an official of the Polish Embassy. Hecht was the only Swiss citizen, and acted as the Swiss representative of the Irgun and its American Emergency Committee.

Despite all the opposition, this small group succeeded in obtaining some support. First they opened communication with Jews in occupied Europe. Then they enlisted the help of Monsignor Phillipe Bernardini (Apostolic Nuntius) as well as that of Alexander Lados, the Polish Minister to Switzerland. Lados turned over to Kuhl one thousand Polish "Aryan" passports that saved some Hungarian Jews.

Kuhl remembers Mayer's reluctance to give any assistance to this committee. At first Mayer even "disbelieved" Kuhl's information about the extermination camps. After that meeting, Isaac Sternbuch consistently refused even to meet Sally Mayer.

Landau related to me that Sternbuch, a Swiss Jew, knew that Mayer had connections with Rothmund and the Swiss police and was plainly afraid of him. Sternbuch maintained till the end of his life that it was Mayer who had asked the Swiss authorities to close the doors to the Jews fleeing Austria. This was in 1938, when the lives of so many could have been saved. Mayer reflected the fear of many Swiss Jews that involvement in rescue activities would be dangerous to them. (This is exactly what Rothmund confirmed.)

*   *   *

Sternbuch was in serious trouble. How could he convince Himmler that the Orthodox Vaad Hatzalah was an influential American Jewish organization?

Time was of the essence, and the whole operation was endangered. Therefore it was explained to the Germans that while the Union of Orthodox Rabbis dealt with political problems, the organization represented by Sally Mayer, though it was important, was of a more philanthropic nature and could not be of any political benefit to the Nazis.

Musy again went to Berlin carrying this statement and a number of clippings from Jewish newspapers in America describing the importance of Sternbuch's organization.

Musy remained convinced that Schellenberg and Gehring "sincerely" believed that it was in Germany's interest to complete the deal. They knew that this was a unique opportunity, that the freeing of Jews had to be unconditional and that they had to be released from all the camps. Thus it was agreed that from twelve hundred to thirteen hundred people, "the first transport," would leave immediately for Switzerland under the personal supervision of Gehring, to be followed by a similar "transport" each week. Four days later, twelve hundred Jews were waiting at the Swiss border near Constance. The Swiss government which, during the first years of World War II had not been very humanitarian (to say the least), must have decided at the last moment not to create any visa difficulties. So the Jews were admitted.

Then a new problem arose. This is how Musy describes it: "Gehring himself confided in me that immediately after the arrival in Switzerland of the train which he himself had taken to the border, rumors were spread in Germany among the Nazi leadership that this freeing of prisoners was the result of a deal according to which two hundred SS leaders would be admitted to the United States at the end of the war. It was said that this report was spread by Sally Mayer himself and that it was delivered to Colonel Becher, a German official whom Mayer had sought out in order to compete with the Orthodox rabbis in saving Jews."

Musy continues, "Becher was a friend of the beast Kaltenbrunner, who in turn went to Hitler himself and complained about this deal. Hitler reportedly became very angry and ordered an immediate stop to the entire operation."

Some newspapers in Switzerland which were against admitting Jews began attacking former president Musy for his role as a fascist in helping the Nazis. The clippings from American newspapers were turned over to Hitler. The Germans who were close to Gehring and Himmler demanded that there be some coverage of this humanitarian effort in the New York press. Some reports did appear, but Radio Atlantik suddenly began broadcasting details about the Musy deal. At this moment, Musy says, Mayer, who was then the leader of the Swiss Jewish community, began an intrigue in order to paralyze the activities of the Montreux committee.

Musy was told in Berlin that if the second train had not yet left for

Switzerland, the delay was caused by Mayer's intrigues: "This was confirmed to me later by Franz Gehring himself."

At that time Mayer started his own activities to liberate Jews from the camps.

Musy did not give up. He went to the International Red Cross which, he admits, had not done anything on behalf of the Jews up until then. For the first time, thanks to this intervention, the Red Cross was allowed to enter some camps.

Himmler gave the order to release from concentration camps a number of Jews whose names were on a list presented to him, socalled rabbis, and to transport them to Switzerland. There were sixty-one Jews on this train.

But somehow the people in Germany with whom Sally Mayer was in touch changed the names on the list and put "their own people" on the train. When the sixty-one arrived, only a few were the ones from the Vaad Hatzalah list. They had been told to state to the press that they had been released thanks to the representatives of Sally Mayer. This horrible publicity stunt, engineered by a Jewish official, hurt the entire rescue program.

In the meantime, the war was coming to an end. Nazi leaders were beginning to panic, but still Schellenberg and Himmler sabotaged Hitler's orders not to free the Jews from the concentration camps. In fact, thanks to this agreement, Buchenwald was not touched and all its prisoners were liberated. Musy promised Himmler that he would personally see to it that the guards of these camps would not be executed by the Allies. This was a promise he had no authority to make, but it worked in favor of the Jews.

At that late hour, the American War Refugee Board became active. Sternbuch, Musy and others met with McClelland, the board's representative. During the last months of the war, the American government relaxed its policy against "buying" Jewish lives from the Nazis. Some funds were released. Recha and Isaac Sternbuch did not stop their activities until the last moment; neither did Hecht, Kuhl and Landau. Hecht, meanwhile, obtained some diplomatic post from a Latin American country as a member of the Hebrew Committee of National Liberation, established by the Irgun Delegation to Washington, D.C.

McClelland surprised Musy by promising to submit to the Allies Musy's committment that if the guards of the camps free the Jews, they will not be executed. Musy promptly informed General Schellenberg about it. Musy, Jr., went to Weimar where Gehring accompanied him to the Buchenwald concentration camp in which many lives were saved, thanks to this intervention. A similar operation took place in Theresienstadt.

The German war machine was breaking down. Gehring disappeared and the young Musy had much difficulty going back home. But the example of the activities in Switzerland had inspired the Jewish communities elsewhere (in Sweden, for example) to emulate the rescue activities.

For the second time, Musy, Jr., returned to Weimar, which was near the Buchenwald concentration camp. However, Gehring, who was supposed to keep the second appointment, did not appear. The road between Berlin and Weimar was cut off. Still, Musy, Jr., was not discouraged. Again he went to Buchenwald and arrived just at the moment when the guards wanted to evacuate the camp and many were being attacked by the fleeing Germans. Musy said he was always afraid of what would happen in the last hours before the German army broke down.

Musy, Jr., returned to Berlin, succeeded in seeing Gehring and Schellenberg again and pointed out that the agreement with Himmler was being broken in Buchenwald. It was clear that Himmler's orders were not being executed; they were superseded by the orders of Kaltenbrunner in the name of Hitler. However, it was a period of disorganization and a new intervention helped save many lives in Buchenwald and Theresienstadt, which Musy, Jr. revisited subsequently. Many of the people for whom he had searched in Theresienstadt were not there anymore. They had been transported to Auschwitz on the last trains. It is remarkable that Gehring continued to negotiate with Musy. Gehring probably hoped that this would be some kind of insurance policy for his life.

In his report Gehring says openly that Himmler and Schellenberg supported the ideas of Musy, and they did save some Jews. Had there been no sabotage, had this activity started before, hundreds of thousands would have been saved. In the meantime, Schellenberg kept his word and liberated all prisoners in the camps in the south of Germany. Hitler was out. Another thousand Jewish women were saved in the neighborhood of Hamburg.

In his conclusion, Musy says: The saddest factor in this entire operation was the "competition" which Sally Mayer saw in this activity. He contacted Becher and Kaltenbrunner. "This perfidious opposition made it impossible for us to save thousands more."

Towards the end Musy, who later became the trustee of the five million francs deposited on behalf of Himmler, returned the money to the committee in full.

*   *   *

When studying this era, time and again we stumble upon the unbelievable fact: whether it was the resistance against the British in Palestine, the activities on behalf of European Jews by the Irgun Delegation in America, or the Vaad Hatzalah in Switzerland, the dedicated, unpaid servants of the Jewish cause were forced to militate against the professional Jews, the New Class. Of course, those in the governments involved preferred the "nice Jews" who were willing to wait until the end of the war rather than disturb the peace of bureaucrats in the State Department, the Foreign Office, the Palestine Occupation Administration or the Government of Switzerland.

In 1953 one of the most sensational trials took place in Jerusalem, then already Israel. Malkiel Greenwald, a Chaplinesque character, an old man, a Hungarian Jew who had immigrated to Israel in 1938 and lost a son in the Irgun revolt, was dragged to court for having "maligned an official of the Israeli government." The plaintiff was the State of Israel because the insulted party, Dr. Rudolf Kastner, was a leading member of the Government Labor Party and editor of *Uj Kelet,* the Hungarian language daily controlled by this political party.

During the war years Kastner was the representative in Budapest of the World Zionist Organization, the Jewish Agency and the American Jewish Joint Distribution Committee. Greenwald, who lost eighteen members of his family during the German occupation, in a widely circulated pamphlet accused Kastner of having cooperated with Eichmann himself in the extermination of Hungarian Jewry. Kastner was also accused of having defended, at the Nuremberg War Crimes Tribunal, Nazi monster Kurt Becher, collaborator of the notorious Gestapo bureaucrat Kaltenbrunner. Allegedly Kastner had defended him because Becher was his partner in crime.

At that time Moshe Sharett was Prime Minister of Israel. He must have felt that he himself was under attack because until this day Sharett's role in another rescue effort has remained a puzzle, to say the least. This questionable role of the late Sharett was often mentioned with the failure of Joel Brand, who was sent by Eichmann to meet with Weizmann and Sharett to suggest the infamous money-for-blood deal. The Nazi was ready to sell a million Jews to the World Zionist leaders. Yet when Sharett met Brand at Aleppo, Syria, somehow British secret agents were there; they arrested him and took him to Cairo where he remained until the end of the war. Brand, who lived in Israel after the war, published a book in which he accused Sharett of having delivered him to the British instead of listening to his story. Brand, however, was never jailed by Israeli officials for defaming a former Prime Minister.

So when Greenwald published his pamphlet against Kastner and the Establishment, disseminating these allegations, the Government of Israel sued him for libel.

A former Irgun commander and brilliant young lawyer, Shmuel Tamir took up the defense of poor Malkiel and succeeded in turning the case into a cause célèbre against Kastner and those who backed him. (Tamir was Minister of Justice in the second Menachem Begin government.) It became the most sensational trial in the history of the Jewish state. At the beginning the government attorney bragged that he would close the case within a week and put Greenwald in jail for maligning a leader of the ruling Labor Party. As it turned out, the deliberations of the court continued for four years — from 1953 to 1957 — and Tamir like a lion stood by Greenwald until the presiding judge stated, toward the end: "Kastner sold his soul to the devil." (Ben Hecht published a book about this case, *Perfidy*.)

*　　　*　　　*

All facts mentioned by Greenwald were substantiated. Not only did Kastner cooperate with the Germans by "drugging" the Jews whose leader he was, and making them believe that the trains to Auschwitz actually were taking them to some ideal town where they would be better fed and obtain better living quarters; Kastner was the only Jew in German-occupied Budapest who lived until the end of the war in luxury: he had a villa, car, private telephone, secretaries, mistress, and was wined and dined by the Nazi killers. He was also the only Jew allowed to leave German-occupied Hungary and return there when he went on a mission to Switzerland together with a Nazi official.

*   *   *

For his services Kastner received a gift: he was given exit visas to Switzerland for 1300 "prominent" Jews, his friends and relatives, while he encouraged directly and indirectly close to 600,000 Jews to travel to the Shangri-La in Auschwitz. So, after the war — a service for a service — Kastner appeared in Nuremberg and in a written document absolved Kurt Becher, who would have been executed, of any guilt in the extermination policies of the Germans. It was also established during the Kastner trial that he performed this mission on behalf of Becher with the concurrence and approval of some officials of the Jewish Establishment in Palestine, and had travelled to Germany at the expense of the Jewish Agency!

In June, 1954, Reuben Hecht, an emissary of the Irgun and the European member of the Hebrew Committee of National Liberation, at one time "one-dollar-a-year" adviser to Prime Minister Begin, testified at the Kastner trial.

Following are a few pertinent excerpts from the official records of the hearings, as translated from the Hebrew:

Q. You (Reuben Hecht) are an industrialist living in Haifa?

A. Yes.

Q. You were active in the Illegal Emigration (Aliyah Bet) movement in 1939 and 1940 in Switzerland, France, Rumania, Hungary, Yugoslavia? You were sent there from Palestine?

A. Yes.

Q. You were a member of the European Rescue Committee of the American Union of Orthodox Rabbis?

A. A member of the Executive and of this Committee.

Q. You were also a member and political representative in Europe of the Hebrew Committee of National Liberation?

A. Yes.

Q. Since the establishment of the Jewish State you are no longer involved in politics; you are only an industrialist?

A. Yes. In 1948 I stopped all my political activities, and since then have devoted all my energies to the economic consolidation of our nation.

Q. How did you become involved with this Rabbinical Rescue Committee?

A. In connection with my rescue activities in Europe I came in contact with Americans, among them Consul General Woods (in Zurich), who at that time was more than Consul General. He suggested that I get in touch with the Sternbuchs. He thought that this connection would be of help to me. I was told by Woods that the Sternbuchs were very active in saving lives from Poland and Hungary.

Q. Thus you worked with the Sternbuchs in order to save Jews from the Nazis?

A. Yes.

Q. A document before this court seems to originate from the American State

Department?

A. Yes. It was important at that time to prove that the Rescue Committee of the Orthodox Rabbis in America was a serious reliable organization. So we received this endorsement from the State Department.

Q. Were you in contact with the Swiss government, the Papal Nuntius and the American Embassy?

A. Yes.

Q. Did you work with a man by the name of Musy? Who was he?

A. He was a Catholic, a Swiss statesman, a former president of Switzerland and, at various times, a member of the Federal Swiss Government . . . his acquaintance with Himmler dated from many years before the war.

Q. Why did you choose an intermediary between you and Himmler?

A. Following our previous experience, we came to the conclusion that we must find a person that would gain the confidence of Himmler.

Q. What were the intentions of Musy, who was neither a member of your Committee nor a Jew?

A. It was impossible at the time to find a Christian personality with an international standing who would consent to intervene with the Nazis on behalf of the Jews . . . we needed someone who could exert some influence and who would be ready to take all risks involved in such trips to Germany . . . Musy was . . . very conservative and reactionary . . . he was known as an extreme enemy of communists . . . that's why we decided that he was the man to be received by Himmler and to gain his confidence . . . my opinion is that he wanted to rehabilitate himself . . . he was then an old man and had second thoughts about his former activities . . . we had heard about one successful intervention of his . . . also he has excellent connections with the Vatican.

Q. Did you trust Musy?

A. At times our situation was such that we did not put our belief entirely in any one man. We had to act fast . . . and the fact was that within fourteen days a reply came from Himmler that he was ready to receive him.

Q. In retrospect do you think he deserved the confidence placed in him?

A. According to my opinion, yes.

Q. Did you try to accompany Musy on his mission to Himmler?

A. I made an application for a permit at the German Consulate General in Berne. (I attached it to an introduction from Musy and from the then Swiss president, von Steiger). Also, Musy tried very hard to have me and Mrs. Sternbuch accompany him to Himmler . . . but permission was refused.

Q. What actually was Musy's mission?

A. It was really a political move . . . to explain to the German circles who understood that their war was lost . . . especially to impose upon Himmler the impression abroad of the extermination of Jews . . . The purpose was to tell him that the reaction could become calamitous (for the Germans) but could become less of a catastrophe if he would save the six hundred to eight hundred thousand Jews in the camps whom Hitler ordered to be liquidated.

Q. Did Himmler ask for an assurance by the Americans that the concentration camp guards not be executed, but treated as prisoners of war?

A. Yes . . . the Americans (following our intervention) agreed to it . . . in fact during the liberation of the Bergen-Belsen camp, Mrs. Sternbuch was already on the way there, in Bregenz.

Q. There was a deal between you and Himmler to desist from further extermination in the camps. Was there also an agreement about special rescue trains to Switzerland?

A. First there was a deal about freeing the last Jews in the camps and allowing them to leave for Switzerland in special trains, each containing between 1,200 and 1,600 people . . . in fact, the first train with 1,200 Jews was brought to Kreuzlingen.

Q. Were there additional trains?

A. No.

Q. Was the Red Cross involved?

A. Yes . . . Through our intervention.

Q. This Rescue Committee of Sternbuch, was it connected with the Agudat Israel?

A. Yes.

Q. The Zionist leaders in Switzerland, did they cooperate with this Committee?

A. No. There was no full cooperation with the Jewish Agency nor with Zionist organizations. Nor did they help us before the war in the Aliyah Bet.

Q. Sally Mayer, was he then the representative of the American Joint in Switzerland?

A. Yes . . .

Q. He did not cooperate with you?

(Hecht then testified under oath that Musy had reported to them that Sally Mayer, because of competition, negotiated with Kaltenbrunner in order to undermine the Nazi's confidence in the Rabbinical Rescue Committee. Sternbuch had made an effort to directly contact the Joint in America to counteract Sally Mayer's obstruction, but to no avail. In fact, from Hecht's testimony it appears that after the first transport of Jews from Germany this rescue operation [through special trains] was discontinued because of Sally Mayer's sabotage . . .)

Q. Since Sally Mayer, according to you, did not cooperate with you, did you find other ways?

A. It was very difficult. The atmosphere was very frigid. The American representative, McClelland, was "cold."

Q. Outside Switzerland was there a possibility of appealing against Sally Mayer's activities?

A. Only in the U.S. — to the Joint.

Q. Did your committee inform the Joint?

A. Yes.

Q. Was it not your duty to show to Sally Mayer Musy's letter of accusation against him and, perhaps, to impress upon him the earnestness of the situation by saying, "we are accusing you of sabotage?"

A. This is not very simple . . . Sally Mayer was convinced that our activities were wrong and his way of doing things was right . . . Therefore we had to part ways . . .

*   *   *

Greenwald's attorney, Tamir, succeeded in turning this trial into a trial of the establishment that neglected to save the Jews from Hitler's Europe.

Isaac Sternbuch, our hero, met Kastner when he arrived in Switzerland on his "mission" during the war, bringing his "prominent" Jews there, and returning to the Nazis. This was in the spring of 1944. Sternbuch could not understand a Jewish leader who was gallivanting in Germany with the Nazis, who wore no yellow star, and who "is active on behalf of a select 1,300 people from among the million who await rescue."

I consider most instructive the text of the letter Sternbuch sent to the presiding judge at the Kastner trial. Sternbuch not only accused Kastner of collaborating with the Nazis, but suggested that an international Jewish tribunal be established in order to look into the guilt of many others who later became "leaders" in Palestine and other free countries. He said he would prefer such a trial to a court in Israel, as he would want such deliberations to take place in a country where there would be no pressure from local politicians to save their skins.

Of course, nothing happened. Sternbuch's documents were filed away; his statements hushed up with the explanation that it would not be nice to present to the world such a sad picture of "leading Jews." This, however, did not satisfy Sternbuch, who remembered that when he and his wife had sent an emissary to Himmler — Jean-Marie Musy, the former President of Switzerland — the establishment in Switzerland became jittery and started "competing" with him.

Musy had a deal. All Jews were to have been released from the camps. Yet after the first "transport" of Jews arrived in Switzerland, Sally Mayer discovered Kurt Becher. Becher went to Kaltenbrunner and told him that the Sternbuchs did not represent influential American Jews but only a clique of old-fashioned Orthodox rabbis, and any political deal with them would be meaningless.

I studied these documents well, and I still have difficulty believing they are true: Mayer contacted Becher; Becher in turn appealed to Kaltenbrunner. Somehow, in Berlin, the news of this deal was leaked to the newspapers. Kaltenbrunner, who did not agree with Himmler that a deal should be made with Jewish leaders, went straight to Hitler, and, as evidenced by the records of that period (unpublished until now), Hitler went into a rage and ordered the entire operation stopped. (Kastner Trial Record).

Kaltenbrunner told Hitler that Himmler was already preparing his own escape from the 1,000-year-old Reich . . . Kaltenbrunner enraged Hitler when he "revealed" to him a "secret": Himmler had received in exchange a written guarantee that he and 300 other S.S. men would be admitted to Switzerland.

In a letter to Dr. Reuben Hecht, one of Tamir's key witnesses at the Greenwald trial, Sternbuch made the following points:

(a) Once and for all the legend must be killed that the Jewish philanthropic organizations in Switzerland supported the rescue efforts;

(b) It is not true that Sally Mayer ever suggested that Sternbuch cooperate with him, or that he would cooperate with Sternbuch's Committee. Quite to the contrary, "we told Mayer that our opponents are absolutely determined not to cooperate with us";

(c) Mayer is only trying to defend the role of the American Jewish Joint Distribution Committee, whose representative he was in Switzerland;

(d) Mayer alleges that the Sternbuchs did not take his advice into consideration. Simultaneously, he contradicts himself by suggesting that he was not opposed to the Musy mission when he first heard about it;

(e) Of course, Mayer and his coterie now try to question the effectiveness of Musy's *démarche,* but Mayer conveniently forgets that because of Musy many were released from concentration camps and saved. Who else but Musy could have obtained a signed document from Himmler about releasing Jews from extermination camps? (Also, Mayer would rather forget that it was Kastner who negotiated with Becher on his behalf.);

(f) Let us not forget that at a very late date the representative of Roosevelt's War Refugees Board, Mr. McClelland and Father Bernardini, the Papal Nuntius in Switzerland, as well as Polish Ambassador Lados and others, finally recognized "our role" (the role of the Vaad Hatzalah);

(g) Mayer was "consistent" in his position — from the very beginning of the persecutions in Germany — that Swiss Jews must lie low, not do anything, not say a word, otherwise they would expose themselves to antisemitism in Switzerland;

(h) Now we know that we could have saved many Jews by *buying lives* — by at least negotiating with the Nazis. Also Mayer's American superiors in turn failed to inform the American government of this opportunity to save lives.

Then Sternbuch reminded his former colleague on the Rescue Committee, Dr. Hecht, "Do not forget that Schwalbe (who was an official of the Jewish Establishment Organizations in Switzerland) told our men after the arrival of the first rescue train in Switzerland: 'Sternbuch will not get more trains out of Germany.' He must have been sure."

In 1947 Sternbuch was urging Hecht to bring into existence an International Jewish Investigation Committee or War Crimes Commission to determine the guilt of certain "leaders." He felt he had to do this, as the organizations were trying to malign him.

*   *   *

I believe that until the last days of his life (Sternbuch died at a relatively young age) he was unable to erase from his memory the battles he had to fight against philanthropists and do-gooders who helped disrupt the small but efficient organization of rescue that he had established. It sounds rather paradoxical, but the fact remains that while many influential Jews still failed to support his unorthodox methods of dealing with an unusual situation — a challenge never before known to civilized man — Sternbuch found allies among many non-Jews. (So did the Irgun delegation in America and the resistance organizations in Palestine.)

*   *   *

Something very strange occurred when the Secretary-General of the World Jewish Congress, Dr. A. Leon Kubowitzki (known as Kubovy when he became Israel's Ambassador to Czechoslovakia), attacked the Sternbuch committee and its role during World War II. This happened in 1948. Kubowitzki by then had become one of the leaders of the establishment and an assistant to Dr. Wise as Secretary-General of the World Jewish Congress. Kubowitzki evidently forgot that more than three years before he made that statement against Sternbuch, he himself had asked Sternbuch to use the connections of the Vaad Hatzalah to try to locate Kubowitzki's missing relatives! Certainly the World Jewish Congress was a "more important" organization, certainly financially and publicity-wise, so why disturb a little man like Sternbuch?

Sternbuch refused to ignore this ignoble attack. On July 5, 1948, in a letter to Dr. Kubowitzki, he expressed his astonishment at the untruths Kubowitzki had enunciated in a statement to the press, in which he deliberately exaggerated the role of the World Jewish Congress and reduced to nil the activities of the Vaad Hatzala.

Sternbuch, always the well-mannered Swiss gentleman, said he had no intention of ignoring the political activities of the World Jewish Congress. Yet, when one measures the activities of the Congress against "our great tragedy," one must state "with regret and pain" that these efforts cannot be weighed against the challenge of the hour.

Sternbuch continued, " . . . We don't publish newspapers or bulletins. We do not believe in publicity; and we cannot compete with American PR methods. Still, we must declare in order to be true to what happened that even in the pursuit of publicity and self-praise one must not lose the sense of proportion."

Sternbuch seemed to have been essentially upset because of Kubowitzki's *post-factum* assault against Jean-Marie Musy.

So, again the question: Why did the Jewish leaders refuse to "gamble," to try to save lives? What could the Jews have lost?

*   *   *

Sternbuch spoke of the strange discrepancy so evident when one compares the "activities" of the "big" organizations on behalf of the hostages to the achievements of the little-known groups.

I believe the discrepancy stems from the refusal of the pompous leaders to degrade themselves into negotiating with Nazi gangsters when human lives were at stake, while men such as Sternbuch were willing to exploit any avenue, explore any opportunity, any possibility in their rescue efforts. The "big" organizations needed publicity, press conferences, speechmaking, in order to give the illusion of importance. So the concern for the little man in danger was lost in this modern PR machinery without which any fundraising outfit cannot endure. The Sternbuchs were just plain people who acted to save human lives, not to save their standing in the community.

*   *   *

In his letter to Kubowitzki, Sternbuch recalls the fact that when Dr. Joseph Schwartz, the J.D.C. executive vice-president, visited Geneva in December 1944, he would not listen to any complaints against Sally Mayer. He also rejected the idea of any support for the Musy *démarche.* "Unfortunately," Sternbuch concludes, "these people succeeded in sabotaging this rescue work and rescue trains were discontinued by the Germans."

Sternbuch was unable to comprehend the "impertinent" statement by Kubowitzki that the World Jewish Congress had saved 190,000 Jews in Hungary, while the records of the activities of the Swiss Consul, Lutz, in Budapest are an open book today. Kubowitzki also conveniently forgets, Sternbuch says, that thanks to his "little Committee in Montreux," the Jews in Hungary and the other countries "were saved by us" because "we supplied them with fake passports." In this effort the Committee was supported not by the World Jewish Congress but by the Pope's Nuntius in Berne, Monsignor Bernardini, Polish Envoy Alexander Lados and others — all non-Jews. *(The savior of these people was Julius Kuhl, the liason between harrassed Jews and the Polish embassy. Kuhl at the time was an attaché at the Polish embassy in Berne. He risked his position to rescue people).*

How is it possible, Sternbuch asks, "to state that *no Jewish organization did as much in the field of rescue as the World Jewish Congress?* To exploit this tragedy for propaganda on behalf of the World Jewish Congress," Sternbuch concludes, "is unheard of after such a calamity!"

Sternbuch reminded Kubowitzki that Stephen Wise was alarmed about the German Final Solution, when the Swiss Vaad Hatzalah sent the famous cable to Rosenheim. Kubowitzki never replied to Sternbuch's suggestion that the leaders appear before an impartial tribunal and submit documents that would once and for all establish the facts.

*   *   *

During World War II, while the World Jewish Congress and similar organizations were busy with politics, the Sternbuch Committee was busy saving lives. Because of official Jewish sabotage it was only in 1944 (a State Department document reveals) that the Vaad Hatzalah in New York had received permission to legally transfer some money for rescue activities. (State Dept. documents and Bunim).

After the war none other that the Apostolic Nuntius, Monsignor Philippe

Bernardini, confirmed in statements to Reuben Hecht and Julius Kuhl the important role played by these little-known men who decided to act instead of crying or calling mass meetings. These men and others, representing the Irgun delegation and Vaad Hatzalah in America, labored incessantly for the rescue of those incarcerated in Hitler's Fortress Europe.

Interesting: They were also engaged in promoting American interests. Alfred R.W. de Jong, the military attaché of the American Legation in Berne, told Dr. Hecht, the Irgun representative, in 1945, when the war terminated: " . . . I know that one day you will get recognition for the way in which you have fulfilled your tasks."

Although some men in the establishment prefer to ignore the historic role of the Sternbuch Committee, Roosevelt's special envoy, Roswell D. McClelland, (who arrived in Europe very late) recognized its role. When the first transport of inmates reached Switzerland, it was the sensation of the day in the American press.

There were more than the number originally announced: seventeen hundred, according to *The New York Times* report.

*   *   *

Sam Woods, the American Consul General who had collaborated with Reuben Hecht for several years, was not the usual foreign service bureaucrat. In fact, according to historian William L. Shirer, author of *The Rise and Fall of the Third Reich,* Sam Woods was thought to be a "genial extrovert." He had a German friend who was the first to inform the Americans that Germany was about to attack Russia. It was Woods who gave the first danger signal to Washington, according to Cordell Hull, then Secretary of State.

When Secretary Hull read the Woods report, he called in J. Edgar Hoover to check its veracity. Hoover judged the information authentic. Woods had suggested that Hecht, because of his service to the American Army in Yugoslavia and Switzerland, be awarded the Medal of Merit. During the war B.R. Legge, a brigadier general, informed Hecht that the United States was aware of the fact that "you have rendered useful and valuable service to us."

Yet this medal was never presented to Hecht because he was a "Zionist" revolutionary. The British government, at that time the Colonial power occupying Palestine, considered him *persona non grata,* and put his name on the black list. Many news items were planted in the press against Hecht because of his role in fighting the British occupation of Palestine for the independence of the Hebrew nation. British propaganda continued to defame Reuben Hecht. London's *New Review Magazine* said he was *the* power behind the "Palestine Terrorists." (However, he was instrumental not only in supporting the resistance in Palestine. Because of him, Dr. Isaac Herzog, the Chief Rabbi of the Holy Land, intervened discreetly and successfully on behalf of the Fighters of the Freedom of Israel who had been imprisoned in Kenya, then a British Colony.)

Thus, the Medal of Freedom which, according to Consul General Sam E.

Woods, "you so richly deserve for the help you gave me in looking after American interned aviators," was never awarded.

Isaac Sternbuch, Recha Sternbuch, Julius Kuhl and Reuben Hecht are "guilty" of saving Jews from Hitler. The Jewish establishment in America and Palestine should be relieved of this stigma: It never, but never, rose to the challenge of the hour. In the rescue efforts it remained virginal, innocent of utilizing any unorthodox methods to save lives.

XVIII
1944-1945
Six Million Too Late

On January 22, 1944, Franklin Delano Roosevelt, the president of the United States, issued an executive order establishing the War Refugee Board. In his proclamation, the president stated that the policy of his government was to take all measures "within its power" to rescue victims of enemy oppression "who are in danger of death." The War Refugee Board included the Secretary of State, the Secretary of the Treasury and the Secretary of War.

Years had passed since the Irgun delegation began pressuring the U.S. government to establish a special agency to save the Jews of Europe — when there was still time to save millions. It took two million dead and more political battles until the Board was finally established.

The president's announcement was made immediately after it became clear that the tremendous pressure of the nonsectarian Emergency Committee to Save the Jews of Europe had succeeded in rallying the House and Senate behind the rescue resolutions.

While the sponsors of the congressional resolutions — Senators Gillette and Ferguson, and Rogers and Baldwin, Members of the House — hailed the establishment of the War Refugee Board, they expressed their regret that the presidential order did not mention "the specific Jewish problem." These legislators, who were supporters of the Irgun activities, spoke out: " . . . Although there are other peoples persecuted in Europe, yet none but the Jews have been officially and specifically marked for total extermination . . ." (*Answer* Magazine).

As late as November 9, 1943, after these legislators had introduced the resolutions demanding the establishment of a government agency to deal with the rescue of Jews, the official Jewish leaders fought this initiative because it had originated with the Irgun delegation. Yet these members of the Senate and House, moved by the Jewish tragedy in Europe, supporters of the "dissenters," ignored "the leaders." They were joined in their battle for the resolution by Christian clergymen, among whom was the Archbishop Athenagoras of the Greek Orthodox Archdiocese of North and South America. (At the time of his death several years ago he was head of the Greek Orthodox Church.) From Jerusalem, Chief Rabbi Isaac Halevy Herzog, ignoring the establishment in Palestine, wired the members of Congress urging them to pass the resolution sponsored by the Emergency Committee. The revered Chief Rabbi implored the legislators:

" . . . Save from Satanic destruction a great, ancient people, the source of the true spiritual ethical values of world civilization!"

Wendell Wilkie, the Republican Party leader, and former Democratic governor of New York, Alfred E. Smith, urged the House and the Senate to pass the resolution. This time the State Department's boy, Congressman Bloom, was unable to continue his sabotage on behalf of the government clique opposed to such activities.

Still, the opponents had one victory to register: A War Refugee Board, not a United States government agency to save the Jews of Europe, was established. A U.S. agency to save the Jews would have been understood much better in Berlin, especially by those Germans who knew by then that the Nazis were finished . . .

Finally, even the *Washington Post* recognized editorially the industrious spadework done by the Emergency Committee to Save the Jewish People of Europe: "The Committee is likewise (sic) entitled to credit for the president's forehanded move."

*   *   *

When Roosevelt became convinced that the resolutions could no longer be blocked in both Houses of Congress, he announced the establishment of the War Refugee Board, although, as the *Washington Post* remarked: " . . . The legislators perhaps would have rephrased the title to exclude the word "refugee," for, after all, the congressional aim was that steps should be taken before the Jews become refugees."

But this was a concession to the State Department and some scared Jews.

*   *   *

The leaders of Jewish organizations who for years had fought tooth and nail, almost hysterically, against the establishment of such an agency, suddenly became interested and hailed the president for his wisdom. Then they aspired to control its activities. One organization, the H.I.A.S. (Hebrew Immigrant Aid Society), announced at a conference in New York that it would support the U.S. government with a subsidy of ten thousand dollars!

Within the Jewish establishment, fundraising groups began to discuss the opportunity to participate financially in this undertaking, so that the poor U.S. government would not have to bear all the expense. This would also enable these groups to continue raising funds "for refugees."

Yet to the impartial observer it became clear that the composition of the War Refugee Board, its personnel, would place stumbling blocks to prevent it from truly fulfilling its mandate. Secretary Morgenthau, who finally became deeply involved with the task undertaken by the Refugee Board, still had to fight State Department bureaucracy each step of the arduous road. The State Department, with the help of some misled, prominent Jews, made sure that the offer of the Emergency Committee to place its personnel at the disposal of the War Refugee Board was not accepted, so that even when the representatives of the Board reached European countries, their operations would be slowed down. In the meantime, the Hebrew Committee continued its pressure, demanding practical steps of rescue.

Hillel Kook reminded the president that "on various occasions" the U.S. government had "warned Germany to refrain from the use of poison gas against either civilian or military populations." He also asked the president if he recalled having warned the Germans that if poison gas were used against the inhabitants of any of the member countries of the United Nations, "the United States would retaliate in kind against Germany."

Referring to Auschwitz and the other extermination camps, Kook stated that "hundreds of thousands of Hebrew people in Europe are being asphixiated through the use of poisonous gases. We therefore suggest that, in accordance with the above-mentioned policy of the United States, a specific statement be issued warning Germany to cease forthwith this practice."

Much earlier, at the beginning of 1944, the Irgun delegation, through producer Billy Rose, succeeded in having Bernard Baruch intervene with the president that in all United Nations countries freed from the Nazis, special camps be established for temporary shelter for about two million refugees. It also pressed for immediate help in order to evacuate the Hungarian Jews. All these demands, however, were conveniently sabotaged by the State Department where officials were busy answering Zionist political statements concerning Palestine.

How "successful" the Zionist leaders were with their political campaign on behalf of Palestine became clear after the war. Britain did not move one inch; nor did Roosevelt. We know that while the president had authorized Stephen Wise to make statements on his behalf in support of the establishment of a free and democratic Jewish Commonwealth in Palestine — and despite the democratic election plank so enthusiastically hailed by Dr. Wise and Dr. Silver — the president and the State Department continually assured the Arabs in secret memoranda and secret conversations that they should not pay any attention to these political statements. The Arabs were told that these proclamations were election-campaign, vote-catching gimmicks, that they were meaningless and did not represent American policy.

Towards the middle of 1944, the Irgun delegation in America strove valiantly to give added impetus to the ultimate effort on behalf of the surviving Jews in Hitler's Europe. Many territories had already been liberated by the Allied armies, and the Irgun felt that some political steps should be strongly advocated in order to obtain *de jure* recognition for the *de facto* Hebrew nation. This, the emissaries of the Irgun believed, would help rescue the remaining hostages and force the United Nations to deal with the problem as an emergency.

While the leading Jews continued to campaign against the Irgun and for postwar aims, prominent non-Jews came forward in defense of the Hebrew Committee. The first step was an appeal to the president by the co-chairmen of the Emergency Committee to Save the Jewish People of Europe, Dean Alfange, Will Rogers, Jr., Sigrid Undset, Louis Bromfield, Ben Hecht, and the Chinese exile, Professor Li Yu-Ying. In the appeal it was suggested that temporary rescue camps for Jews be established immediately, not only in the United States, but also in North Africa, in countries liberated from the Nazis and in Palestine. It was also suggested that those Jews who were rescued be given only a temporary status, that the United Nations publicly announce the establishment of such camps and that individual Germans be encouraged to help Jews flee Hitler-controlled territory.

This was the humanitarian suggestion. The American government was told that the least the Jews could ask for was to be treated like German prisoners of war.

The Irgun emissaries also realized that a political move, again an unorthodox initiative, had to be made to impress the world that from the ashes of Auschwitz a new nation had arisen; that this nation be recognized immediately, not *after* the war, so that homeless Jews in Europe and occupied Palestine could cease being political beggars and, as a recognized nation, be able to take care of their own problems. The author Ben Hecht summarized this new attitude:

" . . . All apologetics have ended in disaster . . . we must counterattack!"

So the Irgun emissaries established, for the first time in Jewish history, a "Hebrew embassy" in Washington, D.C., and proclaimed the existence of the Hebrew Committee of National Liberation. It duly registered with the Department of State, and hoped to obtain support from the Jewish establishment there and in Palestine so that Jews could finally begin to act as a nation.

The Irgun emissaries knew (this was also the opinion of the High Command of the underground Irgun and Fighters for the Freedom of Israel in Palestine who had been consulted in advance) that the old Zionist "Sir, give me a penny!" politics had failed. The Jewish establishment did not succeed in any of its undertakings. It certainly did not bring any closer the recognition of a Jewish nation, nor did it succeed in securing its place among the councils of the United Nations. Mizrachi World President Rabbi Meir Berlin(Bar Ilan), upon his return to Palestine from New York, declared to the press that the only political and humanitarian activities in America on behalf of Jews had been carried out by the Irgun delegation, and that the "Zionists should learn Jewish politics from them."

Many years before the establishment of the Jewish state, the Irgun emissaries understood that, in terms of international law, there was no such entity as a "Jewish people," and that if one demanded the recognition of a Jewish *nation*, a political entity, it had to be made clear that this new nation did not encompass Jews who considered themselves Jews only by religion or by descent. Today, years after the establishment of Israel, it is clear that there is a difference between Israelis and Jews. No one today would expect the government of Israel to speak in the name of Jews who are citizens of the United States, Canada, England or France — no one except those who cling to the old-fashioned, outdated, obsolete organizations such as the World Zionist Organization or the World Jewish Congress, tolerated for the amusement of some amateur politicians and "leaders."

Yet, in 1944, there was a feeling that the different approach, the recognition of a nation of homeless Jews and Palestinians, giving it a name, could help move the problem into the forefront of the Council of Nations. Had the Hebrew Committee at that time been able to issue passports to Jews in camps, the situation might have been changed.

In its proclamation, the Hebrew Committee stated it spoke not on behalf of Jews who considered themselves citizens of free nations, but for the persecuted Jews who were not protected by any government and for the Jews of Palestine who had begun to build a nation and a home for the homeless.

" . . . The Jews who live today in the hell of Europe together with the Jews of Palestine constitute the Hebrew nation . . . there is no other nation to whom they owe allegiance but the Hebrew nation . . . it is as a part of these millions that we exercise the right of self-determination; that we proclaim the existence of the Hebrew nation . . . and its elementary right to be represented by its own sons." (*Answer*, 1944).

The Hebrew Committee of National Liberation clearly indicated that American Jews were not a part of this Hebrew nation as long as they were citizens of the United States. This was something new, another step in the march of the Jewish revolution. Of course, Americans understood that Bernard Baruch, Henry Morgenthau, Jr., U.S. Secretary of the Treasury, and Admiral Hyman Rickover were not "Jewish nationals," but citizens of the United States. But the Zionist establishment considered itself at war with this Committee of "imposters." Perhaps they realized that if America and the other U.N. members were to recognize the Hebrew Committee of National Liberation, the "Zionists" would have been out of business "representing Jews" and begging Roosevelt to state that he believed in the Jewish Commonwealth — in the future. At that time a Hebrew government-in-exile could have helped save the lives of millions, and the Jewish state in Palestine could have been proclaimed four or five years earlier. Certainly England could not have ignored an internationally recognized government-in-exile.

So the revolutionary move of the Irgun delegation, which declared that "Palestine, in its historic boundaries, was the territory of the Hebrew nation by the will of God as defined in the Bible and had been politically ratified as such in 1922 by fifty-two nations which recognized the historic connection between the Hebrew people and Palestine," was attacked by the "leaders."

The Hebrew Committee of National Liberation (established by the Irgun) stressed that Palestine should be a free state in which the Arabs and other non-Hebrew residents should be full and equal citizens, and that the Hebrew nation be recognized as a co-belligerent in the United Nations war against the Axis. It also proclaimed solemnly that the surviving four million Jews in Europe (at that time) were prisoners of war and that the International Red Cross must deal with their problems "as it deals with all other prisoners of war."

This move resulted in an avalanche of abuse by the Jewish establishment, especially the Zionist leaders. They did not understand the meaning of such a sudden but necessary action. The Irgun emissaries were accused in the establishment press, and in all statements emanating from Zionist groups and parties, of "splitting the Jewish people into Hebrews and Jews."

The historic implication was lost.

They never understood Jewish history. Instead of supporting this program that made sense to non-Jews (it pointed the road to a solution of the Jewish problem), many thousands of dollars were spent fighting the Hebrew Committee. I think that the more than thirty Jewish organizations won. The Jews in the camps lost. The march of the Jewish revolution was interrupted, and the Jewish state came into being Six Million too late.

CHRONOLOGY OF THE HOLOCAUST

JANUARY 30, 1933: Adolph Hitler becomes Chancellor of Germany.

APRIL 1, 1933: The Nazi Government proclaims an official boycott of all Jewish physicians, lawyers, all professionals and businessmen as well. Stormtroopers guard Jewish stores against their patronage by Aryans. All "Jewish" books, including works by non-Jewish antifascists are forbidden. The same applies to music and paintings. The Nazis call it "cleansing" (Reinigung) of German Aryan culture. All democratic parties and trade unions are forbidden.

SUMMER 1935: Restaurants, public buildings carry signs forbidding Jews to enter the premises.

SEPTEMBER 15, 1935: The Reichstag (Nazi Parliament) votes laws declaring Jews as second class citizens in adopting the Medieval regulations against soiling German blood by intermarriage and sexual relations between the Jews and Germans. These regulations were officially "the law for the protection of German blood and German honour" later known as Nuremberg laws.

JULY 6, 1938: The Democratic nations under pressure of public opinion organize the first refugee conference, allegedly to rescue the Jews from Hitler. The conference took place in Evian. The conference terminated with the fiasco, as no country was ready to receive Jews whom Hitler at that time was ready to release from captivity. **Examples:** Australia stated she was afraid of creating a racial problem; New Zealand was against liberalizing immigration laws; the British stated that they had no room in the Empire to take in Jewish refugees; Canada declared it had room only for agricultural workers and this excludes Jews. The United States spoke of caution and wisdom which must be applied to its immigration laws.

NOVEMBER, 1938: Official pogrom organized by German Government during the famous Krystallnacht when synagogues were burned and thousands of Jews arrested and sent to concentration camps. Remaining Jewish shops and homes robbed and destroyed.

JANUARY 30, 1939: Hitler, in a speech, declares that in the event of war, Jews in Europe would be exterminated.

SEPTEMBER 1, 1939: Hitler invades Poland. Two days later England and France declare war on the Nazi Empire.

OCTOBER, 1940: German Governor of occupied Poland, Hans Frank, decrees the establishment of ghettos and the beginning of what Germans declared to be "resettlement" of Jews.

"Resettlement" (in German "Ubersiedlung") as explained in an official secret document of the Gestapo dated September 21, 1939, had as objective: the concentration of Jews in the ghettos in the larger towns and cities and that no Jews could hide in villages. At the same time, Jews are ordered to wear a yellow badge for identification.

JULY 22, 1941: Hitler invades the Soviet Union.

JANUARY 20, 1942: The most decisive meeting takes place. The heads of the German Gestapo called a meeting in the Berlin suburb of Wannsee. At this meeting which "was followed by breakfast", the final solution, the extermination of all Jews, was decided by them, and Adolph Eichmann was appointed as executor of this program. The hunt against Jews throughout German occupied Europe begins. The entire German Government machinery is mobilized to help liquidate the Jewish people in Europe.

JULY, 1942: Transportation of Jews to extermination camps begins throughout Poland. From Warsaw alone, 400,000 Jews are moved to the death camps of Treblinka.

FALL, 1942: American Jewish leaders are informed by the representatives of the orthodox Agudat Israel in Switzerland about the final solution and the extermination of Jews in the death camps. Two months later the reports are confirmed by the Department of State to American Jewish leaders.

NOVEMBER 8, 1942: Hitler, in a speech "You will recall . . . when I declared the International World War . . . will be the annihilation of Jewry in Europe . . . they laughed at me . . . they . . . will not be laughing much longer . . ."

SPRING, 1943: Another intergovernmental conference of the Allies, ostensibly to save the Jews of Europe, takes place in Bermuda. Results are the same as that of the Evian conference. No action as American and British governments oppose any steps that would "interfere" with the prosecution of the war against the Nazis.

APRIL, 1943: Warsaw Ghetto Uprising.

MAY 16, 1943: S.S. General Stroop declares: "The German army finally subdued the Jews of Warsaw — the former Jewish Ghetto of Warsaw is no longer in existence."

SUMMER, 1943: The liquidation of the second largest community in Poland begins. Most are expedited to Auschwitz.

JULY, 1944: The Soviet army liberates Maidanek. Worst fears are confirmed.

NOVEMBER, 1944: Germans blow up the crematoria in Auschwitz, destroy the records in anticipation of arrival of Soviet army.

JANUARY 26 1945: Soviet army enters Auschwitz.

FEBRUARY, 1945: Berlin. Eichmann tells his assistant Wisliceny that more than five million Jews were already exterminated.

APRIL, 1945: Allies armies enter Buchenwald and Bergen-Belsen.

APRIL 28, 1945: American army enters Dachau.

MAY 7, 1945: Germany surrenders unconditionally to the Allies.

End of the Second World War.

SOURCES OF REFERENCE
BOOKS & DOCUMENTS

Rabbi Michael Dov Weissmandl: **Min Hamaytzar**, Memoirs of the Years 1942-1945. (Hebrew) Published by Emunah, Brooklyn, New York, 5720 (1969).

The Labyrinth. Memoirs of Hitler's Secret Service Chief with Introduction by Allan Bullock, New York: Harper and Brothers, 1956.

Allen Bullock: **Hitler**, Penguin Books, 1962.

George Lukacs: **Von Neitzsche Zu Hitler** (German) Frankfurt and Hamburg: Fischer Bucherei, 1966.

Albert Speer: **Inside the Third Reich**, New York: The Macmillan Company, 1970.

Benjamin Zeev Hendles: **Am Hatorah**, (Hebrew-Yiddish). Published Privately, New York, 5721 (1961).

American Jewish Yearbook, Vol. 46 (5704, 1944-1945) (Review of the Year 1943-1944). Edited by the American Jewish Committee for the Jewish Publication Society, Philadelphia, Pa., 1944.

Konrad Heiden: **One Man Against Europe**, London: Wyman and Sons Ltd., 1939. A Penguin Book.

Matthew Josephson: **Sidney Hillman**, Garden City, New York, Doubleday and Company, Inc., 1952.

Bernard M. Baruch: **The Public Years**, New York: Holt, Rinehart and Winston, Inc., 1960.

Michael Weichert, **Yiddishe Alaynhilf**, (Jewish Mutual Assistance in the Ghettoes); 1934-1945; (Yiddish) Tel Aviv, Menorah Publishing House, 1962.

Arrows in the Blue, an autobiography by Arthur Koestler, New York; The Macmillan Company, 1952.

Vaadath Ezra Vo-Hazale Be-Budapest
    "Der Bericht des Judischen Rettungskomitees 1942-1945"
        (German) Report marked "Confidential" by author Dr. Rzso (Rudolf) Kastner concerning activities of the so-called "Jewish Rescue Committee" in Hungary directed by Kastner. (Mimeographed)
    "Political Horizons" published by the Fighters for the Freedom of Israel (Stern Group). December, 1948.   (Mimeographed)
    Prof. James MacGregor Burns. "Roosevelt": Harcourt, Brace, Jovenovitch, Inc. "The Soldiers of Freedom" New York, 1970.)
    (Henry Morgenthau Jr. telling the Assistant Secretary of State Breckenridge Long in the presence of President Roosevelt: "You particularly are antisemitic!")
    Foreign Affairs, 1944, Vol. V (Full report of Weizmann discussions with Roosevelt during the war years).
    L'Allemagne et le Genocide, par J. Billig, Editions du Centre, Paris, 1950.

Alfred A. Hesler: **The Lifeboat is Full**, New York: Funk and Wagnalls, 1969.

Menachem Begin: **The Revolt**, Henry Schuman Inc., New York, 1951.

Peter Papadotos: **The Eichmann Trial**, Frederich A. Praeger, New York, 1964.

Eichmann in Hungary, Pannonis Press, Budapest, 1961.

Frank E. Manuel: **The Realities of American-Palestine Relations**, Public Affairs Press, Washington, D.C., 1949.

Haim Lazar-Litai: **Af-Al-Pi (in spite)**, Story of Aliyah Beth (Hebrew) ("Illegal Immigration" to Palestine), Jabotinsky Institute, Tel Aviv, 1957.

Congressional Record (U.S.) Senate, 1943. Pages 4295, 4296, 4297, 4131, 4132, 4133, 4134.

Communications between Emergency Committee to Save the Jewish People of Europe and the International Red Cross in Geneva. (Photostatic Copies).

William D. Hassett: **Off the Record with F.D.R. 1942-1945**, published by Rutgers University Press, New Brunswick, N.J.

Years of War — from the (Henry) Morgenthau (Jr.) Diaries 1941-1945. Houghton, Mifflin Co., Boston, 1967.

New York Times, February 13, 1943, about the Jews in Rumania.

Stefan Zweig: **The World of Yesterday An Autobiography**, The Viking Press, New York 1943.

Pierre Van Paasen: **Days of Our Years**, Hillman-Curl, Inc., New York, 1948. Also by the same author, **The forgotten Ally**.

Nahum Goldmann, Autobiography, Hold, Rinehart and Winston, Inc. New York, Chicago, San Franscisco, 1969.

Ben Hecht: **Perfidy**, Julian Messner, Inc., New York, 1961.

The American Jewish Conférence. Proceedings of the First Session; Proceedings of the Fourth Session. Published by the American Jewish Conference, New York, 1944.

Senator Guy B. Gillette, Co-Chairman Irgun's Emergency Committee replies to American Zionist Emergency Council (Photostat).

Zionist Emergency Council writes to supporters of Irgun, attacking them as "dissenters". (Photostat).

Minutes of historic meeting: Irgun Delegation in America deciding to harness all energies for rescue campaign (April 25, 1943).

Photostatic copies of letters by:

Gizi Fleischmann

Rabbi Dov Michael Weissmandl

Dieter Von Wisliczeny

Franklin Delano Roosevelt

Governor Herbert H. Lehman

Gay Talese: **The Kingdom and the Power**, New York and Cleveland: The World Publishing Company, 1969.

Robert Silverberg: **If I Forget Thee, O Jerusalem**, New York: William Morrow and Company, Inc., 1970.

Henry L. Feingold: **The Politics of Rescue**, Rutgers University Press, New Brunswick, New Jersey, 1970.

Aryeh Morgenstern: The Jewish Agency and Rescue, Essay in **Yalkut Moreshet**, (Hebrew), Periodical published by Moreshet and Sifriat Poalim, Tel Aviv, June, 1971.

Darkness Over Europe: Edited by Tony March for Army Times Publishing Company. Rand McNally and Company, Chicago, New York, San Francisco, 1969.

Leon Poliakov: **Breviaire de la Haine** (French), forward by Francois Mauriac, Paris: Calmann-Levy, 1951.

Essays by Aryeh L. Kubovy and Livia Rothkirchen in **Yad Vashem Studies**, Vol. VI, Jerusalem, 1967.

Report by Lieutenant Colonel Harold B. Hoskins on the situation in Near East in "Foreign

Relations" 1943, Vol. IV, Washington, March 3, 1943, (page 757).

Shmuel Zygelbojm (Arthur) Reports in New York Times, Jewish Dailies, July, 1942.

Desperate Mission, Joel Brand's Story as told by Alex Weissberg, New York: Criterion Books, 1957.

Jews in Nazi Europe, February, 1933 — November, 1940. A study of the Institute of Jewish Affairs. Inter-American Jewish Conference, November, 1941, Baltimore, Md. Auspices American Jewish Congress.

From Evian to Bermuda, published by the Committee for a Jewish Army of Stateless and Palestinian Jews, New York, 1943.

The Autobiography of Sol Bloom, G.P. Putnam's Sons, New York, 1948.

Josef Lettrich: **History of Modern Slovakia, New York: Broderick A. Praeger, 1955.**

Dr. Isaac Lewin: Hurban Ayrope (Destruction Europe); Yiddish; Research Institute for Post-War Problems of Religious Jewry, New York; Vol. 1, 1948; Vol. II, 1950.

Hurban un Retung (Destruction and Rescue), Yiddish. Published by the Vaad Hatzalah, New York, 1957. With a forward by Rabbi Eliezer Silver.

Arthur D. Morse: **While Six Million Died**, New York: Random House, 1967.

Pictorial Review Vaad Hatzala, Germany, 1948.

C.L. Sulzberger: **A Long Row of Candles**, New York: The Macmillan Company, 1969.

Extermination of Jews on Polish Territories during the Hitler Occupation, (Collection of Documents — Polish). Published by the Jewish Historic Institute in Warsaw, 1957.

Photostats of Documents (close to 1200 pages)
From FDR Library in Hyde Park, New York and National Archives in Washington, D.C.
proving:
A. FDR continuously appeases Arabs assuring them there will be "no decision regarding the basic situation in Palestine without full consultation with Arabs and Jews"; Assuring King of Saudi Arabia that Jews will be resettled in Poland;
B. While simultaneously publicizing statements supporting Zionist post-war aims;
C. Collusion between the White House, State Department and British to sabotage rescue efforts on behalf of Jews in Europe;
D. "Official" Jewish leaders constantly flattering FDR following expression of "sympathy" with Jews in Europe;
E. Zionist leader telling State Department, Zionists opposing movement for Jewish Army.

Photostatic Documents (about 1,000 pages) Covering sabotage of rescue in Europe, collusion between Swiss authorities and the Jewish Establishment. (From Dr. Reuben Hecht, Archives, Haifa, Israel)

Rapport Au Comite Suisse de l'Union of Orthodox Rabbis of the United States and Canada par le Dr. Jean-Marie Musy, ancien President de la Confederation Suisse. (Fribourg Suisse), 1945.

Dr. Musy reports (in French) to the Orthodox Vaad Hatzala about the negotiations with Himmler and dwells upon the sabotage of his efforts by the representative of the American Jewish Establishment.   (Confidential, Mimeographed)

Correspondence between Dr. Isaac Lewin and the Polish Minister in New York. (Photostats). Last effort to save remaining Jews in Europe. (Strictly Confidential)

American Jewish Conference Press Release against Irgun's Emergency Committee, December 29, 1943. (Photostat)

Memo circulated by American Jewish Conference against Irgun's Rescue Activities. (Photostat)   (Confidential)

The White Paper Policy in Palestine and the Problem of Saving the Jewish People of Europe. Published by the Committee for a Jewish Army, New York, 1943. (Mimeographed)

The Answer, Monthly Magazine, published by the Irgun Delegation in America. 1943-1946.

The New Judea, August-September 1937, Official organ of the Zionist Organization of America. Report of Weizman's speech at the World Zionist Congress in Zurich, 1937.

Memorandum on the Findings of the Emergency Conference to Save the Jewish People of Europe, July 20th to 25th, 1943. (Mimeographed).

Exterminacja Zydow na Ziemiach Polskich w Okresie Okupacji Hitlerowskiej. (The Extermination of Jews on Polish Territories during the period of Hitler Occupation; (in Polish). Published by the "Jewish Historic Institute", Warsaw, 1957.

A Year in the Service of Humanity, published 1944, by the Emergency Committee to Save the Jewish People of Europe, New York. (Mimeographed)

Memorandum submitted by the Washington Emergency Committee to Save the Jewish People of Europe to the War Refugee Board, February 7, 1944. (Mimeographed)

The American Press and the Rescue Resolution, Emergency Committee to Save the Jewish People of Europe, New York, (1943).

A Jewish Fairy Tale (Manuscript), by Ben Hecht.

A Blueprint For Hebrew Freedom, a letter from Peter H. Bergson to Dr. Ch. Weizmann, 1945, Published by the American League For a Free Palestine, New York.

Munich — 1938, par Genevieve Volette et Jacques Bouillon, Paris, 1964, Librairie Armand Colin.

Trouble in Israel: The Story of the Irgun Ship, (Manchester Guardian, June 26, 1948), by Arthur Koestler.

The Altalena Incident, American League for a Free Palestine, New York, 1948.

The End of the Road, by William Ziff. American League for a Free Palestine, New York, 1945.

Black Paper: British Terror in Palestine. The Answer, New York.

An Answer to Ernest Bevin, by Vladimir Jabotinsky. Beechhurst Press, New York, 1946.

The Concentration Camps, by Hannah Arendt, Partisan Review, Vol. VII, 1948.

DOCUMENTS

1. State Department (August 5, 1939) to the U.S. President concerning negotiations between Myron Taylor and Herr Wohltat.
2. May 4, 1939. Myron Taylor reports on the "splendid work" done by the intergovernmental committee on refugees.
3. April 9, 1943: F.D.R. refuses to endorse appeal for Zionist funds.
4. Letter to American Zionist Emergency Council from Senator Guy M. Gillette, criticizing Zionist establishment for attacking his pro-Irgun stand, and the Irgun delegation. (January 13, 1944.)
5. Sept. 25, 1944 S. Strakacz, Polish Minister Plenipotentiary, transmits to Dr. Issac Lewin confidential memo about possibilities of saving the last Jews in Europe.
6. March 9, 1945. Roswell D. McClelland, American diplomat, in Berne, Switzerland, informs Isaac Sternbuch that the U.S. co-operated with some rescue efforts undertaken by Swiss ex-President Musy.
7. February 8, 1945. New York Post reports in a cable from Switzerland that Swiss Federal Counsellor (ex-President) Jean-Marie Musy had conducted successful negotiations with Himmler, and that the first 1,200 freed Jews had arrived in Berne.
8. April 11, 1945. Red Cross in Geneva informs Dr. Reuben Hecht (representative of the Rabbinical Vaad Hatzalah and the Hebrew Committee of National Liberation) that it succeeded in transmitting food to survivors in Theresienstadt.
9. In a letter from the Continental Hotel, in Istanbul, 1943 famous Belzer Rebbe, Aharon Rokeach, thanks Dr. Julius Kuhl for his rescue from Nazi Europe.
10. November 26, 1943 — Official Congress records of the hearings before the Committee on Foreign Affairs re: "rescue of the Jewish and other peoples in Nazi-occupied Europe."
11. August 6, 1943. U.S. Secretary of State, Cordell Hull, asks Attorney General, Francis Biddle, to investigate Peter Bergson (Hillel Kook).
12. February 24, 1941. Cordell Hull informs American Embassy in Berlin that it is "inappropriate" to furnish information (about Palestine) requested by Montgomery on behalf of the American Jewish Welfare Organization.
13. December 4, 1941. Mizrachi Organization of America asks F.D.R. to endorse a campaign providing matzot for the Jews in the ghettoes. The President refused to endorse the appeal.
14. **New Judea**, August/September 1937, official organ of the Zionist Organization of America, reports from the World Zionist Congress in Zurich:
    WZO president, Chaim Weizmann, warns the Zionist Congress that we cannot bring the Jews from Europe to Palestine, and that their end will be "dust." Of the 6 million, Weizmann predicts perhaps 2 million will survive.
    The Assembly applauded Weizmann, and sang the Jewish National Anthem.
15. January 15, 1971: Israel daily **Ma'ariv** reveals on the basis of documents publish-

ed in London, that in 1940 the British cabinet rejected Jabotinsky's proposal "to mobilise hundreds of thousands of Jews to fight Hitler on all fronts." Reason for refusal? "Jabotinsky is an opponent of Weizmann," and such a move would strengthen politically Jabotinsky against Weizmann's organization.

16. June 15, 1973. **Maariv** publishes sensational documents about Yehuda Arazi (Tannenbaum) who was in charge of the police investigation of the Arlosoroff murder in 1933. Arazi admits that he had lied upon orders; Stavsky and Rosenblatt were innocent, as were the Revisionists. On June 21, 1973, **Ha'aretz** publishes a column by Dan Margalit in which the story of a youngster in the family of a Labour leader is told not to divulge the truth about the real murderers of Arlosoroff.

17. May 26, 1946. The chief Rabbi of the Holy Land, Dr. Issac Halevy Herzog, in a statement in French, commends the work of the committee which supports the underground fighters detained by the British. The statement is sent to Dr. Reuben Hecht by the chief rabbi's son, Yaacov Herzog.

18. June 14, 1944. U.S. Under-Secretary of State, Edward R. Stettinius, writes to the President to do something about consoling Rabbis Silver and Wise on the future of Palestine. Abba Hillel Silver and Stephen Wise then thank Stettinius and express their hope to **"resume the discussion** on Palestine in mid-August."

19. September 16, 1944. Stephen S. Wise urges the President to see to it that the Palestine plank at the forthcoming National Democratic Convention be confirmed "by you personally." Wise also cautions the President that the Republican candidate is making "the broadest and most reckless of promises (on Zionism)."

20. May 14, 1943 — F.D.R. asks the Secretary of State "do not give any unlimited promises (to Jews on the issue of rescuing other Jews)." F.D.R. specifically refers to the Bermuda Conference. He is against sending Jewish refugees to North Africa. "That would be extremely unwise."

21. July 17, 1942. Dr. Israel Goldstein on behalf of the Synagogue Council of America informs Cordell Hull that because of the mass murders of Jews in Nazi-held Europe the Synagogue Council "set aside next Thursday as a day of memorial for the victims." He asks Mr. Hull for a relevant statement to be read in the synagogues. The State Department refuses because "as you know" they did enough already.

22. October 1943, **Bitzaron**, the Hebrew monthly edited by Dr. Wise's close friend Prof. Chernowitz, carries an editorial criticizing the Rabbis for daring to try to see F.D.R. (during the Rabbis' march) and for ignoring "the Jewish key to the White House" (Dr. Wise).

23. September 4, 1945. Philippe Bernardini, the Apostolic Nuncio in Berne, recommends Dr. Julius Kuhl to those who can assist him in his rescue work of Jews trapped by Hitler.

24. 1943. Stephen Wise criticizes Harold Ickes, the Secretary of the Interior for accepting the chairmanship of the (Irgun sponsored) Washington Division of the Committee to Rescue European Jews. (Ickes replies: he resents the fact that Wise dared to tell him which Jewish organization to support).

25. Fall 1943. The American Press and the Rescue Resolution, published by the Emergency Committee to Save the Jewish People of Europe.

26. September 26, 1944. Dr. Stephen Wise and Abba Hillel Silver ask the President to meet with them in order to discuss the problem of Palestine.

27.   January 1944, Magazine *"The Answer"* — The Story of Resolution, Page 7. Contains also names of Congressmen who supported the resolution sponsored by the (IRGUN) Emergency Committee. Chief Rabbi Isaac Halevy Herzog in a telegram to the Congress implores the legislators to pass the resolution sponsored by the Irgun's Emergency Committee.

28.   Manchester Guardian, June 26, 1948. The Story of the Irgun Ship (Altalena) by Arthur Koestler.

29.   May 1, 1945. Confidential Minutes of a meeting between Swiss ex-President Musy and Dr. Hecht.

    Musy states that Jews from Germany could have been legally evacuated if the Americans had declared that they were ready to accommodate them temporarily. He also reports on his last conversation with Himmler and the neglected opportunities of rescue. (German, 2 typewritten pages dated Lausanne).

30.   March 1, 1945. Dr. A. Leon Kubowitzki, (Koubovy) Secretary General of the World Jewish Congress, asks Isaac Sternbuch to help find Dr. K's family.

31.   July 9, 1954. Isaac Sternbuch in an open letter to Justices Haim Cohn and Benjamin Halevy of the Kastner trial demands the establishment of a Jewish court to try a number of wartime Jewish leaders as criminals.

    Sternbuch enumerated all accusations.

    (10 pages, text in German).

    This memo refers to a previous letter addressed to the Attorney General in which Sternbuch enumerates the crimes of Rudolf Kastner.

32.   August 28, 1942. "Israelitisches Wochenblatt" organ of Swiss Jewry, in a front page editorial reports on the efforts to stop the expulsion of Jewish refugees back to Germany.

33.   State Department letter #862:4016:2233. The State Department advises Dr. Wise that it has received a request from Mr. Gerhardt Riegner, Secretary of the World Jewish Congress at Geneva, to the effect that the Germans are trying to exterminate between 3½ to 4 million Jews by prussic acid; however, the American legation in Berne has "no means" to confirm this rumor.

34.   March 20, 1945. Sam. E. Woods, U.S. Consul General in Zurich, commends Dr. Hecht and Mr. Sternbuch for their humanitarian work.

35.   March 7, 1944. Mr. McDermott informs the President that the U.S. government has a commitment to the British government not to undertake anything on behalf of Jewish refugees without British consent.

36.   October 7, 1938. British Prime Minister Neville Chamberlain asks the President of the United States to appeal "to Herr Hitler" on the moral and practical side of the refugee problem. Hitler should be informed that his government's treatment of "emigrants" is a serious obstacle for better understanding. Chamberlain would like to persuade the German government to make a practical contribution to the solution of the problem.

37.   October 10, 1938. Undersecretary of State Sumner Wells is happy to inform the President that the American Ambassador in Berlin will sound out the German government regarding the refugee question.

38.   1943. Memorandum of the American Jewish Conference against The Emergency Committee.   (4 pages)

39.   August 9, 1945. Alfred R.W. de Jonge, U.S. Military Attache in Switzerland, thanks Dr. Kuhl for his wholehearted co-operation.

40. Secret report on Kastner's obstruction of Dr. Hecht's negotiations in Switzerland. There was an agreement with Himmler to rescue people for a price, Kastner undermined it.

41. April 12, 1945. F.D.R. assures Shukri el-Kuwatly, President of Syria, that the government of the U.S. will make no decision on Palestine without "full consultation with both Arabs and Jews."

42. February 14, 1945. Secret memo of conversation between King Aziz al Saud of Saudia Arabia and President Roosevelt in which the American President tells al Saud: "The Germans appear to have killed three million Polish Jews, by which count there should be space in Poland for the resettlement of many homeless Jews."

43. October 13, 1944. General Watson "complains" to the President that while Stephen Wise and Rabbi Silver both signed the letter to the President, only Wise was received and Rabbi Silver is upset.

44. July 15, 1943. The State Department is informed that Congressman Bloom is very angry because Peter Bergson attacked him for his role at the Bermuda Conference.

45. March 27, 1945. Sam Woods, American Consul General, lauds Dr. Hecht for his help in the Allied cause.

46. March 8, 1944. Memo for Stephen Early from Edward R. Stettinius, undersecretary of State. (1) The President wishes that you and Rosenman jointly redraft a statement concerning Jews. He believes that in the original statement "there is too much emphasis on the Jewish situation, and thinks it should be redrafted along more general terms." (2) The President made an additional point: "The statement will have to be clear to the British."

47. April 2, 1941. The Government of the United States refused to ask the British to admit 750 refugees from Bulgaria and Roumania including women and children. The Secretary of State was asked to explain to Senator Robert Wagner why the U.S. cannot intervene.

48. July 24, 1944. The Irgun's Emergency Committee to Save The Jewish people of Europe in a message to F.D.R. repeats its demand that railways and bridges leading to extermination centres should be destroyed by bombing. The extermination camps themselves should be bombed. The American and British governments should threaten with retaliation in kind if the Germans continue to use poisonous gas in Auschwitz and Birkenau.

   (The Allies did bombard the oil fields in Ploesti, Roumania which was much further from London than Auschwitz).

GLOSSARY OF NAMES, PLACES, ORGANIZATIONS

ABDULLAH — First ruler of Transjordan, eastern bank of Palestine, amputated by the British from Palestine in 1920.

ACRE FORTRESS — The most notorious British prison in Palestine up to the extablishment of the Jewish State, where Jabotinsky had been jailed after he organized active resistance to Arab pogroms. Many underground fighters were kept there by the British. The Fortress stems from Napoleonic times.

AGUDAT ISRAEL — A non-Zionist World Organization, established in 1911; also a political party in Israel.

AHAD HAAM — pseudonym of Asher Ginsberg, Hebrew Philosopher who preached the idea of a Jewish spiritual centre in Palestine; as opposed to a political centre.

AHIMEIR, ABBA, DR. — Most outspoken leader of the Zionist Revisionists in Palestine and its leading journalist.

ALIYAH — Hebrew for going up, i.e., emigrating to Israel.

ALIYAH BETH — "Illegal" Aliyah, smuggling Jews to Palestine through the British blockade.

ALLING, MR. — Official of the Department of State.

ALTALENA — A boat purchased by the Irgun delegation in America which carried arms to help liberate Jerusalem — was attacked by Palmach in 1948 under the orders of Ben Gurion. Irgun Commander Menahem Begin ordered the crew not to fire back — but surrender in order to prevent civil war in Israel.

AMERICAN FRIENDS OF JEWISH PALESTINE — One of the organizations created through the initiative of the Irgun in America.

AMERICAN JEWISH CONGRESS — One of several national organizations of American Jewry.

AMERICAN JEWISH JOINT DISTRIBUTION COMMITTEE — Established during World War I as a philanthropic agency to help Jews in distress in Europe and other parts of the world; the most powerful Jewish philanthropic organization. Is one of three organizations composing the United Jewish Appeal, the others being the Organization to Help New Americans and the United Israel Appeal, financing colonization in Israel.

AMERICAN ZIONIST EMERGENCY COUNCIL — Body representing all Zionist groups in the United States. Representative of the official Zionist Establishment in America.

AMIEL, MOSHE AVIGDOR — Chief Rabbi of Tel Aviv; supporter of the Irgun.

ARLOSOROFF, CHAIM — Head of the political department of the Jewish Agency in 1933 who negotiated the Transfer Deal with the Nazis and was murdered in Palestine a few weeks after his arrival from Europe. His murder was the beginning of a split within the world Jewish community of the Zionist movement.

ATHENAGORAS, ARCHBISHOP — Last head of the Greek Orthodox Church. Spent war years in America. Supported Irgun activities.

AUSCHWITZ — Town in South Western Poland around which the Germans constructed during World War II their most infamous camps for slave labour and extermination of their "enemies".

AUSSIEDLUNG — Nazi term for resettlement of Jews in the Ghettos; word used as cover-up for transporting Jews to death camps.

BALDWIN, JOSEPH C. — U.S. Congressman active in the Irgun sponsored organizations.

BALFOUR DECLARATION — In 1917, James Balfour, Great Britain's Foreign Secretary, sent a letter to Lord Rothschild in which he officially undertook on behalf of his Government to help establish a national Jewish home in Palestine.

BARLAS, H. — Labour Zionist emissary in charge of the Zionist rescue activities in Istanbul during World War II.

BARUCH, BERNARD — American financier and confidential advisor of many Presidents of the United States.

BECHER, KURT, COLONEL — Assistant to Himmler.

BEGIN, MENAHEM — Commander-in-chief of the Irgun until the establishment of the State. Former Prime Minister of Israel.

BEN AMI, YITZHAQ — Irgun delegate involved in Aliyah Beth.

BEN GURION, DAVID — Famous Zionist leader and then the most famous Prime Minister of Israel. Leader of the Labour Zionists. Died in 1973.

BERGEN-BELSEN — German concentration camp.

BERGSON, PETER H. — nom-de-guerre of Hillel Kook, Chairman of the Irgun Delegation in America, during World War II.

BERLE, ADOLPH A., JR. — Assistant Secretary of State of the U.S.

BERLIN, MEIR, RABBI — One of the international Zionist leaders during World War II. Head of the religious Zionist movement.

BERMUDA CONFERENCE — International meeting of allied governments held in Bermuda in 1943 for the purpose of helping the victims of Hitler.

BERNARDINI, PHILIPPE, MONSIGNOR — Vatican representative in Switzerland during World War II.

BETAR — Zionist Revisionist Youth Organization.

BEVIN, ERNEST — Second World War Foreign Minister of Great Britain and trade union leader who fought efforts to bring Jews into Palestine and finally, because of armed resistance, announced in British Parliament that his Government would give up its mandate over Palestine.

BIDDLE, FRANCIS — U.S. Attorney General.

BILTMORE CONFERENCE — First International Zionist Conference held during World War II at the Biltmore Hotel in New York City and at which time the Biltmore Program — establishment of a Jewish commonwealth in Palestine — was adopted.

BITZARON — Hebrew publication in America.

BLOOM, SOL — New York Congressman who was the first Jewish chariman of the Foreign Relations Committee of the House of Representatives.

BLUM, LEON — First Jewish Prime Minister of France and leader of French Socialists.

B'NAI B'RITH — International Jewish fraternal organization.

BRAND, JOEL — Head of the Jewish community and delegate of the Jewish Agency in Budapest during World War II years; was sent by Eichmann to negotiate with Zionist leaders abroad the 'money-for-blood deal'.

BRANDEIS, LOUIS DEMBITZ, JUSTICE — Member of U.S. Supreme Court and militant Zionist leader. Friend of Jabotinsky; opposed Weizmann's policies.

BRISCOE, ROBERT — First Jewish Mayor of Dublin; member of the Irgun delegation in America.

BRUNSCHVIG, GEORGE, DR. — Leader of Swiss Jews.

BUCHENWALD — German Concentration Camp.

BUND — Anti Zionist Jewish Socialist Party in pre-World War II Poland. Controlled Jewish trade unions in that country.

BUNIM, IRVING — Leader of Young Israel, largest Jewish orthodox organization in America and one of the leaders of the Orthodox Vaad Hatzalah.

BURNS, JAMES — Secretary of State of the United States.

CANADIAN JEWISH NEWS — A Toronto weekly established January 1, 1960 by the author.

CHALUTZ — Pioneer, i.e., pioneer in Zionist settlements in Palestine.

CHAMBERLAIN, NEVILLE — British Prime Minister known for appeasement policy with regard to Germany.

CHOCHME — Yiddish for clever tricks; Hebrew word means wisdom.

CHURCHILL, WINSTON — Prime Minister of England and leader of the anti-Nazi War Coalition.

COMMITTEE FOR THE JEWISH ARMY — Established upon the initiative of the Irgun delegation and the Zionist Revisionist organization in America during World War II.

COMMITTEE OF THE FOUR LANDS — Eighteenth century representative body of Polish Jews.

CRETZLENU, ALEXANDER — Rumanian Minister to Turkey during World War II.

CZERNIAKOW, ADAM — Last President of the Jewish Community Council in Warsaw.

DACHAU — Concentration camp near Munich.

DALADIER, EDOUARD — A Premier of France.

DAS KAPITAL — Standard work of Marx; "Bible" of scientific socialism.

de HAAS, JACOB — Secretary of Dr. Theodor Herzl, later American Zionist leader and collaborator of Jabotinsky.

DEWEY, THOMAS E. — Republican Governor of New York State during World War II. Also defeated Presidential candidate of the Republican party.

DIASPORA — Dispersion of Jews outside of Palestine. Term applied to all Jewish communities outside of the Land of Israel.

DODDS, HAROLD W., PROF. — Head of the American delegation to the Bermuda Conference.

EICHMANN, ADOLPH — Gestapo official who was charged by the Hitler Government with the Nazi extermination program of the Jews. He was captured, tried and executed by the Israelis in 1961.

EINSTEIN, ALBERT — Nobel Prize Winner, Physics, discoverer of the Theory of Relativity, indirectly father of the atomic bomb.

EL MALEH RAHAMIM — Jewish Memorial prayer.

EMERGENCY COMMITTEE TO SAVE THE JEWISH PEOPLE OF EUROPE — A non sectarian, non partisan group founded in New York in 1943 upon the initiative of the Irgun Delegation in America. Attracted most representative leaders among Americans. Founding Conference was addressed by former U.S. President Herbert Hoover.

ALFANGE, DEAN; BROMFIELD, LOUIS; HECHT, BEN; ROGERS, WILL, JR.; UNDSET, SIGRID; YU-YING, LI, PROF. — Leading members of the Emergency Committee to Save the Jewish People of Europe.

ESHKOL, LEVI — Third Prime Minister of Israel.

EVIAN CONFERENCE — Meeting of Governments which took place in the French town of Evian in 1938 at which intergovernmental committee was established to assist refugees from Nazi Germany.

FEFFER, ITZIK — Soviet Yiddish poet liquidated by Stalin.

FEINGOLD, HENRY L. — Historian; author of book on Roosevelt's role vis-a-vis the efforts to rescue European Jewry.

FEISAL, KING — Ruler of Saudia Arabia

FELLER, ABRAHAM — High official of the UNNRA. Brooklyn, N.Y. lawyer.

FIGHTERS FOR THE FREEDOM OF ISRAEL — (Stern Group) — The extreme underground resistance group against the British in pre-State Israel.

FINAL SOLUTION — Nazi term for the extermination of European Jewry.

FISHMAN, JACOB — Editor of the Jewish Morning Journal and American Zionist leader.

FLEISCHMANN, GIZI — Representative of World Zionist Organization and Jewish Agency in Bratislava in World War II.

FRANKFURTER, FELIX — Jewish member of Supreme Court of the United States and friend of FDR.

FREEHOF, SOLOMON — Famous American Reform Rabbi.

FREUD, SIGMUND — Founder of psychoanalysis.

GALBRAITH, JOHN KENNETH — American diplomat and economist.

GENERAL ZIONISTS — Middle-of-the-road Liberal Party. Formed together with Herut the Likud, the Union of non-Socialist parties led by Menahem Begin, the commander of the Irgun.

GILLETTE, GUY — Senator from Iowa; leader of the Irgun sponsored organizations during World War II.

GLOBKE, HANS, DR. — Author of the infamous Nuremberg laws.

GOEBBELS, MAGDA — Wife of Joseph Goebbels, Hitler's propaganda minister who had been a school pal of Chaim Arlosoroff.

GOERING, HERMANN — Second to Hitler under the Nazi hierarchy.

GOLD, WOLF, RABBI — Leader of Religious Zionists.

GOLDENE MEDINA — Yiddish for the Golden Country, a popular euphemism denoting beautiful America.

GOLDMAN, SOLOMON — Chicago Rabbi, at one time President of the Zionist Organization of America.

GOLDMANN, NAHUM — President of the World Jewish Congress.

GOY — Yiddish for non-Jew.

GREENBAUM, YITZHAQ — Until settling in Israel, leader of Polish Zionists, then member of the executive of the Jewish Agency; later Minister of the Interior of the first Government of Israel.

GRIFFEL, JACOB — Representative of the Agudat Israel in Istanbul during World War II.

GUGGENHEIM, SILVAIN S. — Leader of Swiss Jews.

GUNTHER, FRANCES — Wife of author John W. Gunther and active member of the Irgun sponsored organizations in America during World War II.

HADANI, RAFAEL — Member of the Irgun delegation in America.

HAGANAH — Defence in Hebrew. The first Jewish defence organization established in Palestine in the 20's to face Arab terrorism, later split up in three different groups when the Haganah become the organ of the official Zionist establishment. The dissident organizations were known as Irgun and Stern group.

HALEVY, BENJAMIN, JUDGE — Israeli Judge.

HALPERIN, "IRMA" (JEREMIAH) — Zionist Revisionist leader.

HASHOMER HATZAIR — Main group of extreme leftist Mapam party in Israel.

HASLER, ALFRED A. — Swiss historian of World War II rescue activities.

HASSETT, WILLIAM D. — An assistant of President Franklin D. Roosevelt.

HATZALAH, VAAD — Rescue Committee created by the American Orthodox Jewish Organizations during World War II.

HEBREW COMMITTEE OF NATIONAL LIBERATION — Established by the Irgun in Washington towards the end of World War II. Demanded the recognition of stateless and Palestinian Jews as a nation.

HECHT, BEN — American writer who was most active in promoting and helping organize several non-sectarian and non-partisan front organizations in America supporting the Irgun and its activities on behalf of European Jews.

HECHT, REUBEN, DR. — Irgun representative in Switzerland in charge of rescue activities; former advisor to Prime Minister Begin.

HENDLES, BENJAMIN W., RABBI — Executive head of Agudat Israel in America (an orthodox, non-Zionist world movement extablished in Katowitz, Poland — then Germany — in 1911).

HERUT — Israeli political party established by the Irgun in 1948.

HERZL, THEODOR — Founder of the World Zionist Organization in Basle in 1897. Was first political Zionist.

HILLMAN, SIDNEY — U.S. trade union leader, friend of Roosevelt.

HIMMLER, HEINRICH — Notorious head of German secret police in the Nazi period. Responsible for the worst crimes committed by the Nazi regime.

HINDENBURG, FIELD MARSHALL — President of Germany in 1933 who appointed Hitler as Chancellor.

HIRSCHMANN, IRA — First representative of the War Refugee Board of Istanbul. Headed mission to help save the remnants of European Jewry.

HISTADRUT — Confederation of trade unions in Israel. The most powerful arm of the Labour Zionist movement in Israel. It is both a trade union and the largest owner of industry in the country.

HITLER, ADOLPH — Nazi Dictator of Germany.

HOCHHUT, ROLPH — German author and playwright whose play "The Deputy" created a controversy in the 60's.

HOLOCAUST — Term used to define the extermination of the Jews in Europe during World War II by the Nazis.

HORTHY, ADMIRAL — Last ruler of Hungary during World War II.

HOZ, DOV — A commander of the Haganah and Labour Zionist leader.

HULL, CORDELL — Secretary of State, United States.

ICKES, HAROLD — FDR's Secretary of the Interior.

IRGUN — Short for Irgun Zvai Leumi, Hebrew for National Military Organization, the dissident Jewish underground army led resistance against British occupation authority in Palestine preceding the establishment of the Jewish State. Its last commander was Menahem Begin.

ISRAEL, STATE OF — Proclaimed by the World Zionist Organization and representatives of the Jewish community in Palestine in Tel Aviv on May 14th, 1948. In its proclamation of Independence, Israel declared it was to be the home of every Jew throughout the world who has the inalienable right to go and settle there.

JABOTINSKY, ERI — Son of Vladimir. Member of the Hebrew Committee of National Liberation and Irgun representative in Constantinople during World War II. Arrested by the British. At his passing, Professor of Mathematics at Haifa Technion.

JABOTINSKY, VLADIMIR — Founder of the Jewish Legion in World War I. Was expelled by the British from Palestine in the 20's, and returned when he organized the defence groups against Arab pogroms. Founder of the original Haganah, Irgun, and head of the opposition World Zionist Revisionist organization established in 1933 when the World Zionist movement split into militant and conservative parties. His remains were brought for reinterment to Israel by Israel's third Prime Minister in 1964.

JELENKO, MARTHA — Author of records published by American Jewish Committee Year Book.

JEWISH AGENCY — According to the Mandate of the League of Nations, the Jewish Agency was established to represent Jewish Communities throughout the world in the field of assisting in the rebuilding of the National Jewish Homeland in Palestine. Most of its members are comprised of the executive of the World Zionist Organization. It also includes representatives of non-Zionist International Jewish groups. It controls the funds collected by the Young Israel Appeal, a beneficiary of the United Jewish Appeal.

JEWISH AGENCY EMERGENCY RESCUE COMMITTEE — In Hebrew Vaad Hatzalah. Was established by the Jewish Agency and the representatives of all Jewish political parties in Palestine during World War II with the purpose to rescue Jews from Nazi Europe.

JEWISH LABOUR COMMITTEE — American non-Zionist group.

JEWISH LEGION — Jewish fighting force established by Jabotinsky and Trumpeldor during World War I. Fought with the British against Germany in Galipoli in 1915 and in Palestine in 1917. Was the first Jewish fighting force since the destruction of the second temple.

JOSEPHUS, FLAVIUS — Roman Jewish historian and famous author of work on the destruction of the second Jewish commonwealth.

JUDENRAT — Council of Jews which the German occupation forces established in each ghetto by nominating leading members of the community as an "advisory board" to collaborate with them.

JUEDISCHE RUNDSCHAU — Official newspaper of the Zionist Organization of Germany which was tolerated by the Nazis until the outbreak of World War II.

KADDISH — Hebrew prayer for the dead.

KALTENBRUNNER — Assistant to Himmler.

KAPLAN, ELIEZER — Labour Zionist leader in Palestine, Treasurer of the Jewish Agency before the establishment of the Jewish State, later first Secretary of the Treasury of the State of Israel.

KASTNER, RUDOLPH — Labour Zionist leader who was tried by an Israeli court for wartime collaboration with the Germans in Budapest and who was told by Justice Halevy that he had "sold his soul to the devil." The Kastner trial was the first occasion at which the Establishment was accused in court of neglecting to save the Jews of Europe. Kastner was killed by a fanatic.

KATZNELSON, YOSEF — Representative of the Irgun in Europe.

KISHINIEV BLOOD BATH — Russian Government organized pogrom against Jews in 1905 in the Bessarabian city of Kishiniev. Was the bloodiest Jewish riot and influenced the beginning of the large scale emigration of Jews from Russia.

KLARMAN, JOSEPH — Representative of the Irgun and Zionist Revisionists in Istanbul during World War II.

KLATZKIN, JACOB, DR. — Recognized philosopher of National Jewish Renaissance, probably most important Hebrew historian, supportor on Kantian philosophy.

KLAUSNER, JOSEPH — Famous Israeli historian; supporter of the Irgun.

KNESSET — Parliament of Israel.

KOESTLER, ARTHUR — Author and novelist; an early collaborator of Jabotinsky.

KOOK, ABRAHAM ISAAC — First Chief Rabbi of Palestine.

KOOK, HILLEL — (Better known as Peter Bergson) Delegate at Large and Commander for the Diaspora of the Irgun Zvai Leumi, the underground Jewish organization which fought the British occupation of Palestine until the establishment of th Jewish State. Kook became famous in the United States during World War II as the head of the Irgun activities for establishing a Jewish army and urging the United States to save the Jews from Hitler.

KOTLER, AARON — One of the foremost Talmudic scholars; was prominent in rescue.

KUHL, JULIUS, DR. — Was attache at the Polish Embassy in Berne, Switzerland during World War II. Used his position to save thousands of Jews. Died in Miami in 1985.

KULTUSGEMEINDE — Jewish community.

LADOS, ALEXANDER — Polish Ambassador to Switzerland.

LANDAU, HERMAN — Now resident of Toronto, Canada. Was secretary of the orthodox Vaad Hatzalah in Switzerland during World War II.

LANKIN, ELIYAHU — Member of the Irgun delegation in Europe.

LASH, JOSEPH — Author of biography of Eleanor D. Roosevelt.

LAVAL, PIERRE — Prime Minister of the Vichy pro-Nazi Government.

LEAGUE OF NATIONS MANDATE — After World War II, the League of Nations confirmed Britain as Mandatory of Palestine with the purpose of helping establish the National Jewish home in the Holyland. In 1940, Mandate mission of the League of Nations stated that Great Britain did not live up to its undertaking vis-à-vis the Jews.

LECHI — Short for Lohamey Herut Israel, i.e., Stern Group.

LE HAND, CAT (MISS M.A.) — FDR's Secretary.

LEHMAN — Famous American Jewish family. Herbert H. Lehman was the first Jewish Governor of New York and a friend of FDR.

LELYVELD, ARTHUR J. RABBI — Leader of the American Jewish Congress, and the organizations that opposed Irgun activities during World War II.

LERNER, MAX — First chairman of the Emergency Committee to Save the Jewish People of Europe; Professor, Brandeis University.

LETTRICH, JOSEF — President of the only democratic Slovak national council during World War II. Fled to America after the Communist coup.

LEVENTHAL, DOV — Member of the presidium of the Union of Orthodox Rabbis of the United States and Canada during World War II.

LEVIN, ISAAC MEYER, RABBI — Agudat Israel leader; Israel's first Minister of Social Welfare.

LEVITT, MOE (MOSES) — Executive Secretary of the American Jewish Joint Distribution Committee during World War II.

LIPSKY, LOUIS — Prominent American Zionist leader and leader of the Weizmann wing of the World Zionist Organization.

LONG, BRECKENRIDGE — Assistant Secretary of State during Roosevelt administration. Was accused by Henry Morgenthau Jr. of anti-semitism. Long was in charge of the task dealing with admitting refugees from Hitler to the United States.

LOTHIAN, LORD — British Ambassador to the United States during World War II.

LUBAVITCH, REBBE, (SCHNEERSON, MENACHEM MENDL) — Leader of the largest Hasidic sect in the world.

MACDONALD, JAMES G. — First American Ambassador to Israel.

MACDONALD, RAMSEY — First Socialist Prime Minister of Britain, remembered in modern Jewish history for his first White Paper against Jewish emigration to Palestine.

MACK, JULIAN W. — Judge and American Zionist leader.

MAIDANEK — Town in central Poland which contained a vast extermination camp for Jews during World War II.

MAIMON, YEHUDA LEIB, RABBI — Israel's first minister of religion and leader of Mizrachi who attacked Ben Gurion for his role in the Altalena.

MANN, THOMAS — German novelist and anti-Nazi (non-Jewish).

MANUEL, FRANK E. — Historian of American Zionist movement.

MARGALIT, DAN — Member of the editorial board of Israel's foremost daily, Haaretz.

MARGOSHES, SAMUEL, DR. — Editor of New York Yiddish daily "The Day"; Zionist leader.

MARSHALL, LOUIS — Leader of American Jewish Committee.

MASARYK, JAN — Last Foreign Minister of free Czechoslovakia, allegedly killed by communists during the coup of 1947.

MAYER, SALLY — Representative of American Jewish Joint Distribution Committee in World War II and Swiss Jewish community leader.

McINTYRE, MARVIN — FDR Presidential Secretary.

McLELLAND, ROSWELL D. — Representative of the War Refugee Board in Switzerland.

MEIN KAMPF — Hitler's programatic work.

MEIR, GOLDA — Labour Zionist leader and a prime minister of Israel.

MERLIN, SAMUEL — Organizer and ideologist of the Irgun activities in America during World War II.

MI BEROSH — Talmudic expression denoting the urge of frustrated people striving for "honours and recognition."

MIKHOELS, SHLOMO — Liquidated by Stalin. Head of the Jewish Art Theater in Moscow.

MIZRACHI — Religious Zionist Organization, now National-Religious party in Israel.

MONSKY, HENRY — Leader of B'nai B'rith and head of the American Jewish Conference during World War II.

MONTOR, HENRY — Was head of the United Palestine Israel Appeal during World War II; known for his violent campaign against supporting Aliyah Beth.

MORGENSTERN, ARYEH — Israeli historian of Zionist rescue activities during World War II.

MORGENTHAU,, HENRY, JR. — Roosevelt's Jewish Secretary of Treasury.

MUNI, PAUL — Famous American actor who participated in the pageants organized by the Irgun delegation.

MUNICH CRISIS — General term used for the meeting in the fall of 1938 in Munich, Bavaria where British Prime Minister Neville Chamberlain, French Premier Edouard Daladier, Italian dictator Benito Mussolini and German dictator Adolph Hitler met for the first division of Czechoslovakia.

MURRAY, WALLACE — U.S. Diplomat and State Department official.

MUSSOLINI, BENITO — Fascist dictator of Italy.

MUSY, JEAN-MARIE — A former President of Switzerland who negotiated with Himmler for the rescue of Jews on behalf of the orthodox Vaad Hatzalah.

NANSEN DOCUMENT — Passport issued to stateless persons. Named for Norwegian philanthropist Nansen.

NATIONAL JEWISH COUNCIL — Jewish Branch of the Emergency Committee of the non-Sectarian Committee to Save the Jewish People of Europe.

NAZIS — Short for National Socialist German Workers Party, a German post World War I movement which openly declared as one of its aims to eradicate the influence Jews throughout the world. Came to power in 1933 and its leaders, according to the verdict of the Nuremberg tribunal, were responsible for World War II and for the extermination of six million Jews in Europe under their authority.

NEUTRA (NEITRA) — Town in Slovakia.

NEWMAN, LOUIS I., RABBI — New York rabbi who supported the Irgun and Aliyah Beth.

NORDAU, MAX — Collaborator of Herzl, famous militant Zionist and extremely influential author at the turn of the century.

NUREMBERG TRIALS — Following the German surrender, the Allies established a War Crimes Tribunal. The trials began in the winter of 1945 and continued for several years. They took place in the German city of Nuremberg.

NUSSBAUM, MAX, DR. — American Zionist leader.

OCHS, ADOLPH — Publisher of the New York Times.

OLIM — Emigrants to Israel.

PAILEY, JOHN — Head of the War Refugee Board.

PALESTINE FOUNDATION FUND — A component of the United Palestine Appeal.

PALMACH — The striking arm of the Haganah.

PAPPENHEIM, WOLF — Head of the orthodox Jewish community in Vienna.

PATTERSON, COLONEL — Commander of the Jewish Legion in World War I. Supporter of the Irgun.

PERL, WILLIAM, DR. — Irgun delegate in Europe, now a resident in Washington, D.C.

PETAIN, MARSHALL HENRI — Notorious for his collaboration with the Nazi occupants of France. Was titular head of the pro-German regime installed at Vichy during World War II.

PROSKAUER, JOSEPH — President of the American Jewish Committee — a non-Zionist organization during World War II.

RAMUZ, C.F. — French-Swiss Nobel Prize winner, author of "Farinet".

RAZIEL, DAVID — Commander of the Irgun.

REPARATIONS DEAL — Agreement negotiated between Dr. Nahum Goldmann and post World War II German Chancellor Konrad Adnauer according to which West Germany agreed to pay individual Jews and the State of Israel reparations for expropriation of Jewish property by the Nazis prior to and during World War II.

RIEGNER, GERHARD — Representative of World Jewish Congress in Geneva during World War II.

ROGERS, WILL, JR. — U.S. Congressman active in the Irgun sponsored organizations.

ROOSEVELT, ELEANOR — Wife of FDR. Known for her sympathy for the Zionist Movement.

ROOSEVELT, FRANKLIN DELANO — President of the United States, 1933-1945.

ROSE, BILLY — Famous American Theatrical producer and promoter.

ROSE, SAMUEL B. — Friend of Ben Hecht and public relations director of the Irgun organizations in America during World War II.

ROSENBERG, ISRAEL — Member of the Presidium of the Union of Orthodox Rabbis of the United States of America and Canada during World War II.

ROSENBLATT, TSVI — Only survivor of the Arlosoroff Affair; was accused with Stavsky as one of the murderers of Arlosoroff. Later rehabilitated.

ROSENHEIM, JACOB — International President of World Agudat Israel, lived during World War II in America. Deceased.

ROSENMAN, SAMUEL T. — New York Judge, FDR's speech writer and close collaborator.

ROSH HASHANAH — Hebrew New Year.

ROTHENBERG, MORRIS, JUDGE — New York Zionist leader.

ROTHMUND, HEINRICH, DR. — Chief of Swiss police in charge of foreigners during World War II.

RUBLEE, GEORGE — American diplomat.

SAMUEL, HERBERT, VISCOUNT — First British High Commissioner in Palestine after World War I. Outstanding British Jew.

SANHEDRIN — Highest court in ancient Palestine.

SATZ, LUDWIG — Famous Yiddish actor.

SAUD, IBN — King of Saudi Arabia during World War II.

SAWICKI, JERZY — Attorney General of post-World War II Poland.

SCHACHT, HJALMAR — Hitler's financial wizard.

SCHELLENBERG, WALTER, SS GENERAL — Assistant to Himmler.

SCHMIDT, JOSEF — Jewish singer; The "Frank Sinatra" of Europe in the years preceding World War II.

SCHWARTZ, JOSEPH — Executive head of the American Jewish Joint Distribution Committee during World War II.

SCHWARTZ, MORRIS — Most famous American Jewish showman and theatrical director.

SHARETT (SHERTOK), MOSHE — Second prime minister of Israel and for many years her foreign minister. Was accused by Brand of turning him over to the British during World War II.

SHABBOS GOY — Yiddish term for one doing dirty work for his master.

SHERTOK, (SHARRET) MOSHE — For many years head of the political department of the Jewish Agency and World Zionist Organization, later on foreign minister to Israel and also its second prime minister.

SHTETL — Yiddish for little town. Denotes a compact traditional Jewish settlement in Eastern and Central Europe in the years preceding World War II.

SILVER, ABBA HILLEL, DR. — Cleveland rabbi; one of the two most prominent Zionist leaders in the United States during World War II. (The other was Dr. Stephen Wise.)

SILVER, ELIEZER, RABBI — Chief Rabbi of Cincinnatti, Ohio and foremost orthodox Rabbi in the United States during World War II.

SILVERMAN, SIDNEY — British Jew, a leader of the Labour Party.

SKULNIK, MENASHE — Famous Yiddish actor.

SMERTENKO, JOHAN, PROFESSOR — Leading member of the Emergency Committee.

SNEH, MOSHE — Leading Zionist and later head of the Communist Party in Israel.

SOCIALIST ZIONIST GROUPS — Also known as Labour Zionists, political parties which later united as the strongest force in world Zionism and became the most powerful political force in Israel. The Labour Zionists consisted of three main groups: the moderate Socialist Mapai, whose most famous leader was David Ben Gurion; the middle of the road Socialist Ahdut Avodah; and the extreme leftist, Marxist and, at times, pro-Soviet Mapam. When Ben Gurion became a leader of the opposition, he split away and together with Moshe Dayan established the Rafi party. Some of its members later rejoined the Labour Alignment which became the largest political concentration in Israel.

SOKOLOW, NAHUM — One of the presidents of the World Zionist Organization.

STAVSKY, ABRASHA — Wrongly accused by Palestine establishment as murderer of Arlosoroff. Later rehabilitated. Died in 1948 on the Altalena when Ben Gurion ordered that this boat carrying arms for Palestine be sunk by the army.

STEINBERG, ISAAC NAHMAN — Leader of Russian Liberal Socialists. He was an orthodox Jew and Lenin's first Commissar of Justice. Later broke with the Communists and escaped to the West. Died in New York during World War II.

STEINHARDT, LAWRENCE A. — U.S. Ambassador to Turkey and Czechoslovakia.

STERN GROUP — Most extremist underground fighting the British in Palestine. Officially known as Lohamey Herut Israel; named for Yair Stern, a poet who was its first commander and who was killed in cold blood by the British.

STERNBUCH, ISAAC — Swiss representative of orthodox Jewish organizations in America; headed rescue operations in Switzerland during World War II in co-operation with his Belgian born wife Recha.

STETTINIUS — Secretary of State of the United States.

STONE, HARLAN, — Chief Justice of the U.S. Supreme Court.

STRICKER, ROBERT — Austrian Zionist Revisionist leader.

SULZBERGER — Famous American Jewish family especially known for its ownership of *The New York Times*.

SULZER, WILLIAM — A governor of New York at the beginning of the century.

SWOPE, HERBERT BAYARD — Famous American journalist.

SZYK, ARTHUR — Famous illustrator and leading member of the Emergency Committee.

TALMUD — The legal code containing Jewish religious laws; the authoritative legal compendium of the Jewish religion.

TAMMANY HALL — Corrupt Democratic political machine in New York City.

TAYLOR, MYRON C. — Roosevelt's delegate in Europe to the Intergovernmental Committee of Refugees.

TEHOMI, AVRAM — First commander of the Irgun.

THERESIENSTADT — German concentration camp in Czechoslovakia.

TRANSFER DEAL OF 1933 — In the spring of 1933, the Jewish Agency entered into an agreement with Nazi authorities, according to which part of the capital of Jews emigrating to Palestine was transferred to Palestine in the form of German goods.

TRANSNISTRIA — Province of Rumania.

UNITED JEWISH APPEAL — Overall organization for fundraising comprising the American Jewish Joint Distribution Committee, the U.J.A., and United Service for New Americans.

UNNRA — United Nations Relief and Rehabilitation Administration.

UNITED PALESTINE APPEAL — Forerunner of United Israel Appeal.

USSISCHKIN, MENAHEM — Palestine Jewish leader.

VAAD HATZALAH, ORTHODOX — Not to be confused with the Vaad Hatzalah of the Jewish Agency Emergency Rescue Committee. It was established during World War II in the United States by all orthodox Rabbinical and lay organizations to rescue

Jews from Hitler and sustain refugees. It was in permanent conflict with the established Jewish organizations because it opposed the 'business as usual' methods of the big Jewish organizations during World War II.

VERSAILLES PEACE CONFERENCE — First post-World War I meeting of victorious powers at Versailles, near Paris.

VOELKISCHER BEOBACHTER — Leading newspaper of the German Nazis.

VON KILLINGER, HERR — German Ambassador in Rumania.

VON PLEHVE, WENZEL — The Czar's Minister of Interior who was accused of encouraging pogroms against Jews.

VON STEIGER — President of Switzerland.

WADSWORTH, GEORGE — American diplomat; Consul General of the United States in Jerusalem during World War II.

WANNSEE CONFERENCE — At this Conference, in the Berlin suburb of Wannsee, the Final Solution, the extermination of **all Jews**, was decided upon by the German government. (January 20, 1942.)

WAR REFUGEE BOARD — Established by FDR in 1944 with the purpose of rescuing Hitler's victims.

WDOWINSKI, DR. DAVID — A leader of the Warsaw Ghetto Uprising and President of the Zionist Revisionists in Poland, later professor of the New School for Social Research in New York.

WEDGEWOOD, LORD — British Labour leader and friend of Zionism.

WEILL, KURT — Famous American musician and theatrical figure.

WEISSMANDL, MICHAEL DOV — Head of Yeshiva in Neitra, who negotiated with Nazis during World War II the money-for-blood deal in Slovakia. Died in New York.

WEIZMANN, CHAIM — World Zionist leader; first President of Israel; opponent of Jabotinsky; believed in cooperation with British.

WELLS, SUMNER — Assistant Secretary of State of the United States.

WERFEL, FRANZ — German Jewish novelist, born in Prague.

WHITE PAPER — The British document first issued by Prime Minister MacDonald limiting Jewish emigration to Palestine. Considered breach of British commitment under the Palestine Mandate.

WHITE, WILLIAM ALLAN — American publisher.

WILLKIE, WENDELL — Republican presidential candidate who opposed FDR in 1948.

WISE, STEPHEN S. — Most famous Reform rabbi in the United States during World War II. Considered most influential Jewish and Zionist leader; was a confidant of President Roosevelt.

WISLICZENY, DIETER VON — Second to Eichmann in charge of extermination program of European Jews.

WOHLTAT — High Nazi official who dealt with Jewish affairs.

WORLD JEWISH CONGRESS — Established 1936 in Geneva by American Jewish Congress and a number of European Jewish Organizations.

WORLD ZIONIST CONGRESS — "Parliament" of the World Zionist Organization. First Congress took place in Basle, Switzerland in 1897 when the World Zionist Organization was established.

WORLD ZIONIST ORGANIZATION — Established in 1897 in Basle, Switzerland by Dr. Theodor Herzl. Its purpose was to organize Jews throughout the world for resettlement in Palestine and the subsequent establishment there of a national Jewish homeland.

YESHIVA UNIVERSITY, NEW YORK — Largest Jewish academy of higher learning in the world combining rabbinical seminary with university and medical school.

YOM KIPPUR — Day of Atonement, holiest day in the Hebrew calendar.

YOUNG ISRAEL OF AMERICA — Largest and most influential non-political organization of orthodox Jews in the United States and Canada which established during the last sixty years most of the modern orthodox synagogues on the North American continent. It is non-partisan and was the first orthodox Jewish movement to use English in its synagogues.

ZAAR, ISAAC — Active member of the Irgun sponsored organizations of America.

ZIFF, WILLIAM B. — American author and publisher, and leader of the Zionist Revisionist movement: supporter of the Irgun.

ZIONISM — Stems from the word Zion. Term was coined by Nathan Birnbaum, first modern Zionist philosopher who later left the Zionist movement to become leader of the Orthodox Agudat Israel.

ZIONIST ORGANIZATION OF AMERICA — Group representing the Liberal Zionists, a liberal non-socialist center Zionist party in Israel.

ZIONIST REVISIONISTS — Militant wing of the World Zionist Movement which in 1935 became an independent organization under the name "New Zionist Organization".

ZWEIG, STEFAN — Famous German Jewish novelist who committed suicide during World War II because of the German persecutions.